Food Process Cooking-Naturally

Food Processor Cooking-Naturally

Laura Ramsay

Contemporary Books, Inc.
Chicago

Library of Congress Cataloging in Publication Data

Ramsay, Laura.
   Food processor cooking—naturally.

   Includes index.
   1. Food processor cookery.   I. Title.
TX840.F6R35   1983   641.5'89   82-22089
ISBN 0-8092-5726-2

Copyright © 1983 by Laura Ramsay
All rights reserved
Published by Contemporary Books, Inc.
180 North Michigan Avenue, Chicago, Illinois 60601
Manufactured in the United States of America
Library of Congress Catalog Card Number: 82-22089
International Standard Book Number: 0-8092-5726-2

Published simultaneously in Canada by
Beaverbooks, Ltd.
150 Lesmill Road
Don Mills, Ontario M3B 2T5
Canada

Contents

Guide to Tables

The purpose of these tables is to spark your ideas for creative cooking, as well as for reference.

Introduction

Here's a delicious idea: cooking with natural food and a food processor. Natural food processor cooking teams up the ideal foods for health with the best kitchen gadget to come out since the electric icebox.

As a group, food processor users must surely be among the world's most sophisticated cooks. Yet, surprisingly, many have yet to discover the benefits of natural food. If you are one of these people, it's quite possible you've tasted a few rather bland natural food meals, and therefore chose to steer clear of this type of cooking (until now). It is true that natural food prepared without imagination does not inspire the palate. Yet, as this book will show you, meals need *not* be tasteless just because they are comprised of whole, unrefined foods. Some of the flavors of natural food may be different and may take some getting used to, but so did wine and fine cheese, remember?

For the sake of health, it makes sense to experiment with natural foods. But for the sake of life, let's affirm the need for variety and imagination. Surprise yourself. Discover what natural food really can be: a cuisine of honest vitality, replete with vivid tastes and textures. With the recipes in this book, you can prepare natural foods that are as sophisticated as you wish to make them.

A different set of surprises awaits the not-yet-processing natural food cook. Many dedicated natural food cooks have told me they dread turning their wholesome kitchens into frantic, fast food operations. Like the myth that natural foods must be dull and bland, the fear that using a processor will detract from the wholesomeness of foods is unfounded.

How will the processor change your kitchen? In the first place, it can bring a deeper appreciation of many natural foods. Technology opens up possibilities. Think, for example, of broccoli. Stems that have been discarded in the past can now be sliced paper thin and steamed for a new, delicate taste. The cooked flowers grated fine add delightfully feathery bits of flavor and texture to what was once an ordinary quiche.

Second, the processor will bring more efficiency into your kitchen. You'll gain freedom to experiment with recipes that otherwise would have been too complex or time consuming to be practical. Keep in mind that this doesn't mean you will become an automaton who has lost all personal contact with food. If you enjoy chopping, you can still, of course, use your favorite knives when you have the time and the inclination. On the other hand, you will also have the satisfaction of knowing that dishes that require time you *don't* have can remain in, or be added to, your repertoire.

Speed of preparation can actually bring a nutritional bonus, because fresher vegetables contain more nutrients. Later you'll read detailed information about nutrient preservation through intelligent cooking methods and food processor use. Here, I'll present an example of freshness you can appreciate based on your own past experience: coleslaw.

Have you ever tasted freshly grated cabbage? The texture, flavor, and moistness signal that the food has maximum value. Vitamins such as ascorbic acid and thiamin are perishable. You may not be able to taste their presence directly, but you can recognize the vitality.

Compare that vitality to the wilted washout found in typical coleslaw. The grating method takes perseverance, courageous knuckles, and time; grated slaw can't be buzzed up in five minutes just before serving. Processor efficiency saves you both nutrients and flavor.

The third, and most exciting, result of food processor use is the promise of self-sufficiency.

It becomes feasible to free yourself from dependence on expensive convenience foods. In minutes you can prepare every eatable that goes onto your table, from bread to spread, from staples to special treats. This book will give you the know-how and the processor will supply your technical needs.

The combination of the food processor and natural food can throw humdrum cooking out of any kitchen permanently. To me, boredom in cooking is inexcusable, as awful as living without a sense of humor. Natural food processor cooking got my meals out of a rut because it showed me many new ways to use the foods I'd always used. I know it can do the same for you. In fact, should my dream for this book come true, every recipe given here will inspire you to create another dish that is equally delicious, invigorating, and satisfying.

1 | How to Use This Cookbook

Appearances can be deceiving, they say. Maybe a fairer statement is this: appearances can be limiting. On the surface, you have opened a recipe book. And you will find recipes here, plenty of them. Yet, depending on what you want, you can also find other things of interest to you as a cook.

After using this book, you can expect to really understand and use both the processor and natural foods. Beyond that, the format of both the book and many of the recipes has been designed to encourage you to experiment. You will learn to improvise in a way that only the combination of processor and natural food cooking makes possible.

Food Processor Use

Chapter 3 provides systematic but brief instructions for the novice food processor user. Veterans will also benefit from a review of this material, plus a look at the list of recipe terms, because these will clarify exactly what terms are used in the recipe instructions. So that there is no confusion, these terms indicate which blade to use and so forth. Whether you're a beginner or a pro with the food processor, the idea in this cookbook is to learn to use this wonderful aid to its best advantage. Once processor use becomes second nature, you can learn the secrets of Problem Solving with a Processor (see Chapter 14), and discover how to use the processor to handle special tasks in the kitchen. In short, the food processor can extend your creativity.

Natural Food Knowledge and Nutrition

Everything you need to know to become a natural gourmet is included in this book, whether you're just beginning to use natural foods or you're a longtime natural food cook. In Chapter 2 you will find a definition of natural food and tips on buying it at a reasonable cost. Throughout the book, specific techniques for preparation of various foods are given, including information on nutritional content of natural foods. The sections on how to adapt recipes to natural food standards and how to keep a natural kitchen (see Chapter 14) will help you relate the principles to all other cooking experience.

Nutritional Conscientiousness

Unfortunately, nutritional conscientiousness does not necessarily go with the use of natural food. In fact, very few cooks know the scientific facts about nutrient conservation. The information in Appendix I can lead to a big improvement in the nutritional value of the meals you prepare. Concern about nutrition underlies the design of all the recipes in this book. To ensure the accuracy of my recommendations, the book was reviewed carefully by Steven Royce, who received his doctorate in nutrition from the University of Illinois in Urbana. Dr. Barbara P. Klein of the Department of Foods and Nutrition at the University of Illinois in Urbana supplied me with detailed information on nutrient conservation.

Protein Combining and Menu Planning

Do you want to become a part-time or full-time vegetarian? This book can show you how to do so without jeopardizing your health or radically altering your lifestyle. You'll find essential information in Chapter 14, in the section on protein combining. For effective meal planning, Chapter 15 also gives pointers on combining compatible dishes and also lists recommended menus for various occasions. Preparation of balanced meatless meals can seem to be an overwhelming task, while actually it entails little more than establishing a good routine. The Recipe for a Cook's Routine in Chapter 16 will show you how easily things can be managed.

How to Use Recipes

T *Transformation Recipes*

The way the processor enables you to change textures of food almost instantly is truly magical. *Transformation recipes* preceded by the symbol T are those that can be transformed, with the aid of a food processor, into one or more related recipes in the cookbook. So when you connect with a taste you love, you can make it do double (or triple) duty.

F *Flexible Recipes*

Here you will find opportunities to improvise without risk. Each *flexible recipe* preceded by the symbol F supplies a carefully balanced framework and allows you to choose the variations and nuances. The section on improvising with confidence (Chapter 4), is especially noteworthy. It contains instructions for changing flavor and texture when you bake—an achievement made much more foolproof by the use of the processor.

• *Storehouse of Tips*

A good cook collects information about the properties of different foods. To help you find them, these bits of information are set off from the recipe instructions by the symbol •. Tips include insights into nutrition as well as facts about food preparation and storage.

Conceptual Tables

Are you fascinated by the principles underlying cooking and recipes? Do you relish the creative aspect of cookery? If your answers are yes, the tables are for you.

Each table will help you understand and give you guidelines for improvisation on a certain type of recipe. Beyond the practical application, you can take the concepts as far as you like. For instance, Whole Grain Flour Resources starts as a recipe for using different types of flour to thicken a cream sauce. Use the same knowledge

to thicken other types of sauces, make puddings, prepare breakfast porridges—all with a variety of whole grain flours, not just the standard white flour and cornstarch thickeners. Since these tables are intended to instill in you the spirit of experimentation, only a limited number of examples are listed. So I've included space at the end of each table for you to list your own.

A GUIDE TO RECIPE TERMS

Check after x minutes: Cooking times are expressed this way rather than as a guarantee that the food will be ready. I think this is a realistic way.

Choices—optional, or, and substitute: Natural food being perishable and budgets being finite, I've thought it best to note alternative ingredients whenever possible. To do this, I have come up with three different terms. An ingredient marked *optional* should be used whenever possible. It is, however, not necessary for a recipe to succeed. Alternatives (x *or* y) can be considered interchangeable. *Substitute* indicates a compromise ingredient. Use of the substitute will give you an acceptable, if not ideal, result.

Drop through the feed tube: See *Pour through the feed tube, Drop through the feed tube.*

Main dish servings: See *Serves x, x main dish servings.*

Oil a pan: Oil a pan (for baking pans only) by using a small amount of liquid lecithin or salad oil. Rub it on with your fingers or a brush, spreading it as thin as possible.

Optional: See *Choices—optional, or, and substitute.*

Or: See *Choices—optional, or, and substitute.*

Oven at x: Preheat the oven to x degrees. Check the real temperature against an oven thermometer and adjust the heat setting if necessary. *In accordance with convention, baking temperatures are presented for metal pans. If you use glass instead (and I hope you will), set the temperature 25 degrees lower.*

Packed: The ingredient should be crammed into the cup before being measured. (Usually an ingredient is loaded loosely into the measure.) For quick, accurate measurement of dry ingredients, scoop with the measure and level off with the edge of a knife.

Pack food sideways and push it through: The food is loaded sideways into the feed tube before being pushed through the slicing disc.

Pour through the feed tube; Drop through the feed tube: These are the only exceptions to a prime safety rule for using the metal blade: always keep the pusher in place. Here you start to run the machine with the pusher in. Then you take out the pusher and either pour in a stream of liquid or drop in a chunk of solid food. You continue to add food through the tube until the desired texture is reached. This technique allows you to control the amount of liquid used in making a puree, frosting, or other mixture.

Process; Process for 5 seconds; Process for 10 seconds: Using the metal blade, run the machine a certain number of seconds and then repeat until a specific result is reached. Typically, you will find the instruction, "Process 10 seconds. Scrape down. Repeat until the mixture is uniform." In other words, stop the machine after 10 seconds of processing. Remove the lid of the workbowl. Examine the contents and scrape down food as necessary. If the mixture still does not look uniform, replace the lid and repeat the whole procedure. Continue until the mixture is uniform (see explanation of "uniform" befow).

This method differs from the instructional format with which you may be familiar, in which directions specify *three* 10-second processings," and so forth. While I will, of course, provide all the essential guidelines you will need to successfully complete each recipe, I strongly believe that the cook must be encouraged to use sensory judgments and self-referral. Furthermore, a mechanical approach is undesirable even in the interest of precision. It is when cooking becomes a matter of counting and timing, instead of watching and tasting, that the biggest mistakes can be made.

Pulse: Use the pulse control. If your machine doesn't have one, turn the machine on and off. Each on-off counts as one pulse. Use the metal blade.

Process until the mixture is smooth; Process until the mixture is uniform: You already know what a smooth mixture is—no lumps. What about uniform? Some ingredients can never be processed totally smooth. Uniform means the smoothest texture you can get. Use the metal blade.

Processor sift: Use the food processor as a flour sifter. Process, using the metal blade, continuously for 10 seconds to sift the flour. The term "processor sift" may seem redundant, because it is often done to ingredients you have already mixed by processing. Processor sifting is quite valuable, though; it fluffs up flour just as an old-fashioned sifter does. Just as a non-processor recipe might call for twice-sifted ingredients, the recipes in this book ask you to process ingredients and then processor sift them. Unlike old-fashioned sifting, however, this extra step adds a mere 10 seconds to mixing time. It's a worthwhile investment in texture.

Pulse until barely mixed: This means that although the batter is fairly uniform, you still can see clumps of flour or inconsistent moistness. Flour batters are barely mixed because otherwise gluten is developed, which toughens the final product. Spreads and other combinations of food may need to be mixed barely because the metal blade chops while it mixes. Further pulsing could break down the shape of ingredients in an undesirable way.

Push food through the slicing, shredding, or french fry disc: Insert the appropriate disc. Pack food upright in the feed tube. Turn on the machine. Push the food through. Remove the food from the workbowl.

Push through chunks, quarters, and so forth: Before you load the feed tube, cut the food into pieces. Use the slicing disc.

Push through the slicing disc twice: The first time you push the food through it is loaded upright into the feed tube. The second time the slices are stacked together horizontally.

Rinse out the workbowl: Water usually works

fine. Sometimes a little scrubbing with a sponge is needed. Also rinse the lid, if necessary. Note that unless this instruction is given, you don't need to rinse out the machine between uses. Usually, though, rinsing should be done between one recipe and another. When a cooking session is over, wash the processor thoroughly according to the manufacturer's instructions.

Scrape down: Use a rubber spatula on the bottom of the workbowl to break up lumps of food and uncover puddles of liquid near the blade. Also use the spatula to guide scattered food down from the top of the metal blade, sides of the workbowl, or inside of the lid.

Serves x; X main dish servings: The serving sizes recommended in this book are not based upon arbitrary volumes; you will not find one standard-size portion repeated for each recipe. In each case, the amount needed for a serving is based on balancing several factors: calories, amount of protein, visual appearance, and function in the meal. A *main dish serving* is more generous than a regular serving.

Substitute: See *Choices—optional, or, and substitute.*

Transfer batter into a baking pan: Use a spoon or other implement of your choice to move the batter. Do it at once, since the chemical reaction we call "leavening" starts as soon as the baking powder or soda is moistened. And immediately after pouring, quickly and lightly smooth the surface of the batter with the back of a spoon. Or, when using muffin compartments, run a forefinger around the surface of each mound of batter. Use a gentle circular motion. Why? Whole grain batters, especially muffin batters, tend to be denser than those made with white flour and so they are more apt to clump. Smoothing before baking evens out the clumps.

In general, you will find that whole grain flours do not rise to give the familiar appearance of full-blown white flour bakings. Just compare the looks of a 100-percent whole wheat loaf with "balloon bread." So if you find your bakings seem a bit flatter or grainier, don't think something has gone wrong. It goes with the ingredients.

Trim: This is a more controversial procedure than one might suppose. Basically it means to pare or peel away the inedible portions of the food in question: to discard cores, corn silk, seeds, and so forth; to cut away discolorations, if you think they indicate aging or decay. The controversy involves how different people define *inedible.* Habits of vegetable washing and trimming can become matters of deep-seated conviction. The instruction to peel a potato, for instance, appalls me. The opposite command would have horrified my grandmothers to an equal extent. Therefore, I leave decisions about the fine points of trimming, washing, and scrubbing vegetables to you unless a specific procedure is critical for a particular recipe. Only then are instructions given in detail.

Until al dente: At al dente, pasta tastes just cooked. It still has some bite, and hasn't been reduced to a mush. The most reliable way to determine this is by sampling the pasta as it cooks. I've heard that some cooks throw pasta against a wall. When it is done, it sticks. Personally, I don't recommend this method unless you regularly feed your walls.

Until almost al dente: Testing by taste rather than by its adhesion to plaster also gives you a more reliable guide to "almost al dente," which means the pasta is underdone by a couple of minutes.

Until heated through: Sometimes you can tell at a glance whether this stage has been reached. If you are not sure, use a knife to swipe a taste from the edge of the pan (stick the knife all the way to the bottom). See what it registers on your tongue.

Until fork tender: We learn to use this test for doneness through experience as eaters, not only as cooks. Who hasn't had practice at sticking in a fork and noticing the give of a vegetable? *Tender* is a subjective term that signifies whatever you mean by ready to eat. Our family likes vegetables crisp; yours may prefer them softer. It's a matter of taste; however, a family's definition of "tender" can have nutritional implications (see Appendix I).

Until barely fork tender: This signifies a little more firmness than the vegetable would have when fully cooked.

Until the bottom browns: Lift the item in question completely out of the pan or high enough to take a look. Cooks are not required to have X-ray vision. As far as "golden" brown versus dark brown, go by your preference.

Until a tester comes out clean: For a tester, use a wooden toothpick, a clean length of broom straw, or a paring knife. Poke it into the center of the pan. Pull it out and examine it. The tester will be sticky or crumbs will adhere to it if the batter has not baked enough.

Until the surface springs back to the touch: Lightly press on the top of the baked item with a forefinger. When a visible indentation remains, more baking is needed. When no indentation is left or it closes rapidly, this is what is called *springing back.* In my early days as a baker, I looked for something more visibly athletic. This rather passive "springing" is easy to overlook. Other clues to look for include the cake pulling away from the sides of the pan and the absence of visible moist patches.

EQUIPMENT

The equipment you will need to prepare the recipes in this book falls into three categories: the food processor; other essentials; and optional equipment.

The Food Processor

Any model of food processor should produce acceptable results with the recipes in this book. There are jobs which high quality processors perform better than less expensive models, most notably kneading bread; thorough mixing of dense, sticky substances such as peanut butter; and grating Parmesan cheese (or other very hard cheeses) with a metal blade. Nonetheless, even these tough functions are possible in most models (none of the many models I have worked with have posed a problem), provided that the manufacturers' instructions are closely read and carefully followed.

Other Essentials

a good paring knife
a sturdy cleaver for chopping
a cutting board
accurate measuring spoons and cups
an oven thermometer
a rubber spatula
a metal spatula
assorted mixing bowls
a cake cooling rack
stainless steel pans with covers
skillets: 1 large, 1 small (preferably cast iron)
ovenproof baking dishes: at least 1 9-inch
    square, 1 pie pan, 1 2-quart casserole with
    cover (all preferably glass or earthenware)
1 loaf pan (8½″ × 4½″ × 2½″)
1 muffin pan, 3-inch-diameter compartments
a baking sheet

Optional Equipment

Other items that I find useful could be replaced with a little ingenuity or extra effort. Frankly, they are matters of style as well as convenience.

a serrated bread knife
an electric mixer
a swivel-blade vegetable peeler
a rolling pin
wax paper
biscuit cutters
a wire whisk
some wooden spoons
a slotted spoon
a tea strainer
a collander
plastic ice cube trays and plastic storage bags
a plastic funnel
a pillowcase (see page 43)
a cast-iron dutch oven
a double boiler
attractive bake-and-serve dishes, both large
    and those that hold individual servings
nonmetal airtight containers for storage in
    assorted sizes (glass jars are my top choice)
attractive jars to display and store grains and
    beans
an electric yogurt maker
sprouting containers

One unexpectedly useful gadget, a ⅛-cup measure, is not included in most sets of measuring cups but can be included as the smallest cup in your set of measures. It corresponds to 2 tablespoons.

2 | Natural Foods to Safeguard the Quality of Life

The longer you eat natural food, the more you appreciate how important it is to do so. The health effects are long term, with the more subtle benefits taking years to work their way to the surface.

How many people have you heard advocate junk food with the rationale, "I've been eating this way all my life"?

Such logic misses the essential point: the *quality* of life. Mere survival doesn't guarantee a fully human existence. In reality, every human being is born with astounding potential—for profound appreciation of knowledge and people, for vivid and delightful perception through the senses, for brilliant intelligence and boundless vitality, for fulfillment of spiritual aspirations.

Admittedly, diet alone will not bring about the fulfillment of life. Yet a balanced diet of natural food vastly increases the likelihood that you will use your potential.

Although health awareness is steadily increasing, too many people who consider themselves healthy are still walking around with undernourished bodies (not necessarily underweight) and perpetually irritated digestive systems. There is absolutely no excuse for it, not in our affluent nation. As the median age of our population shifts upward, more and more of us may voice the following sentiment, which I read once on a plaque in a health food store:

If I had known I would live this long, I would have taken better care of myself.

NATURAL INGREDIENTS

To be a little more specific about natural ingredients, I mean food free from preservatives, whole food that has not been unnecessarily refined. Natural ingredients are also the freshest foods possible, because many vitamins are lost otherwise.

All the recipes in this book have been designed to present food that enhances the overall quality of life. That includes preparing the food deliciously so that it will be a pleasure to eat.

How do these recipes promote a high quality of life?

Recipes are high in fiber. Roughage aids in digestion and may help prevent certain types of cancer. Fresh vegetables and fruit contribute fiber. So do unrefined grains. A high percentage of fiber is easily consumed with natural ingredients. Did you know that, on the average, vegetarians ingest three or four times as much fiber as nonvegetarians? The obvious explanation is that vegetarians tend to eat a higher proportion of fresh fruit, vegetables, and whole grains—the main sources of dietary fiber. You can do this too, even if you have no intention of becoming a vegetarian. Serve the meatless recipes in this collection however you like, alone or with filet mignon. Either way, you will be assured of plenty of dietary fiber.

Vitamins and minerals are conserved as much as possible, with the B vitamins running rampant. The complex of B vitamins is much harder to come by than most people realize and much more vital for physical and psychological health. These vitamins, in the right balance, are needed by every cell in the human body. Deficiencies have been linked with mental depression and stress, hypoglycemia, allergies, kidney malfunction, blemished skin, and arthritis.

In this book you will see occasional references to some of these vitamins. Not all of the names are instantly recognizable as B vitamins: thiamin, riboflavin, niacin, pantothenic acid.

Although the need for B vitamins has come to be fairly common knowledge, a very important aspect has gone virtually unpublicized. The B vitamins are a complex; they work together.

Natural foods such as brewer's yeast and wheat germ represent a rich and safe source of B vitamins, in many ways a better source than synthetic supplements. For instance, adding synthetic vitamin B$_1$ to white flour may seem like a step in the right direction, but it actually may constitute a step backward. When just a few of the B vitamins are furnished in large quantities, they increase the need for those not supplied. In other words, supplements of some B vitamins can cause a deficiency in others. Thus, a "part smart" approach to nutrition can produce worse results than indifference.

This creates quite a dilemma. Health-conscious individuals cannot ignore nutrition, but prudence dictates that they dare not be dilettantes either. So must everyone have a Ph.D. in food science? I think not. A diet of natural food, prepared according to the guidelines in this book or other reliable sources, can ensure nutritional balance without a lot of fuss.

Recipes are low in fat. According to the 1982 report of the American Heart Association, we should decrease our intake of fats. Today, 40 percent of the typical American's total daily calories comes from fats. For certain groups in society, such as businessmen, the percentage is even higher—50 percent or more, according to nutritionist Dr. Jean Mayer.

The heart association urges that the percentage be cut to 30 percent. Furthermore, it recommends a change in the ratio of saturated to unsaturated fat. Instead of the cholesterol-producing fats that come from animal products and hydrogenated fats (such as shortening), the association says we ought to be consuming more of the polyunsaturated products from vegetable, legume, and other nonanimal sources (such as corn, soy, and sunflower oils). It is worth noting that hydrogenation turns polyunsaturates into saturates. Generally speaking, you can identify a saturated fat by its solid consistency at room temperature.

The rationale for recommending polyunsaturates is that they counteract the production of cholesterol, which has been associated with hardening of the arteries.

At the same time, however, research has turned up reasons to apply health warnings to polyunsaturated fats as well. Studies have linked these fats to cancer and premature aging.

So butter and eggs are not necessarily any worse for you than safflower oil. One thing is certain, however. Hydrogenated fats have never been touted by medical experts as health foods. The hydrogenation process may give fats a longer shelf life, but it either destroys essential fatty acids or alters them into an unhealthful form.

Essential fatty acids, like the amino acids, are dietary requirements which much be supplied on an ongoing basis. The body cannot store them or synthesize them. These acids help form the membranes which are part of every cell in the human body. In addition, the acids are an important source of fat soluble vitamins E and A. Finally, the fatty acids work to form hormonelike compounds called Prostaglandins, which are involved in the inflammatory response and muscle contraction.

The saturated fats in my recipes come from dairy products, eggs, and a little optional margarine. Unsaturated fats come from cold-pressed oils.

Sweeteners are used conservatively. I have chosen to use brown sugar, because it contains more nutritive value than white sugar. Be aware, however, that the value still doesn't amount to much. Brown sugar is fortified with 11–13 percent molasses. It contains traces of some B vitamins, and small amounts of iron, calcium, phosphorus, and potassium. Honey has similar nutritional strengths—not overwhelming but better than white sugar which contains virtually no vitamins or minerals. Sugar is worse than empty calories because, like chocolate, digestion of it robs the body of B vitamins. Yet the typical consumption of white sugar for the average American exceeds 100 pounds each year. My recipes also use honey, a luscious food that nevertheless should not be consumed to excess, because it's still basically sugar.

Salt is used sparingly. Excesses of salt have been implicated in high blood pressure and kidney malfunction. All the dietary sodium we need can be obtained without adding any salt to our foods, yet the typical American overdoses to the extent of 10 times the necessary amount. That overdose represents a health hazard.

Fortunately, the passion for salt is largely a matter of habit. Cut down week by week and eventually you won't have to struggle over whether or not to reach for the shaker. The thought won't even occur to you.

In the interest of lower salt intake, recipes here are quite conservative. Add salt, if your taste demands. Later on, as the desire for salt ebbs, you may choose to dispense with even the small amounts of salt in the recipes.

Balance among the ingredients is all-important. In the baked recipes, for instance, you will find unusually low ratios of fat and sweetener to flour. Now that doesn't make Favorite Carrot Cake ideal for a reducing diet; cake is still cake. Instead, the idea is that if you're going to eat cake, why not make it a cake with the greatest possible nutritive value?

Cake can contribute protein, fiber, complex carbohydrates, minerals, and vitamins when ingredients include whole grain flour, eggs, milk, and even vegetables. In the typical cake made with refined products, the amount of grease and sugar, combined, exceeds the amount of flour. The nutrient density is very low.

Balance also refers to the calorie trade-off in recipes. These days just about everyone is calorie conscious, but many of us forget that watching what we eat has a purpose beyond weight control. Empty calories are no bargain.

The approach in this book is to choose foods with a high nutrient density per calorie, rather than to focus on the number of calories. Cottage cheese (at 260 calories per cup) is used more frequently than sour cream (464 calories per cup), but not only because of the lesser amount of calories. Sour cream derives most of its calories from fat. Each gram of protein "costs" 68 calories; each tenth of a milligram of niacin costs 227 calories. With cottage cheese the calorie trade-off is much more advantageous: 8 calories for a gram of protein, 130 for a tenth of a milligram of niacin, plus nutrients the sour cream doesn't even have—vitamins B_{12}, B_6, and iron.

Because of the importance of protein, amino acid complementarity has figured in recipe design. (For an explanation of protein combining, see Chapter 15.)

Carbohydrates used are complex, not refined.
The way in which grains are milled to make flour has become a subject of concern to consumers. Ground from the starchy inner portion of the wheat berry, white flour has lost more than its bulk. It has lost its protein, its vitamins, and its taste as well.

For starters, consider the loss in white flour of 98 percent of the manganese, 80 percent of the iron, 80 percent of the thiamin, 75 percent of the niacin, 50 percent of the pantothenic acid, and 50 percent of the calcium. Although, by current law, the white flour sold in our country must be enriched with synthetic vitamins, many nutrients are never restored, including manganese and essential amino acids.

The most useless white flour of all is the "all-purpose" product that has been chemically bleached. One questions what "purpose" the manufacturers had in mind. Isn't one of the major purposes of food supposed to be nourishment?

No food additives are used. Food additive scares have become a routine result of some laboratory experiments. Many of us are confused, wondering just how important it is to avoid what. Frustratingly, the evidence is not black and white, even for trained scientists.

Regarding preservatives in food, Americans might be wise to take a cue from the British, who have legally banned BHT on the basis of its harmful effects. Other research has linked MSG to brain damage, BVO to degeneration of the heart and testicles, and saccharin (as a sweetener) to cancer.

Recipes are meatless. Although Americans have traditionally thought of meat as the cornerstone of a healthful diet, attitudes are changing. Many scientific studies have shown large quantities of meat to be unnecessary for good health, and even detrimental.

I offer meatless menus exclusively, not to dictate the way you should eat, but to increase your choices. Many people who would like to experiment with occasional vegetarian meals don't know exactly how to start. If you would like some guidelines in this area, see Chapter 15, "Meatless Meals; Meatless Menus." My emphasis throughout this book, though, is on healthful (not *necessarily* vegetarian) cooking and eating. If you wish, you may even add meat to many of the flexible recipes. Please keep the quantities down, however, and watch out for hidden fats.

I do heartily encourage you to experiment with at least a few meatless meals each week—for your health and for your culinary enjoyment.

Care is taken to provide many recipes for a *recognizable main dish*. Why? When a steak or a piece of chicken is served on your plate, you know you've been given an entree—that's a satisfying sight. Even if you could get just as many nutrients from several side dishes, a main dish makes any meal, but particularly a meatless meal, seem more substantial.

The food processor has provided me with

considerable help in creating recipes that adhere to the criteria discussed above. For example, cottage cheese of the large curd variety, when pureed in the processor, functions as mayonnaise in some recipes, as cream in others. Even more surprising, cooked soybeans and chick-peas make marvelous thickeners with a high-protein bonus.

Experimenting with the processor, I have discovered some unconventional uses for broccoli, rice, artichokes, and many other foods. These uses are unusual in terms of cooking technique. The potential of natural food prepared with the processor is tremendously exciting. Imagine concocting a delicious candy based on pureed blanched almonds and turning it into a frosting at push-button speed.

SOME TIPS ON BUYING NATURAL INGREDIENTS

How sad it is that some people are afraid to change their eating habits because of the mistaken belief that healthy food costs more. Ironically, the knowledgeable natural food shopper pays less for better food. Natural food costs less because you don't have to pay as much for labor, machinery, packaging, advertising, and other corporate services. Plain whole wheat flour can be manufactured more easily than wheat derivatives sold separately, such as bleached, enriched white flour; wheat bran adulterated into a sugary breakfast cereal; and wheat germ. A simple loaf of commercial whole wheat bread often contains a host of chemical additives, a lot of unnecessary sweetening, and even white flour (rather than whole wheat) as the primary ingredient. Guess who pays for those unwanted extras? You can bake your own Daily Bread (see recipe) for less than half the price of commercial whole wheat breads.

If you shop wisely, you're bound to save. I'll summarize some shopping guidelines here.

It's important to realize that the best food does not invariably come from the health food store, any more than the best bargains come from the supermarket. It pays to comparison shop for quality, freshness, and cost. For example, you already know where to go for the best dairy products and eggs in your neighborhood, right? Unless you develop a hankering for raw milk products, no change in buying location is needed.

For fresh fruit and vegetables, the produce stand or supermarket is your best source, assuming that you don't have a garden in your backyard. Frozen ingredients can be used in emergencies, such as when you have a craving for corn in February. Since tomatoes are truly in season for a very short time, I consider canned tomato products worthwhile. But buy tomato juice and other products canned in glass rather than in metal. Tomatoes are acidic, and when stored in unlacquered cans, tin leaks into the food at a significant rate. A one-pound can of tomato sauce or juice could give you a hefty serving of tin—67,500 micrograms. High levels of dietary tin have been associated with gastrointestinal distress and have been found to disrupt the metabolism of calcium and zinc. Tomatoes canned in glass won't contain more than 1 microgram of tin.

The supermarket usually is also the best source for stone-ground whole wheat flour, fresh nuts, toasted wheat germ, and even legumes. But grains in today's average supermarket are unnecessarily refined (degermed cornmeal, bah!), so supply yourself from a health food store. You'll find more detailed information on beans and grains starting on page 52, on nonwheat flours starting on page 105. These could become major food discoveries for you.

The health food store or co-op is also the place to find cold-pressed oils (otherwise vegetable oils are filtered and bleached, losing nutrients and flavor). Really zingy cold-pressed oils include corn, wheat germ, and sunflower. Yet depending on the brand you purchase, some cold-pressed oils can taste just as innocuous as the supermarket varieties. If you get stuck with an insipid brand, you have one consolation. Sometimes low-profile oils can be an asset in a recipe; when they are preferable or acceptable I refer to them as salad oil. Sea salt, herbal teas (which can also be used as cooking herbs, peppermint being especially versatile), nutritional yeast (it comes as brewer's yeast and torula yeast—ask around for a brand with good taste and use that for cooking), seeds (including those for sprouting), soy nuts, blackstrap molasses, raw honey, and delicious carob flour are also available at the health food store or co-op. If you're lucky, you'll also find economical herbs, spices, and baking yeast.

Two valuable health food store finds are especially useful in some food processor recipes: lecithin and noninstant nonfat powdered milk. The former is sold as a nutritional supplement because it's supposed to aid in digestion of fats. However, you've probably been eating it for years. Lecithin is commonly added to commercially processed foods that contain fat, such as candy bars and cookies. It is probably used because it improves food texture, rather than for purposes of nutritional altruism, but you can use it for both reasons. Lecithin is sold in two forms. The liquid variety is excellent for "greasing" pans without oil (see page 4). The granular variety is used to improve food texture.

Two little known kinds of sweetener are used in some recipes. One sweetener, Hain's bottled Fruit Concentrate, can be found in a bevy of flavors at the health food store. Frozen juice concentrate is a common purchase, generally used as the start for orange juice, apple juice, and so forth, but you can also keep an opened, covered container in your freezer and use it undiluted as a sweetener. (Incidentally, another supermarket freezer juice is also an excellent product for convenience and economy—Minute Maid frozen lemon juice.)

Occasionally I also refer to some prepared seasonings: Dijon mustard and Liquid Smoke (from the supermarket), soy sauce (from the health food store), and vanilla extract (find Watkins brand if you can—it's reasonably priced, good quality—look in the Yellow Pages). I generally use cider vinegar. Unlike wine or white vinegars, where acetic acid predominates, cider vinegar gets its punch chiefly from malic acid. Therefore, it is much less harsh on the digestive system.

3 | Making the Most of Your Food Processor

Suppose that one day you went into your kitchen and discovered that someone had hired you an absolute treasure of a servant, a first-rate, precise, tireless helper—the equivalent of Lord Peter Wimsey's Bunter, or better.

Well, that's your food processor. Whatever brand and model you happen to own, I'm sure you have heard the manufacturer's claims about the wonders it can perform—vegetables chopped or shredded in seconds, perfect pastry at push-button speed, shorter preparation time with almost any recipe. You have heard that once you get used to using the processor, it becomes an indispensable time-saver.

All this is true. Yet as far as I'm concerned, the most important reason to use a food processor still hasn't been mentioned. What is the effect of food processor cooking on the cook?

Every cook is a decision maker. What distinguishes a first-rate cook from the rest is the quality of those decisions. For instance, at each step of a recipe a cook must evaluate to some degree: Are the ingredients prepared properly (vegetables cut to the right shape and so forth)? Are measurements exact? Does the texture need adjustment? Any final corrections of seasoning needed?

How good a decision can you make when you also have to work as a drudge? Spend an hour pushing pieces of carrot through a pesky grater and see how responsive you are to the niceties of carrot cake batter. Laboriously cut butter into flour, using a pastry blender or other antiquated equipment, and see how attentive you are to the fine points of pastry.

As much as some people like to cook, everyone's stamina has a limit. Often the last person to realize this is the cook. After several hours of continuous food preparation, or 15 minutes of drudgery, most cooks start to feel tired. Even if the cook isn't conscious of fatigue, impatience shows in the quality of decision making. Careless mistakes are made, corners

are cut that shouldn't be, a splendid finishing touch becomes a mediocre adjustment. Drudgery widens the gap between what a cook could be and is.

In contrast, imagine yourself in a setting where your culinary talents can really shine. Perhaps you are recognized as one of the greatest cooks in the world. Your kitchen staff has been chosen accordingly.

Cooking is different now. You have an idea for a recipe and give your sous chefs their orders. They carry out your instructions instantly. You supervise their work, making fine adjustments as needed. Using a minimum of effort and a maximum of skill, you produce real delicacies.

This is what happens when you cook with the food processor.

The rest of this chapter is devoted to food processor technique. Even if you already know how to use your processor, please read through Food Processor Tips and A Guide to Recipe Terms, on pages 17–18 and 4–7.

GETTING STARTED

Learn to identify the parts of the food processor. Start with the workbowl and lid, with its built-in feed tube. Because these parts of the machine are made of clear plastic, it is easy for you to see what is happening to the food, provided, of course, that you stop the machine first.

Find the plastic pusher, which in some models doubles as a measuring cup. Practice inserting the S-shaped metal blade, the shredding disc, the medium-thick slicing disc. All of these are standard equipment.

In some recipes you have the option of using the french fry disc. This is automatically supplied with many food processor models. Many other brands offer the disc as an option; I think you will find it a good investment.

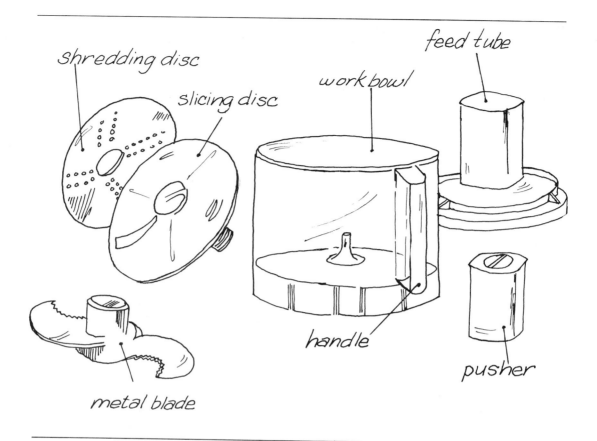

shredding disc

slicing disc

workbowl

feed tube

handle

pusher

metal blade

Before you operate the machine it is very important to learn the safety rules for your model. Read through the instruction manual that came with your machine. Memorize all safety instructions and follow them.

Also learn by heart the capacity of your machine. Overflowing loads are messy and wasteful. Loads should always be sized to your machine; break down batches into smaller sizes if necessary.

To help you visualize machine capacity, insert the metal blade and add the quantity of water that corresponds to your machine's capacity for dry ingredients. Look at the level on the workbowl and memorize it. Even better, mark the level inconspicuously with a dot of nail polish. Repeat for liquid capacity.

Now, let's start to use the machine. Anyone new to the processor should master basic technique before tackling a food processor recipe. The prospect may seem formidable at first—those blades are sharp, and everything moves very fast. Be assured, though, that you can get used to it.

Why not become an expert right now? Equip yourself with several pounds of carrots, about half an hour of time, and the following instructions. Afterward you can make Simply

Carrot Soup·or an outrageous multitextured carrot salad.

Basically, there are two different ways to use the food processor, and the language in this book reflects this. While many people use the word *process* to mean anything done with the food processor, I always use it to indicate *use of the metal blade.* The second way to use the machine is *to push food through one of the discs.*

PROCESSING FOOD WITH THE METAL BLADE

Two things matter when instructions say to use the metal blade: how long to run the machine and how you put the ingredients into the workbowl. For instance, you will discover that carrots cut into one-inch pieces process more uniformly than pieces of assorted size. And the texture of the food will determine what processing really does to the food. Solid food gets chopped. Liquids get mixed. Powdered food (such as flour) gets sifted.

For now, start with solid food. Trim a couple of carrots and cut them into one-inch chunks. Transfer them to the workbowl. Put on the lid and place the plastic pusher in the feed tube.

To process the carrots, turn on the machine and let it run. After about 15 seconds, turn it off. Repeat until you feel comfortable with processing. Experiment with 10-second and 5-second processings.

Next, pulse the machine. A *pulse* indicates the minimum amount of time that the machine can run. Some models come with a special control for pulsing. With other models, pulse by turning the machine on, then immediately off. Repeat until you have the idea.

When processed or pulsed, solid ingredients such as carrots are chopped to progressive degrees the longer the machine is on. The stages solid ingredients reach are *coarsely chopped, chopped medium fine,* and *minced.* There is a second, parallel progression with liquids, soft moist ingredients (such as berries), or combinations of solid and liquid ingredients (such as cake batters): *barely mixed,* to *uniform,* and in some, but not all, cases to *smooth.*

Whether ingredients will be chopped or mixed, the progression of processing can be compared to a train ride taken with a one-way ticket. When you miss your stop you find it impossible to backtrack. And the process works so fast that it's easy to go too far. Pause long enough to drink a glass of water, for instance, and your veggies could be chopped all the way to San Francisco instead of Des Moines.

In fact, the single biggest problem that people have in using the food processor is adjusting to its speed. Physical coordination helps. It isn't necessary, however, to be an Olympic-caliber athlete.

Mostly, I suspect, the problem of overprocessing has to do with the cook's expectations. This is where it can help to think of the food processor as an uncommonly talented assistant.

The instruction "Chop this cup of mushrooms" means five seconds of Bunter's time. Admittedly this job would take 10 minutes or longer with the old-fashioned method using a knife and cutting board. Even 1 minute of processor chopping will mean disaster (an unsalvagable brownish puree).

When you're not used to such efficiency, it can require some adjustment, but it's a pleasure to cope with this kind of problem.

REMOVING FOOD AFTER PROCESSING

1. Make sure the processor has come to a complete stop.
2. Take off the lid.

Now you have a choice. In most cases, the best method is to remove the metal blade first, then take out the food. Sometimes, when working with liquid ingredients, it is more convenient to keep the metal blade in place with one hand while, with the other hand, you tilt the workbowl so that the mixture can pour out. (To get the last few drops, go back to the first method.)

Try the standard method with your processed carrots. Return them to the workbowl and remove them with the alternate method.

Congratulations! You have now processed your first food.

PUSHING FOOD THROUGH THE DISCS

The purpose of using different discs is to cut food into various shapes. As you would expect, the slicing disc, shredding disc, french fry disc, and other optional discs all produce different results.

The possibilities just begin here, however. Other factors that affect the results are the way you stack the feed tube, the shape of the ingredients before you push them through, and the internal structure of the food (e.g., compare layered foods like onions to solid foods like carrots).

After you get the hang of this you may feel like a magician. Meanwhile, let's start with the basic method for using the discs.

Cut your remaining carrots into two- to three-inch lengths. Insert the slicing disc. Put the cover in place. Now insert the carrots into the feed tube.

You packed them in upright, didn't you? That's the easiest way to go about it. Unless instructions in this book say otherwise, food to be pushed through the discs should always be placed in the feed tube in a vertical position.

Now that the machine is set up, turn it on. Guide the carrots down with the pusher. When the food meets the disc it gets cut and falls into the workbowl. Once the feed tube is empty, turn off the machine.

To remove the carrots, remove the lid and lift out the disc. Either spoon out the carrots or detach the workbowl from the base of the machine and upend the bowl so that the food falls out.

Before you continue to practice, here are a couple of tips.

Fine Points of Packing the Feed Tube

For the most uniform results, the feed tube should be packed quite full. It is more important for pieces to fill the width of the tube rather than to stand tall. Cut lengths of food short, if necessary. Otherwise food wobbles as it chugs its way down, so that it is slanted by the time it hits the blade. With the shredding disc, this makes little difference. With the other discs, however, good packing is vital for precision cutting.

Pressure

Some cooks make an issue of how much pressure to exert when pushing food through the discs. I believe, however, that the matter is overemphasized. As a beginner, just don't force the machine to the point where you jam it. (If this happens, release pressure immediately.) Simply strive for an amount of pressure that feels natural. Usually that means less than you think. Remember, the pusher serves as a guide, not as a hammer.

As your expertise grows, you may experiment with using more pressure for slightly thinner slices, less for slightly thicker slices. With the shredding or french fry discs, always use a comfortable degree of pressure.

What about Strays?

Occasionally, when using the discs, you will find that a small amount of food gets wedged on top of a disc. (This is especially apt to happen if the feed tube has not been packed properly.) Since this stray food never gets pushed through the disc, it does not end up having the same shape as the other pieces. Many cooks unthinkingly throw such rejects away.

Belonging as I do to the "waste not, want not" school, I think it's worth mentioning that these scraps of food can be salvaged. Perform a little quick surgery with a paring knife and cutting board. Usually the scraps can be trimmed so they fit in with the rest.

Back to pushing carrots through the discs. Practice with the slicing disc, shredding disc, and (if you have one) french fry disc.

What happens in each case? The slicing disc gives you a cross section of the shape it cuts. For example, an upright carrot turns into circles (or discs). The shredding disc gives you shreds. For an upright carrot it is cutting against the grain, so the shreds are short. The french fry disc gives you shards of carrot cut crosswise. More unpredictably shaped pieces come from a layered food such as onions. For illustrations, see page 17.

Variations on Pushing Food through the Discs

Pack Sideways and Push Through

To produce a different effect, insert the carrots horizontally into the feed tube. The tube need only be three-quarters full. Turn on the machine and guide the food down with the pusher.

What happens? The slicing disc gives you a cross section, as usual, but this horizontally cut carrot turns into wedges. The shredding disc gives you longer shreds, because now it cuts along the grain. The french fry disc provides longer matchstick pieces. From this angle, the pieces actually are shaped like french-fried potatoes.

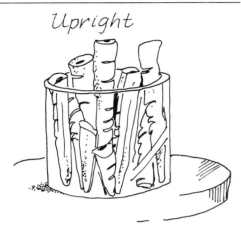

Upright

discs:
slicing   *shredding*   *french fry*

Sideways

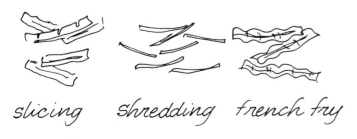

slicing   *shredding*   *french fry*

Push through Chunks, Quarters, and So Forth

Sometimes recipes ask you to cut the food in a certain way before pushing it through a disc. Sometimes a particular shape is specified (e.g., apple quarters). When no particular shape is specified the idea is just to cut food into pieces small enough to fit into the feed tube.

Whenever you push through a piece of vegetable or fruit with skin on one side, stack pieces in the feed tube so that the skin faces the back of the machine (the motor). You'll get a cleaner cut. Experiment with eggplant, cucumber, and apple.

FOOD PROCESSOR TIPS

- Whenever you work with flour batters or doughs, be especially careful not to overprocess. For a light touch, be stingy with processing time.
- Nuts gum up unless you start with a scrupulously dried workbowl and blade.
- All dry mixtures—pastry dough, flour to be sifted, etc.—also gum up, but to a lesser extent.
- The texture of cheese can suffer. Aside from starting off with a dry machine, it is also good to begin your chopping with pulses before you process for several continuous seconds—kind of a running start for the machine.

  Very hard cheese, such as Parmesan, should only be minced, and only with the metal blade. Cut it into one-inch cubes first.

  Medium-hard cheese, such as cheddar, can be either shredded or minced.

  Softer cheese, such as mozzarella, should be put into the freezer for five minutes before machine grating. Then use the shredding disc.

- The softer the texture of what you chop, the more careful you must be not to overprocess. Beware of turning mushrooms into mush, pickles into brine. Pulse; don't process continuously. And don't even attempt to chop ripe avocado unless you're aiming for a puree; use a knife instead.
- Here's a dramatic example of the effect of the shape of food before processing: chopping hard-boiled eggs. For best results, cut three eggs in half lengthwise, place in the workbowl, and pulse a few times. That way the pieces of egg come out quite uniform and attractively sized. In contrast, whole eggs process into a hodgepodge of

fragments, ranging from partially slashed ovals to unprepossessing crumbs—a pretty cruel fate for a good egg.

- To keep dates from getting gooey, either pulse them with flour or pulse them into an already smooth mixture (see Date Nut Spread).

- Don't try to mash cooked potatoes, sweet potatoes, or yams with the metal blade. Their starch turns into unimaginable glue. For a workable method, see Mashed Potato Mashterpiece.

- Good news: butter and cream cheese don't have to be softened to room temperature to process them smooth (otherwise known as creaming). If presoftened, they may even spatter, so use them straight from the refrigerator.

- To make julienne green beans, trim them and load sideways into the feed tube. Push through once. You'll find many uses for julienned beans when cutting them is so easy.

- Thanks to the food processor, beets are neat. Just be sure to leave each beet root with about six inches of stem. Cook or parboil as desired. Then hold beets under cold running water. Cut off the stem at one end and the button at the other end. Skins pare off easily.

  Beets can then be pushed through the shredding, french fry, or slicing disc. Once you don't have to worry about ruining your clothes, this brightly colored vegetable becomes wonderfully versatile.

- I have had the best results with the following foods when using an old-fashioned knife:

  tomatoes

  green peppers (unless they are raw and being processed into a dressing; see Smiling Succotash)

  melons

  strawberries or other very soft fruit (unless they are being processed into a mixture; see Strawberry Tingle)

4 | Baking with Confidence

Why on earth do people buy mixes for baking? I've wondered about this many times while walking by all the packaged products in the supermarket. There is plenty of time to reflect, since there are shelves full of boxes for instant cake and quick breads, freezers full of cookie dough rolls and heat-and-serve ready-mades. I've considered the pros: promises of time saved, simple preparation, interesting flavors. I've kept coming back to the cons: white flour and other nutritionally inferior ingredients, artificial flavors, and extra cost.

Eventually I concluded that the best thing about mixes is that they give the cook confidence. If someone feels hesitant about baking from scratch, a few packaged ingredients might provide a feeling of security.

Well, why not have the time-saving feature of convenience food and the low price and freshness of homemade? That's why I developed Confidence, an all-purpose, whole grain baking mix.

CONFIDENCE MIX

Because it is natural food, with fresh wheat germ in the flour and no preservatives, this mix will not stay fresh forever. I recommend that you mix up only what you will be able to use in a couple of months. Store Confidence in an airtight container in the coolest place that is convenient (including the refrigerator, but refrigeration is not necessary).

3½ cups whole wheat flour
½ cup toasted wheat germ
¼ teaspoon salt
4 teaspoons baking powder

With a dry workbowl and metal blade, process 15 seconds. Scrape down. Repeat until uniform. Store airtight in a cool place.

Yield: 4 cups

IMPROVISING WITH CONFIDENCE

To the creative cook, baking can seem like a stifling exercise in leveling measurements. Where is the opportunity to throw in a pinch of this or a smidgen of that?

It seems discouraging that proportion is the name of the baking game. All it takes is a few disasters to persuade you that *any* kind of improvisation in baking is a risk.

Well, it is true that some elements of baker's recipes must remain fixed for dependable results: flour, leavening, shortening, sweetener, liquid. But flavorings and other additions can successfully be added and combined according to your own original ideas.

Consult Framework for Improvisation (Table 1) for guidelines on how to add to baked goods in proportion. Then look at individual recipes for specific instructions.

Due to the variability of whole wheat flour, as well as texture properties in some of the additions, you can expect to find different degrees of moistness in some batters. An experienced baker will note if a batter appears somewhat dry. Pulse in small amounts of the liquid used in the recipe (usually milk). Conversely, an overmoist batter can be corrected by adding a bit more wheat germ or Confidence. If you aren't an experienced baker, don't fuss with batters at all; you still should get a satisfactory product.

Table 1 lists ingredients that I have had success in using. Blank space is left on this chart (and others like it throughout this book) so that you can experiment with your favorite ingredients and then record the results for future reference.

Because of the complex properties of food, you may not find that all your experiments succeed. For instance, orange juice concentrate doesn't just sweeten baked goods; it also densifies them, sometimes changing the texture in a way you may not find appealing.

How can you keep yourself from adding clunkers to your table? First test how your ingredient works in one Confidence recipe. If the experiment succeeds, record on the table exactly what you added. If a unit of sweet additions works when you make muffins, there's no reason it shouldn't do exactly the same thing for cakes. That's the value of learning how to improvise with Confidence.

Ⓕ CONFIDENCE PANCAKES

For one of my cooking classes, I had students compare these pancakes with pancakes made from a commercial mix (the nation's best-seller, according to the package). The experiment may be worth repeating in your kitchen to introduce your family to the difference between many commercial foods and home-processed natural food.

The cotton-candy-like pancake did taste good to most people, but the whole grain product had a more distinctive flavor and a more interesting texture. I think one man said it best: "The Confidence kind has character."

1¼ **cups Confidence**
1 **egg**
1 **tablespoon salad oil**
1 **cup milk**
Optional: ½ **unit of chewy addition (page 22)**

Prepare Confidence mix, if you don't already have some on hand. Processor sift and set aside.

Prepare any chewy addition that must be chopped. Set aside.

Process the egg, oil, and milk until smooth. Pulse in the other ingredients until barely mixed.

Heat a heavy skillet over medium heat until water dropped on the surface spatters. If well-seasoned cast iron is used, it is not necessary to oil the cooking surface.

Drop the batter onto the skillet by ⅛-cup measures. When bubbles begin to appear on the surface of the pancakes, flip them over with a metal spatula. When the bottoms brown, the pancakes are done.

Yield: a dozen pancakes

- To keep them hot you may choose to stack the cooked pancakes on a plate, wrapped in a cloth napkin, and serve the whole batch at once.
- Whole grain pancakes hold up relatively well when frozen, so if you have leftover batter, cook the pancakes anyway. Wrap leftovers airtight in plastic and stick them in the freezer. Thaw in the oven or toaster or at room temperature—they make good snacks.

- For blueberry pancakes, wash and trim fresh berries. (Individually frozen berries, thawed to room temperature, can also be used.) Have them handy while you cook the pancakes. Just before you turn over each one, position 6–8 berries on the surface. Then flip the pancake for final cooking.
- Do not use a chewy addition when making blueberry pancakes.

Ⓕ BUTTERMILK PANCAKES

These are the lightest whole wheat pancakes you've ever tasted.

1¼ **cups Confidence**
¼ **teaspoon baking soda**
1 **tablespoon salad oil**
1 **cup buttermilk or Instantly Soured Milk (see box)**
Optional: ½ **unit of chewy addition (page 22)**

When you *processor sift* the Confidence (after initial processing to prepare the mix), include the baking soda. Otherwise prepare exactly as for regular Confidence Pancakes.

Yield: a dozen pancakes

Instantly Soured Milk—A substitute for buttermilk in baking.

For each cup soured milk needed, place one tablespoon lemon juice or cider vinegar in a one-cup measure. Add enough fresh milk to fill the measure. Let the mixture stand 15 minutes before using.

TABLE 1: FRAMEWORK FOR IMPROVISATION WITH CONFIDENCE

Sweet Additions

1 unit equals any one of the following:

½ **cup raisins or currants**
½ **cup dates or dried apricots***
1 **cup grated carrot**
1 **cup grated zucchini**
½ **cup grated raw apple**
Substitute apple cider for milk
½ **cup pureed cooked apple****
½ **cup pureed cooked winter squash****
½ **cup pureed cooked chestnuts****
½ **cup pureed soaked apricots****

My Discoveries:

_____

*Measure, then chop by pulsing with the Confidence needed for that recipe. Set the fruit and flour aside, to add when indicated in the recipe.
**Process 10 seconds. Scrape down. Repeat. If necessary, add water, 1 tablespoon at a time, until the mixture is smooth.

Chewy Additions

1 unit equals any one of the following:

½ **cup coarsely chopped walnuts, pecans, cashews, hazelnuts, almonds, or brazil nuts. Almonds and hazelnuts may be blanched before chopping. For stronger flavor, pan roast all nuts except brazil nuts.***
½ **cup sesame seeds or sprouts**
½ **cup sunflower seeds or sprouts**
⅓ **cup sunflower meal**
2 **teaspoons poppy seeds**
½ **cup grated coconut**
½ **cup Grape Nuts cereal**

My Discoveries:

_____

*Measure nutmeats, then pulse with the Confidence needed for that recipe until coarsely chopped. Set nuts and flour aside, to add when indicated in the recipe.

Flavoring Additions

1 unit equals any of the following:

1 **teaspoon vanilla extract**
½ **teaspoon lemon extract + 2 teaspoons grated orange or lemon zest (counts as 2 units)**
1 **teaspoon grain coffee or instant coffee (or however much is required for 1 cup brewed coffee)**
1 **teaspoon ginger**
½ **teaspoon cinnamon + ½ teaspoon nutmeg + ¼ teaspoon allspice**
½ **teaspoon ginger + ½ teaspoon cinnamon**
¼ **teaspoon cinnamon + ⅛ teaspoon powdered clove + ¼ teaspoon nutmeg**
¼ **cup carob flour + 1 tablespoon water + 2 teaspoons salad oil**
Substitute coconut milk for liquid*
Substitute medium-brewed, well-strained peppermint tea for liquid*

My Discoveries:

_____

*If the recipe contains buttermilk, do not use this option

Ⓔ CONFIDENCE WAFFLES

Any waffles are a treat for the tongue, with all those nooks and crannies. Nutritionally, though, they should amount to more than a resting place for syrup. Compare the ingredients of Confidence Waffles with what goes into commercially packaged or frozen waffles.

1½ **cups Confidence**
½ **teaspoon baking soda**
2 **eggs**
1¾ **cups buttermilk**
½ **cup salad oil**
Optional: ½ **unit of chewy addition**
Optional: 1 **unit of flavoring addition**
Optional (for a dessert waffle): ½ **unit of sweet addition—but do not use a substitute for the buttermilk.**

Prepare Confidence mix, if you don't already have some on hand. Processor sift with the baking soda and set aside.

Prepare any chewy addition that must be chopped.

Separate the eggs. Process the yolks for 15 seconds. Add the buttermilk and oil. Add the optional flavoring addition if desired. Process smooth. Distribute the Confidence and optional additions over the top and pulse in.

In a grease-free bowl, preferably made of copper, beat the egg whites until they form stiff peaks. Use a gentle, circular motion to fold the batter into the egg whites. Do not overmix; bits of egg white should be visible in the batter.

Cook in a waffle iron, according to manufacturer's directions.

Yield: Approximately 5 round waffles with a 7-inch diameter

- For a delicious open-faced sandwich, shred enough cheddar cheese to top a waffle generously. Heat on a baking sheet in a 350° F. oven until the cheese melts.

CONFIDENCE BISCUITS

Confidence biscuits aren't just for butter. Split them in half and fill them with sandwich spreads or serve them split and topped with hot steamed vegetables and your favorite sauce.

Whole grain biscuits have more substance and flavor than their white flour counterparts. If you especially prize lightness in a biscuit, be sure to try the buttermilk version that follows.

2 cups Confidence
¼ cup frozen butter, cut into 4 pieces
⅔ cup cold milk
Additional milk as needed

Preheat oven to 425° F.

Prepare Confidence mix, if you don't already have some on hand. Processor sift, and then pulse in the butter by processing 3 seconds and then stopping, repeating for a total of 5 or 6 times. Scrape down the bottom of the workbowl

and check to see that the mixture is uniformly granular. If not, do a couple more 3-second processings and check again. Repeat as needed.

Pour in the milk and pulse twice. Scrape down. Pulse again.

Turn the dough out onto wax paper or a floured surface and knead it with a few strokes. If the dough is too dry to form a ball, sprinkle additional milk, a tablespoon at a time, on top. Repeat as needed. Avoid overworking the dough or producing a dough too sticky to handle. If the dough gets too sticky, add a little more flour.

Roll out the dough. Now comes the fun—you must choose the size, thickness, and shape of the biscuits. Thicker dough (½ inch) produces fluffier biscuits; thinner dough (¼ inch) makes crunchier ones.

For a round shape, cut the dough with a biscuit cutter or the rim of a drinking glass. In one batch of biscuits you may vary the diameter of the circles; in fact, circles of several different sizes can add eye-catching variety to your breadbasket. Be careful, though, to make all biscuits the same thickness if not the same size, so that baking time remains constant.

Easier and quicker than circles are squares or diamonds. Use a long knife to cut the dough into 2-inch strips. Cut 2- or 3-inch lengths from these strips.

Remember to make clean cuts. When edges are sawed back and forth, biscuits cannot rise properly.

If you have a few dough scraps left over, the simplest thing to do is to roll them into circles between your palms and flatten them to the desired thickness.

Transfer cut biscuits to an oiled cookie sheet (using a metal spatula can help). Bake on the middle rack until the bottoms brown. (For ¼-inch-thick biscuits, check after 10 minutes. For ½-inch-thick biscuits, check after 12 minutes.)

Yield: 15 biscuits (thick dough), 30 biscuits (thin dough)

BUTTERMILK BISCUITS

2 cups Confidence
¼ teaspoon baking soda
¼ cup frozen butter, cut into 4 pieces
⅔ cup buttermilk, more as needed

Processor sift the Confidence (after initial processing), adding the baking soda. Otherwise prepare exactly the same way as Confidence Biscuits.

- Whichever biscuit recipe you use, and whether you cut round or square shapes, make clean cuts. When edges are sawed back and forth, biscuits cannot rise properly.

Yield: 15 biscuits (thick dough), 30 biscuits
    (thin dough)

Ⓕ CONFIDENCE MUFFINS

Bran muffins don't have a monopoly on natural fiber. Any way you improvise with Confidence Muffins, you'll be adding bulk to your diet when you serve them.

2 cups Confidence
4 tablespoons butter (substitute margarine)
1 tablespoon corn oil (substitute other salad oil)
1 egg
1 cup milk
Optional: **1 unit flavoring addition**
Optional: **1 unit chewy addition**

Preheat oven to 400° F.
Prepare Confidence mix, if you don't already have some on hand. Processor sift and set aside. Prepare any chewy addition that must be chopped. Set aside.
Process butter and oil for 10 seconds. Scrape down. Repeat until smooth. Add the egg, half the milk, and any optional flavoring addition. Process smooth.
Add all remaining ingredients. Pulse until barely mixed.
Transfer into oiled muffin tins, filling them two thirds full. Bake on the middle rack until a tester comes out clean (check after 18 minutes). Cool on a rack.

My favorite Confidence muffin so far is flavored with cinnamon, cloves, and nutmeg.

Yield: at least 10 muffins

Ⓕ CONFIDENCE QUICK BREAD

This is quick to mix and also quick to disappear from the plate.
When you use a moist sweet addition, such as pureed apple, the texture is on the moist side. Otherwise the quick bread has a crumbly texture. I prefer the latter; in fact, my favorite version so far has just two flavoring addition units of ginger. The resulting loaf is reminiscent of graham crackers.

3 cups Confidence
½ teaspoon baking soda
2 eggs
⅓ cup corn oil (substitute salad oil)
⅓ cup honey
⅔ cup buttermilk
2 units flavoring addition
Optional: **1 additional unit of flavoring, for a stronger flavor (If you combine 2 different flavorings, be careful in making your selection.)**
Optional: **sweet and chewy additions to total 3 units (but do not substitute for buttermilk)**

Preheat oven to 350° F.
Prepare Confidence mix, if you don't already have some on hand. Processor sift with the baking soda. Set aside in a large mixing bowl.
Prepare any additions that must be chopped or pureed. Set aside.
Process the eggs for 10 seconds. Add the oil, honey, buttermilk, any other liquid additions or flavoring extracts, and any spices. Process smooth. Pulse in the chopped or pureed additions.
Pour this mixture over the Confidence. If there are any remaining additions, add them to the bowl. Stir with a fork until barely mixed.
Transfer to an oiled 8½″ × 4½″ × 2½″ loaf pan and bake on the middle rack until a tester comes out clean (check after 45 minutes). Let the loaf cool in the pan 15 minutes, then loosen sides with a knife and remove to cool on a rack.
If a shinier crust is desired, after placing the loaf on a rack, rub top and sides with butter.

Yield: 1 loaf

F CONFIDENCE COOKIES

*These are hearty, wholesome snacks.
Because of the healthful ingredients, we'd like to
see plain Confidence cookies replace sugar
cookies as a cookie jar tradition.*

2 cups Confidence
¼ cup corn oil (substitute salad oil)
½ cup honey
**½ cup milk (or use peppermint tea or apple
    cider, counting it as your second optional
    flavoring addition)**
1 unit flavoring addition
Optional: **a second flavoring addition**
Optional: **1 unit chewy addition or ½ cup raisins**

Preheat oven to 375° F.
Prepare Confidence mix, if you don't already
have some on hand. Processor sift (after regular
processing) and set aside. Prepare any chewy
addition that must be chopped. Set aside.

Process the oil, honey, milk, and flavoring
addition(s) for 10 seconds. Pulse in the
Confidence and optional chewy addition until
barely mixed.

Drop by ⅛-cup measures onto an oiled cookie
sheet, 2 inches apart. Bake on the middle rack
of the oven until the bottoms brown (check after
13 minutes). Remove from pan and cool on a
rack.

My favorite Confidence cookie so far has
coconut and is flavored with vanilla and ginger.

Yield: 18 cookies or more

F CONFIDENCE CAKE

*Cakes made without white flour or white
sugar have a chewier crumb. The flavor is subtly
sweet. People often find that they feel more
satisfied after eating a cake made with whole
grain flour. It has more of a "stick to your ribs"
heartiness.*

2 cups Confidence
⅓ cup butter (substitute margarine)
½ cup brown sugar, packed
2 eggs
¾ cup milk
1 unit flavoring addition

Optional: **a second unit of flavoring addition**
Optional: **up to 2 units sweet or chewy additions
    (but not 2 units of the same item, e.g., do use
    1 cup carrots + ½ cup coconut; don't use 2
    cups carrots)**

Preheat oven to 375° F.
Prepare Confidence mix, if you don't already
have some on hand. Processor sift (after regular
processing). Set aside.

Prepare any additions that must be chopped,
grated, or pureed. Set aside.

Cream together butter and sugar. Process 10
seconds and scrape down. Repeat until the
mixture is uniform.

Add eggs, milk, and flavoring addition(s) one
at a time. Process each 10 seconds and scrape
down. Repeat until the mixture is uniform.

Distribute over the mixture any sweet or
chewy addition(s) and the Confidence. Pulse
until barely mixed.

Transfer the batter to oiled and floured
pan(s). You can use one 8″ × 8″ × 2″ or 9″ × 9″ ×
2″ layer for a square cake, or 1 round 9-inch
layer, or two 8-inch round pans for a layer cake
(in which case you must double the recipe,
preparing it in 2 batches to avoid overloading
the processor). Bake on the middle rack of the
oven until a tester comes out clean (check after
25 minutes for a square or 1-layer cake; check
after 17 minutes for 2 round 8-inch layers.

Allow the cake to cook in the pan for 10–15
minutes. Then loosen edges with a knife and
invert onto a rack to cool completely.

Frosting of square cakes is optional. If you do
frost, be sure the cake is completely cool. It may
be refrigerated or frozen before frosting. Before
applying the frosting, brush off all loose crumbs.

My favorite Confidence cake so far uses 2
coffee flavoring additions and a sweet addition
of chopped dates.

My favorite Confidence layer cake is flavored
with coconut and vanilla, filled with Papaya
Delight Cake Filling (see Index) and frosted with
Pineapple Flexible Frosting (see Index).

Yield: 1 square or round 1-layer cake
    or half of a 4-layer cake

Note: The 2 round layers produced from 1 batch
of Confidence are thin, so for a festive layer
cake, prepare a second batch of batter.
Assemble the 4 layers into 1 cake.

- Whole wheat-based cakes are not going to be as high as white flour ones. For a higher cake use any or all of the three following methods. They are listed in increasing order of additional time required.

1. Add an extra egg to the batter.

2. Be especially sure to start baking with all ingredients at room temperature.

3. Use a more elaborate method of mixing: Separate the eggs. Beat the whites until stiff peaks form.
   Process egg yolks into the butter and brown sugar. Pulse the Confidence into this mixture. Add the sweet or chewy addition(s) at this time.
   Gently fold the batter into the egg whites. Do not overmix. Little patches of egg white should be visible in the final batter.

F CONFIDENCE BANQUET CAKE

If you need a huge cake for a special occasion, this is the ticket.

3 cups Confidence
½ cup butter, cut into 8 pieces
¾ cup brown sugar
⅓ cup corn oil
3 eggs
1¼ cups milk
2 or 3 units flavoring addition
***Optional*: up to 3 units chewy addition (but not more than 2 units of the same item; e.g., do use 1 or 2 cups carrots + ½ cup coconut, but don't use 3 cups carrots)**

Preheat oven to 375° F.
Prepare Confidence mix, if you don't already have some on hand. Processor sift (after regular processing). Set aside in a large mixing bowl.
Prepare any additions that must be chopped, grated, or pureed. Set aside.
Cream together butter and sugar by processing 10 seconds; scrape down. Repeat until uniform. Add oil and eggs and process 10 seconds. Scrape down, then add milk and flavoring additions.

Stir this mixture into the Confidence just until mixed. Quickly stir in any additions until mixed. Transfer to an oiled 13½″ × 8½″ × 2″ pan and bake on the middle rack until a tester comes out clean (check after 25 minutes).

Yield: 1 large layer cake

F CONFIDENCE CUPCAKES

Cupcakes give you a chance to decorate really creatively. If you frost with Flexibility (see Index), you can easily create an assortment of little cakes with icings that taste (not just look) different.

1½ cups Confidence
2 tablespoons butter (substitute margarine)
⅔ cup brown sugar, packed
1 egg
¼ cup corn oil (substitute salad oil)
½ cup milk
1 flavoring addition
***Optional*: a second unit of flavoring addition for stronger flavor (If you combine 2 different flavorings, be careful in making your choice.)**
***Optional*: 1 unit sweet or chewy addition**

Preheat oven to 375° F.
Prepare Confidence mix, if you don't already have some on hand. Processor sift (after regular processing). Set aside.
Prepare any additions that must be chopped or pureed. Set aside.
Process butter and sugar for 10 seconds. Scrape down. Repeat until uniform. Add egg, oil, milk, and flavoring addition(s). Process 10 seconds. Scrape down. Repeat until smooth.
Distribute the Confidence and any sweet or chewy addition over this mixture. Pulse until barely mixed.
Transfer batter to fill oiled and floured muffin compartments two thirds full. Bake on the middle rack until a tester comes out clean (check after 20 minutes). Remove from the pan and cool thoroughly on a rack before frosting.
My favorite Confidence cupcakes so far are apricot, with vanilla flavoring and Peanut Butter Frosting (see Index).

Yield: at least 9 cupcakes

5 | Spreads and Dressings

Fats are great combiners. They add richness to taste, body to texture, and gloss to appearance. No one wants to cook à la greasy spoon, of course. The trick is to use as little fat as necessary.

A food processor can help you get maximum effect from oil and butter because, in its own way, it also is a great combiner. Incorporate oil thoroughly into a recipe and you will need much less of it.

All the recipes in this chapter feature fats used for maximum effectiveness. If you have a processor, there is no reason *not* to save money by preparing staples such as Unadulterated Mayonnaise, Butterstretchers, and Peanut Butter. The recipes for these foods are included at the start of this chapter, but the real purpose of the chapter is to introduce you to lesser-known conveniences: fats combined with nutritious ingredients to form spreads. In turn, each spread can be adapted in seconds to become a distinctive salad dressing.

Spread recipes have been scaled to the smallest possible quantity. This is to facilitate error-free small servings, for it is safer to multiply in cooking than to divide.

These tiny batches also show off one of the advantages of the processor: waste is eliminated thanks to easy removal from the workbowl. Compare what happens when you try to get a small batch of dense food out of a blender. Most of these spreads couldn't even be made in a blender, much less quickly removed.

Should you prefer to make a large batch, scale it up according to the yield you desire. To do this, multiply the whole set of recipe ingredients up to four times—but measure precisely; the balance of ingredients is critical to these spreads.

Many of the recipes may surprise you with their versatility. If your initial reaction is that spreads are only for sandwiches, think again:

- Hearty salads can be created with spreads rather than dressings. Several examples are given in Chapter 7.
- For a festive application of spreads, try using them as stuffings. Team up spicy spreads with mushroom caps, large or cherry tomatoes (slice off the top and remove the seeds first), 2-inch lengths of celery stalk, or cucumber (peel, cut lengthwise, and seed before adding the spread).

- Most spreads can be used as dips with crackers or crudités. For party food, make crackers from a sweet Flexible Pastry (see Index) dough to serve with Date Nut Spread or Bingo (see Index). To create crudités, trim raw vegetables and cut them into dippable pieces, such as carrot sticks or thin slices of potato.
- Thick, smooth spreads can be squeezed out through a pastry tube for elegant hors d'oeuvres. To prepare hors d'oeuvres in advance, first seal in the texture of the bread by spreading with Butters for the Table, Unadulterated Mayonnaise, Avocado Spread, Zesty Spread, Nut Butters (see Index), cream cheese, or tahini. Finally, decorate with a spread squeezed through a pastry tube. Suitable spreads for this are Gorgeous Orange, Pepper Cheese, and Garlic (see Index).
- Many spreads can be used to recycle leftover cooked grains in a delightful way. Bring brown rice, wheat berries, rye berries, or barley to a boil in a saucepan, using a minimum of water. Right before serving, stir in a spread and heat through. Try Gorgeous Orange (see Index) with rice for breakfast, Olives Plus (see Index) with barley for dinner. (Note: Do not boil spreads that contain yogurt or cottage cheese.)
- Spreads also can revitalize plain leftover legumes. For an example, see Sunny Split Peas (see Index).
- The low-fat makeup of these dual purpose spreads has one potential disadvantage. Since they won't seal bread the way concentrated fats do, sogginess is a danger. (Sealing is the purpose of smearing conventional sandwiches with butter, mayonnaise, and so forth. Mustard, the apparent exception, is used with self-contained slabs of food that don't seep into bread or with oily salads.)

The best sandwiches and salads are always prepared just prior to serving to avoid sogginess. For appetizers, then, it's best to serve spreads in a bowl with crackers, toast, or crudités for do-it-yourself sandwiches that won't wilt. To pack sandwiches or salads for brown bag meals or picnics, pack the spread or dressing in a separate container. Add it right before eating.

GENERAL TIPS FOR OILS AND FATS

- Tahini tends to separate when stored for a long period of time. When you buy a new jar of it, transfer the contents to the workbowl and process until smooth. The consistency will be improved tremendously.
- Cold-pressed olive, sesame, wheat germ, and corn germ oils are especially flavorful. Yet they have no more calories or fat than the more innocuously flavored oils. Sometimes the sparing substitution or addition of one of these distinctive oils can enhance an entire dish. But remember not to use these distinctive oils when a recipe calls for salad oil.

CLARIFYING BUTTER

- The difference between clarified butter and regular butter is the difference between superb and very good. To clarify butter, melt a pound of it (preferably unsalted) in a saucepan over low heat. Watch it carefully to prevent scorching. Let the butter cool for a few minutes. White impurities separate from the golden liquid. Skim them off with a spoon. Warm the butter, cool, and skim a second time. To store it, pour the clarified butter into an airtight container and refrigerate it. And don't try to get every last drop of butter out of the saucepan. Any residual impurities will cling to the sides of the pan, so leave them there.

  Actually, what I call *impurities* are a natural part of butter. The white particles consist of milk solids and high melting fat, and they are really impure only in taste.

  Clarified butter tastes much better than unclarified. And dispensing with the milk solids also has a practical advantage: it reduces the likelihood of scorching when the butter is melted. Many recipes using butter also call for a small amount of oil for stovetop cooking. This is not necessary with clarified butter.

⊤ UNADULTERATED MAYONNAISE

Commercial mayonnaise is loaded with sugar and other flavoring additives. This recipe isn't.

You can add seasonings as appropriate to the particular use for the spread.

1 egg
1 tablespoon cider vinegar
¼ cup soy oil (or other bland salad oil)
¾ cup soy oil

Add the first three ingredients to the workbowl. Process 60 seconds. With the motor running, pour in 1 tablespoon of the remaining oil through the feed tube. After 10 seconds, pour in the remainder, pouring in the thinnest of thin streams. Refrigerated in an airtight container, Unadulterated Mayonnaise keeps for 1 week.

- Since slow pouring of the oil is essential for creamy mayonnaise, I like to balance a plastic funnel in the top of the feed tube and keep the measure of oil in the funnel. Dripping is thus directed to the place it should go—otherwise slow pouring is apt to be messy.

Yield: 1¼ cups

⊤ AMAZING MAYONNAISE

Although you can often substitute it for regular mayonnaise, this spread contains no eggs and not a drop of oil. The recipe started out as a courtesy for a non-egg-eating friend, but its clean taste commends it to anyone.

The only disadvantage of this high-protein food is its perishability. I recommend that you make it in small batches and use it within 24 hours.

⅓ cup tofu, cubed
⅓ cup large-curd cottage cheese
1 teaspoon lemon juice
1 tablespoon yogurt or sour cream
Optional: **¾ teaspoon curry powder (Curried Mayonnaise) or**
Optional: **1 tablespoon poppy seed + 1 tablespoon yogurt or sour cream (Poppy Spread) or**
Optional: **2 tablespoons chopped parsley or raw spinach + 1 tablespoon onion (Green Mayonnaise)**

Drain tofu carefully. Add to the workbowl along with the other ingredients and process 10 seconds. Scrape down. Repeat until the mixture is uniform.

To create Curried Mayonnaise, Poppy Spread, or Green Mayonnaise, include the appropriate optional ingredient(s).

Yield: at least ½ cup

BUTTERSTRETCHERS

Despite all those margarine commercials, I believe no table spread tastes better than butter. The processor helps you get your money's worth from "the higher priced spread" by stretching it out with other ingredients. In four of the five following recipes, extra flavor is added to complement (never mask) the sumptuous buttery taste.

BUTTER FOR THE TABLE

Homemade margarine *doesn't quite do justice to this all-natural spread. Margarine conveys economy and spreadability well enough. More important, though, this convenience food tastes like butter because it is primarily butter. Serve it at the table and save money deliciously.*

½ **cup butter**
¼ **cup soy oil or other salad oil**
Optional: ⅛ **teaspoon lecithin granules**
Optional: **yellow food coloring**

Cut the butter into 8 pieces. Process with the oil and optional lecithin until smooth. Pulse in enough food coloring, drop by drop, to produce an attractive color (otherwise the color is not unattractive; it just looks like mayonnaise).

Once chilled, the mixture solidifies, but it spreads easily. Store in the refrigerator.

Yield: about ¾ cup

PEANUT BUTTER FOR THE TABLE

This is a sophisticated version of the stuff that sticks to the roof of your mouth. The taste is richer than regular peanut butter, but the texture is lighter.

¼ **cup Butter for the Table (see preceding recipe)**
½ **cup roasted peanuts (see Index)**

Process butter and peanuts 30 seconds. Scrape down and repeat until smooth. Store in the refrigerator.

Yield: at least ½ cup

BREAKFAST BUTTER FOR THE TABLE

For folks who like a little something sweet first thing in the morning, this spread is ideal. Keep it on hand for the easiest, tastiest cinnamon toast ever.

½ **cup butter, cut into 8 pieces**
½ **cup honey**
2 **tablespoons salad oil**
½ **teaspoon cinnamon**
Optional (but strongly recommended): **2 tablespoons noninstant milk powder**

Process all ingredients together for 30 seconds. Scrape down and repeat until smooth. Store in the refrigerator.

Yield: 1¼ cups

MUSTARD BUTTER

This spicy condiment goes especially well with tofu. (Try pan frying a slice of tofu in it. Tofu cooked in Mustard Butter also can be processed into a flavorful sauce. Thin it with lemon juice.) Mustard Butter also tastes wonderful on steamed cabbage, broccoli, or cauliflower.

½ cup butter, cut into 8 pieces
¼ cup salad oil
2 teaspoons Dijon mustard
Optional: ⅛ teaspoon lecithin granules

Process ingredients together for 30 seconds. Scrape down and repeat until smooth. Store in the refrigerator.

Yield: ¾ cup

MAPLE NUT BUTTER

Its creamy texture, flecked with nuts, also makes this spread valuable as a cake filling. It should always be served at room temperature for the best consistency.

Of all the spreads I've ever tasted, this one is the hardest to stop eating.

¼–⅓ cup hazelnuts (substitute walnuts or
    pecans)
½ cup butter, cut into 8 pieces
¼ cup maple syrup
¼ cup salad oil
¼ cup noninstant powdered milk
Optional: brown food coloring

Pan roast the nuts. Chop fine with the metal blade and set aside. Process the butter, syrup, oil, and powdered milk until smooth. Scrape down the workbowl after 10-second processings. Pulse in food coloring until the mixture turns tan. Pulse in the nuts. Store in the refrigerator but serve at room temperature.

Yield: 1⅓ cups

To pan roast nuts or safflower, sunflower, or sesame seeds:

Place 1 layer of nuts or seeds in a heavy skillet (preferably cast iron—otherwise you may need to protect the pan with a preliminary coating of oil). Roast over medium heat, stirring every minute or so. Taste for doneness—browning and aroma are also clues to doneness.

⊤ BASIC PEANUT BUTTER AND VARIATIONS

My brother-in-law, Doug, wouldn't touch most "health food" with a 10-foot fork. Peanut butter, though, is one of his favorite edibles. On one occasion I presented him with a gift of assorted peanut butters. Some were quite unusual, all of them were indisputably wholesome.

By using the optional soy nuts, you can reduce the percentage of fat, improve the amino acid balance—soybeans supply different amino acids than peanuts—and cut down on cost.

1 cup roasted peanuts or ¾ cup roasted
    peanuts + ¼ cup roasted soybeans,
    commercially known as soy nuts
1 tablespoon peanut oil or salad oil (or more as
    needed)
1 tablespoon butter (substitute margarine)
Salt to taste

To roast peanuts, spread the shelled nuts out on a baking sheet and warm in a preheated 300° F. oven. Stir every few minutes. Taste after 20 minutes to determine if they are done.

Process the nuts for 30 seconds. Add the oil. Process 10 seconds. Scrape down. Add the butter. Scrape down. Process in 1 additional teaspoon oil at a time, scraping down between additions, until the desired consistency is reached. Process in salt to taste, adding ¼ teaspoon at a time.

Refrigerated in an airtight container, the spread will keep for 2 weeks.

For best results, do not double the recipe. Making this size batch of peanut butter is hard enough work for the processor.

Yield: ⅔ cup

VARIATIONS

DUSKY PEANUT BUTTER: Process into Basic Peanut Butter (see preceding recipe) 6 drops of Liquid Smoke and (if desired) 2 tablespoons dark brown sugar. The nutty flavor deepens to give a meatier taste.

PEANUT HONEY BUTTER: Process into Basic Peanut Butter (see preceding recipe) 3 tablespoons honey.

SUNFLOWER NUT BUTTER: Substitute ¼ cup raw Sunflower Meal (see Index) or roasted sunflower seeds for ¼ cup of the peanuts in Basic Peanut Butter (see preceding recipe). You can still use the optional soy nuts in making the recipe. The peanut taste predominates in the blend of nutty flavors.

PB WITH EXTRA B: Process into Basic Peanut Butter (see preceding recipe) 2 teaspoons brewer's or torula yeast. Most people will not even notice the supplement of B vitamins unless forewarned that the taste is different.

⊡ OTHER NUT BUTTERS

1 cup roasted almonds, cashews, or walnuts
1 tablespoon salad oil (more as needed)
1 tablespoon butter (more as needed)
Salt to taste

Pan roast (see page 31) or oven roast (see page 37) the nuts. Process 30 seconds.

Add 1 tablespoon each of oil and butter. Process 10 seconds and scrape down. Add additional butter or oil, first 1 tablespoon at a time and then, as you get close to the desired texture, 1 teaspoon at a time. Process 10 seconds after each addition. Repeat until the desired consistency is reached. Process in salt to taste, adding ¼ teaspoon at a time.

Butter produces a creamer spread than oil and is especially delightful with cashews.

Yield: about ⅔ cup

- For an utterly delicious sauce, start with cooked yellow or green split peas. Process in the nut butter of your choice to taste. Water may be processed in to thin the sauce.
- Home-processed peanut butter tends to have a somewhat grainy texture. I feel that this is amply compensated for by its superior freshness. If greater smoothness in these spreads is desired, substitute butter for oil.

⊡ AVOCADO SPREAD

A luxurious green delight.

¾ cup ripe avocado pulp (from 1 medium avocado)
¼ cup lemon juice
1 egg
¼ cup salad oil
¼ teaspoon salt
⅛ teaspoon black pepper
¾ cup salad oil, 2 tablespoons of which can be olive oil
Optional: **dill weed or cumin to taste**

Process the avocado and lemon juice until uniform. Scrape down between 10-second processings. Add the egg, ¼ cup oil, salt, and pepper. Process 60 seconds. Add the remaining oil in the thinnest of thin streams, poured through the feed tube, as for Unadulterated Mayonnaise (see Index).

Yield: 2 cups

Note: The batch given for this recipe is rather large because emulsified egg is necessary to thicken the spread. The amount given is really the minimum quantity that should be made in one batch. However, this spread keeps well for 2 days or longer—it shouldn't go to waste.

AVOCADO DRESSING

Broccoli boosts the avocado flavor while it gives the spread a higher nutrient density.

1 cup Avocado Spread (made without the optional dill or cumin) (see preceding recipe)
1 cup broccoli
2 tablespoons vinegar
¼ teaspoon cumin
¼ teaspoon powdered mustard
¼ teaspoon raw onion—a small slice
Salt to taste

Prepare the Avocado Spread. Steam broccoli until very tender. Cut pieces to measure the needed amount. Drain well.

Process with the other ingredients for 10 seconds. Scrape down. Repeat until the mixture is smooth. Pulse in salt to taste.

Yield: 2 cups

☐ STROGANOFF SPREAD

This rich stovetop pâté delights meat eaters and vegetarians alike. Serve it with bread or crackers.

2 tablespoons minced onion
2 tablespoons butter (melted) (substitute margarine)
½ cup (1½ ounces) mushroom pieces
1 tablespoon butter (substitute margarine)
2 tablespoons whole wheat flour
Soy stock (from cooking soybeans) or other stock, as needed
½ cup cooked soybeans, drained
¼ teaspoon paprika
Salt to taste

Put pieces of peeled onion in the workbowl and pulse until minced. Measure the needed amount. Rinse the workbowl. Sauté onion in the melted butter until transparent. A large cast-iron skillet is recommended.

Wipe mushroom pieces clean with a towel. Separate caps and stems. (Although you could use the caps for this spread, why not reserve them for a recipe that will show them off?) Pulse the mushrooms until minced. Measure the needed amount. Add to the cooked onion, stirring together until the mushroom darkens. Remove the mushroom and onion with a slotted spoon, leaving as much butter as possible in the skillet. Set aside.

Rinse out the workbowl.

Add the remaining butter and the flour to the skillet. Bring the stock within reach of the stove.

Cook the flour over low heat, stirring constantly as it forms a paste. Cook for a total of 5 minutes, adding small amounts of stock if needed to keep the flour from sticking. Aim for the thickest possible paste. (What happens here is that you exchange a floury flavor for a savory taste.)

Process together the cooked flour, soybeans, paprika, and salt. Scrape down the workbowl between 10-second processings. When the mixture is uniform, pulse in the mushroom mixture. Thin if desired with additional stock. (*Note:* If you're working on a large batch and your processor has a small capacity, play it safe by doing this final step in 2 loads.)

Yield: ⅞ cup

STROGANOFF DRESSING

Adorn lettuce with this to create a salad worthy of your best company.

¼ cup Stroganoff Spread (see preceding recipe)
¼ cup sour cream (substitute yogurt)
1 tablespoon vinegar
1 tablespoon salad oil
¼ teaspoon paprika
Pinch salt

Process all ingredients, scraping down as necessary, until uniform in texture.

Yield: ½ cup

☐ OLIVES PLUS SPREAD

Enjoy the fruit of the olive tree along with some extra nutrition. (Soybeans and yogurt improve the nutrient density.) Add this recipe to your repertoire of hors d'oeuvres; it's a festive way to top crackers.

¼ cup cooked soybeans, drained
1 ounce cream cheese
1 tablespoon yogurt
¼ teaspoon basil
¼ teaspoon paprika
¼ cup (1 ounce) pitted olives: black or green, may be stuffed

Process together all ingredients but the olives. After 10 seconds, scrape down. Repeat until the mixture is uniform.

Sprinkle the olives evenly over the mixture. Pulse twice. Check the texture: the goal is to have the olives mixed into the spread but not chopped into liquid. Alternate single pulses and checking until you have it.

Yield: ½ cup

OLIVES PLUS DRESSING

This is the dressing for salad at an Italian banquet.

¼ **cup cooked soybeans, drained**
1 **ounce cream cheese**
¼ **cup yogurt**
¼ **teaspoon basil**
¼ **teaspoon paprika**
¼ **cup olive oil**
¼ **cup salad oil**
¼ **cup vinegar**
¼ **cup pitted olives: black or green, may be stuffed**

Process together all ingredients but the olives. After 10 seconds, scrape down. Repeat until the mixture is uniform.

Sprinkle the olives evenly over the mixture. Pulse twice. Check the texture: the goal is to have the olives mixed into the dressing but not chopped into liquid. Alternate single pulses and checking until you have it.

Yield: 1 cup

⊤ GARLIC SPREAD

Sentiments about garlic run strong. If you're a garlic lover, you'll adore this spread.

Although Garlic Oil (see Index) is the most reliable way I know to keep fresh garlic on hand, sometimes you do get stuck with some heads of fresh garlic. You'll find this spread a good way to make use of them.

2 **heads of garlic (plus or minus a few cloves)**
2 **tablespoons olive oil**
2 **tablespoons chopped fresh parsley**
1 **cup cooked soybeans, drained**
3 **ounces cream cheese**
⅛ **teaspoon salt**
½ **teaspoon tarragon**
¼ **teaspoon black pepper**

To release the individual cloves of garlic from their skins, bring a saucepan of water to a rolling boil. Separate the garlic into individual cloves. Drop them into the water and let them cook 1–2 minutes. Pour them into cold water and you can easily nudge off the skins. Trim away any discolorations.

In a large skillet (one that you won't mind smelling garlic in for some time afterward), warm the oil over medium high heat. Sauté the garlic, stirring often, for 5–8 minutes (longer for a milder flavor).

With the metal blade, chop the parsley. Measure and set aside. Place drained soybeans, cream cheese, salt, tarragon, and pepper in the workbowl. Pour in the garlic and oil. Process 20 seconds. Scrape down and repeat until the texture is uniform. Pulse in the optional parsley.

• I always like to serve garlicky food with sprigs of fresh parsley, meant for chewing, not just decoration. It does a pretty good job of neutralizing garlic breath.

Yield: about 1⅛ cups

GARLIC DRESSING

This creamy white dressing has a bold taste.

2 **tablespoons Garlic Spread (see preceding recipe)**
2 **tablespoons yogurt**

Process ingredients together until uniform.

Yield: ¼ cup

⊤ LICORICE LOVER'S SPREAD

Bored with cottage cheese? Try this. It perks up whole grain toast to a memorable extent.

⅓ **cup large-curd cottage cheese**
⅛ **teaspoon black pepper**
⅛ **teaspoon tarragon**
¼ **teaspoon aniseed**
1 **tablespoon salad oil**
1½ **teaspoons vinegar**
2 **tablespoons buttermilk or yogurt**

Process 10 seconds. Scrape down. Repeat until the mixture is smooth.

Yield: ⅓ cup

LICORICE LOVER'S DRESSING

For a tasty, low-calorie cucumber salad, this is the dressing to use. The slicing disc prepares suitably thin slices to offset the subtle, clean tasting dressing.

⅓ **cup Licorice Lover's Spread (see preceding recipe)**
Dash cumin
Buttermilk or yogurt as needed

Process the cumin into the spread for 10 seconds. Add 1 tablespoon buttermilk. Reprocess and scrape down the workbowl. Repeat until the desired consistency is reached.

Yield: about ⅓ cup

⊤ PEPPER CHEESE SPREAD

This transformation of ordinary cottage cheese is surprisingly tasty. Enjoy it as a household staple. After you try the combination of spices and herbs given here, invent others featuring your favorites.

⅓ **cup large-curd cottage cheese**
⅛ **teaspoon black pepper**
⅛ **teaspoon basil**
⅛ **teaspoon sage**
1 **teaspoon olive oil (substitute salad oil or buttermilk)**

Process all ingredients together for 10 seconds. Scrape down. Repeat until the mixture is smooth.

Yield: ⅓ cup

PEPPER CHEESE DRESSING

Slice some good tomatoes and stack them up, spread with this dressing. They look like round, triple-decker sandwiches. Just don't try to pick up those stacked up slices; give them the benefit of a knife and fork. One tomato sandwich, served over lettuce, makes a festive light appetizer or individual salad.

⅓ **cup Pepper Cheese Spread (see preceding recipe)**
1 **tablespoon olive oil**
1 **teaspoon lemon juice**
Salt to taste
Optional: **buttermilk as needed**

Process spread, oil, and lemon juice for 10 seconds. Scrape down. Repeat until the mixture is smooth. Add salt sparingly to taste and, if a thinner dressing is desired, process in buttermilk 1 teaspoon at a time until the desired consistency is reached.

Yield: about ⅓ cup

⊤ SPREADABLE CHEDDAR SPREAD

Use the yellow-colored variety of cheese, if you can. Chewy little morsels add interest to the spread's texture, and if those morsels stand out as golden, so much the better.

½ **cup (1½ ounces) sharp cheddar cheese**
¼ **cup large-curd cottage cheese**
1 **tablespoon salad oil**
⅛ **teaspoon Dijon or dry mustard**
Dash cayenne

Mince the cheese in the processor and measure the needed amount. Set aside. Process the other ingredients until smooth. Pulse in the cheese.

Yield: ½ cup

SPREADABLE CHEDDAR DRESSING 1

¼ cup Spreadable Cheddar Spread (see
    preceding recipe)
1 teaspoon salad oil
¼ cup large-curd cottage cheese
Garlic Oil (see Index) to taste
Sour cream, half and half, cream, whole milk, or
    low-fat milk as needed

Process the spread, oil, and cottage cheese
10 seconds. Scrape down. Repeat until uniform.
Thin to a smooth consistency with sour cream.
Pulse in Garlic Oil to taste.

Yield: about ½ cup

SPREADABLE CHEDDAR DRESSING 2

¼ **cup Spreadable Cheddar Spread (see Index)**
1 teaspoon salad oil
¼ **cup large-curd cottage cheese**
¼ **teaspoon dill weed**
1 teaspoon raw onion—a small slice
Sour cream, half and half, cream, whole milk, or
    low-fat milk as needed

Process all but the sour cream until smooth.
Thin to desired consistency with sour cream.

Yield: about ½ cup

⊡ PUCKER UP SPREAD

*You don't have to be a sourpuss to love the
tartness of this spread. Use it as a fascinating
icing for toast or put it in a sandwich along with
slices of hard-boiled egg. Don't let the thin
texture of the spread deceive you—it's strong.*

1 tablespoon tahini
¼ **cup cooked soybeans, drained**
1 circular slice of fresh lemon, ¼ inch thick
¼ **cup Unadulterated Mayonnaise (see Index)**
1 tablespoon lemon juice
Pinch salt
Optional: **yellow food coloring**

Process all ingredients but the optional
coloring together for 10 seconds. Scrape down
and repeat until the mixture is uniform.
(Regarding the lemon, include all the rind and
pulp; remove only the pits. This sounds unusual,
but try it. The lemon flavor gets set off by a
sharp undertaste, a real match for the earthy
tahini.)

To use food coloring, pulse in a drop at a time
until the spread just turns a yellow tint.

Yield: ½ cup

PUCKER UP DRESSING

This is a delightful accompaniment to salad.

¼ **cup Pucker Up Spread (see preceding recipe)**
¼ **cup yogurt**
¼ **teaspoon dill weed**

Process all ingredients until smooth.

Yield: ½ cup

⊡ ZESTY SPREAD

*Exactly what is margarine good for?
Margarine beats butter as a money saver in
baking. Nutritionally it's superior to
hydrogenated vegetable shortenings, which
contain such a high percentage of saturated fat
that they don't even need to be refrigerated.
Nonetheless, a better solution than margarine
for the butter-shy baker is simply to use an oil-
based, rather than solid-shortening-based,
recipe. Especially if you bake with cold-pressed
corn oil, the product can be as tasty as
something made with butter. Margarine doesn't
have much going for it as a table spread either.
Not when you can process your own Butter for
the Table—fresh, economical, and preservative
free.*

*So what is margarine good for? I've found
one superb use for it. Margarine teams up
magnificently with nutritional yeast. At any rate,
the combination must be tasted to be believed:
savory and hearty.*

Zesty Spread on whole grain bread makes an

excellent snack, giving you a little B vitamin boost at the same time. Try a little over hot chick-peas or brussels sprouts.

1 stick margarine, cut into 1-tablespoon pieces
⅛ teaspoon cayenne
3 tablespoons brewer's or torula yeast
Optional: **1 tablespoon toasted wheat germ**
Optional: **additional yeast**

Process the margarine, cayenne, and yeast for 10 seconds. Scrape down. Repeat until the mixture is smooth.

Pulse in the wheat germ, if desired. Taste the spread on a cracker or something and decide if you'd like a stronger yeast flavor. Process in additional yeast 1 teaspoon at a time, to taste.

Refrigerated, the spread keeps for 2 weeks.

Yield: about ½ cup

ZESTY DRESSING

When my friend, Sylvia Burnes, told me to try brewer's yeast on salad, I thought she was joking. But I love it. I think you will, too.

2 tablespoons Zesty Spread (see preceding
    recipe)
2 tablespoons salad oil
1 tablespoon vinegar
⅓ cup chick-peas, cooked and drained
Pinch salt
⅛ teaspoon oregano
¼ teaspoon basil
2 tablespoons sour cream or yogurt (substitute
    mild stock)

Process all ingredients for 10 seconds. Scrape down. Repeat until the mixture is uniform.

Yield: ½ cup

⊡ DATE NUT SPREAD

Do you ever get a craving for the delicious taste of cream cheese with date nut bread? Here's a relatively low-calorie equivalent of that binger's delight.

¼ cup walnuts
1 ounce cream cheese
¼ cup large-curd cottage cheese
1 tablespoon brown sugar, packed
⅛ teaspoon cinnamon
¼ cup pitted dates, quartered

Optional: Oven roast the nuts and let them cool to room temperature.

Pulse the walnuts (no more than 1 cup at a time) until chopped medium fine. Set aside.

Process the cream cheese, cottage cheese, sugar, and cinnamon for 10 seconds. Scrape down and repeat until smooth.

Add dates and process 30 seconds. Scrape down. Repeat until smooth.

Distribute the nuts evenly over the mixture. Pulse twice and scrape down the workbowl. Repeat until uniform.

Yield: ½ cup

**To oven roast nuts or safflower,
sunflower, or sesame seeds:**

Spread them out on a baking sheet in a preheated 350° F. oven. If you have a reliable nose, remove from oven the instant you start to smell the delicious aroma of roasted nuts. Otherwise, check after 5 minutes and every 2 minutes thereafter. When they darken slightly, they are done.

DATE NUT DRESSING

Here's a deceptive appearance. The slightly brown bloom on the milky-colored dressing represents tiny chunks of date and nut, which pack quite a wallop. Swirl this dressing onto lettuce and lemon-dipped apple slices for an exceptional Waldorf-type salad.

¼ cup Date Nut Spread (see preceding recipe)
¼ cup large curd cottage cheese
¼ cup Unadulterated Mayonnaise (see Index)
1 tablespoon salad oil
3 tablespoons orange juice
Pinch salt

Process all ingredients until smooth. Scrape down the workbowl as necessary.

Yield: ¾ cup

⊤ PINEAPPLE CREAM SPREAD

This naturally sweet mixture is a family favorite. Don't limit your use of it to spreading on bread. Try it on tofu or slices of semisoft cheese.

1 ounce cream cheese, cut into 4 pieces
1 teaspoon vanilla extract
⅛ teaspoon cinnamon
½ cup pineapple chunks, fresh or canned in its own juice
½ cup cooked brown rice
Yellow food coloring as needed

Process the cheese, vanilla, and cinnamon for 10 seconds. Scrape down. Add *half* the pineapple. Process 10 seconds. Scrape down. Repeat until the mixture is smooth.

Pulse in the remaining pineapple and the rice until uniform. Pulse in food coloring drop by drop until the spread is pale yellow.

Yield: about ¾ cup

PINEAPPLE CREAM DRESSING

Try this dressing on cubed carrots. It brings out the best in both—sweet flavors and beautiful colors. This dressing is also the base for the FP Fruit Salad (see Index).

¼ cup walnuts
¼ cup Pineapple Cream Spread (see preceding recipe)
¼ cup Unadulterated Mayonnaise (see Index)
Yellow food coloring as needed

Pulse the walnuts until coarsely chopped. Set aside.

Process the spread and mayonnaise until smooth. Add food coloring, drop by drop, to achieve a pale pineapple shade. Pulse in the nuts.

Yield: ½ cup

⊤ HIGH-PROTEIN CURRY SPREAD

This unusual sweet spread tastes especially refreshing on apple slices. If you don't plan to eat the slices at once, keep them looking fresh longer by dipping them into 1 cup water mixed with 1 tablespoon lemon juice, then assemble them on the serving dish and refrigerate. Plan to eat them within an hour.

¼ cup dried fruit (raisins, pitted prunes, apricots, pears, peaches—alone or in combination)
2 tablespoons minced onion
½ cup soy stock (substitute water)
2 teaspoons curry powder
½ cup cooked soybeans, drained
1 tablespoon lemon juice
1 tablespoon salad oil
1 tablespoon yogurt, buttermilk, or sour cream
Salt to taste

Place the dried fruit, onion, stock, and curry powder in a saucepan. Cover and bring to a boil, then simmer until the liquid is absorbed (check after 5 minutes). Transfer the fruit to the workbowl. Add all other ingredients. Process 10 seconds. Scrape down. Repeat until smooth.

Yield: ¾ cup

HIGH-PROTEIN CURRY DRESSING

Drizzle this over cooked, chilled green beans and sprinkle with some cashews. On a hot day it makes an invigorating appetizer.

½ cup High-Protein Curry Spread (see preceding recipe)
¼ cup yogurt, buttermilk, or sour cream
1 tablespoon salad oil
1 tablespoon vinegar
Pinch salt

Process all ingredients together until the mixture is smooth. Scrape down as needed.

Yield: ¾ cup

⊞ GORGEOUS ORANGE SPREAD

This spread is a sight for sweet-loving eyes and tastes as sumptuous as it looks. For extra protein, try it on slices of tofu, not just bread.

1 tablespoon honey
2 ounces cream cheese
2 tablespoons orange juice concentrate

Process all ingredients together until smooth. Scrape down as needed.

Yield: ¼ cup

GORGEOUS ORANGE DRESSING

This makes a delicious base for fruit salad, especially melon slices.

¼ cup Gorgeous Orange Spread (see preceding recipe)
2 tablespoons Unadulterated Mayonnaise (see Index)
Optional: **⅛ teaspoon ground cardamom**
Orange food coloring

Process or stir the spread, mayonnaise, and optional cardamom until smooth. Add the food coloring, drop by drop, to create a subtle orange glow.

Yield: ⅓ cup

⊞ APRICOT LARK SPREAD

Jam made from beans? No, it isn't conventional, but maybe it ought to be. Imagine the texture and sweetness of good-quality apple butter. Now color it apricot. Team it up with cream cheese and dark bread and you'll get a taste as good as apple butter, with a good deal more protein (soybeans complement the amino acids in the bread).

¼ cup dried apricot or fresh apricot, peeled and pitted
1 tablespoon dark brown sugar, packed
¼ cup orange juice
1 tablespoon honey
½ cup cooked soybeans, drained
2 tablespoons apple cider, more as needed

Stir the apricot, sugar, and orange juice in a saucepan over medium heat. Cover and simmer until the apricot is fork tender (check after 5 minutes).

Transfer to the workbowl. Add all other ingredients and process until smooth, scraping down as necessary. For a thinner texture, add more apple cider by the teaspoon until the desired consistency is reached.

Yield: about ¾ cup

APRICOT LARK DRESSING

Here's another idea that may seem odd at first: Russian dressing made with beans and apricots. But is it any stranger to eat the typical mixture of white sugar, tomato, and additive ridden mayonnaise?

1 medium dill pickle
¼ cup Apricot Lark Spread (see preceding recipe)
½ cup yogurt
Pinch salt
½ teaspoon paprika

Rinse off and dry the pickle. Cut it into pieces no longer than 1 inch. Pulse into coarse chunks. Set aside. Rinse out the workbowl.

Process other ingredients until smooth, scraping down as necessary. Stir in the chopped pickle.

Yield: about 1 cup

⊤ A PERFECT MARRIAGE SPREAD

What goes together as well as peanut butter and jelly? Tahini and honey. The soybeans in this spread add nutritional substance and extra chewiness. Try it on an open-faced sandwich.

½ **cup cooked soybeans, drained**
2 **tablespoons tahini**
2 **tablespoons honey**

Process all ingredients until uniform, scraping down as necessary.

Yield: ¾ cup

A PERFECT MARRIAGE DRESSING

Try this memorably zesty topping on lettuce or sprouts.

¼ **cup A Perfect Marriage Spread (see preceding recipe)**
1 **tablespoon tahini**
1 **tablespoon sesame oil (substitute salad oil)**
3 **tablespoons lemon juice**
1 **teaspoon raw onion, cut small enough to measure**
¼ **teaspoon dried peppermint or spearmint leaves**
Freshly ground pepper to taste
Salt to taste

Process everything but the pepper and salt until smooth. Scrape down as needed. Pulse in freshly ground pepper and salt to taste.

Yield: ½ cup

⊤ TAHINI 3 SPREAD

Here's another tahini treat, a pungent, chewy spread if ever there was one. Stuff it into celery, dab it onto thin slices of radish, or heap it onto tofu.

1 **tablespoon tahini**
¼ **cup cooked brown rice**
¼ **teaspoon ground ginger**
1 **teaspoon soy sauce**

Process all ingredients until smooth. Scrape down after 10-second processings.

Yield: about ¼ cup

TAHINI 3 DRESSING

This light dressing, the color of coffee ice cream, works especially well on Chinese cabbage. The low fat content may be of interest to you. This dressing gets body not from additional fats but from rice and stock, stretching out the rich taste of the tahini.

¼ **cup Tahini 3 Spread (see preceding recipe)**
¼ **cup soy stock or other stock**
Garlic Oil (see Index) to taste
Soy sauce to taste

Process spread and stock until uniform. Pulse in other ingredients to taste.

Yield: ½ cup

⊤ BINGO SPREAD

Five very different ingredients line up to produce a winner.

2 **tablespoons walnuts, pecans, or almonds**
¼ **cup cooked soybeans, drained**
1 **tablespoon tahini**
2 **tablespoons frozen apple juice concentrate**
⅛ **teaspoon ground coriander**

Pulse the nuts until chopped fine. Set aside.
Process the other ingredients 10 seconds. Scrape down. Repeat until uniform. Pulse in additional juice concentrate as needed.
Distribute the nuts over the top. Pulse. Scrape down and repeat until the mixture is uniform.

Yield: ⅓ cup

BINGO DRESSING

This dressing brings out something wonderful in raw green cabbage.

¼ cup Bingo Spread (see preceding recipe)
¼ cup Unadulterated Mayonnaise (see Index)
¼ teaspoon lemon juice
Salt to taste

Process all ingredients until uniform.

Yield: ½ cup

6 | Spontaneous Salads

When you first owned a processor you might have found it hard to believe that using the processor could actually improve salad. By now, however, you probably have a good idea of the versatility the food processor exhibits in contributing to your salad repertoire. No doubt, you've discovered that the processor is ideal for salads with grated, sliced, or finely cut ingredients. The difference in taste between salads prepared just before serving and those assembled after laborious cutting, done hours earlier, is amazing. By decreasing the time needed for pesky jobs such as shredding cabbage, the processor also encourages you to do such jobs often. This chapter contains five recipes that use shredded or finely cut carrot— more than you'd probably try without a processor. And the flexible recipe for the FP Salad at the end of this chapter may inspire you with dozens of uses for finely cut vegetables— creative uses that are also very convenient.

Using the processor to cut vegetables in ways you wouldn't attempt without it, such as shredding beets for Dramatic Cucumber Salad, enables you to expand your knowledge of vegetables by introducing you to tastes and textures that would otherwise go unnoticed.

Finally, the processor is indispensable for preparing dressings which can make otherwise ordinary salads dazzling. For example, the green pepper processed right into the dressing in Smiling Succotash (see Index) adds wonderful color and flavor. The juiciness of the vegetable also dilutes the dressing to a suitable texture. Spreads can also be the basis for composed salads. The example given here, Cold Cauliflower Buffet, may inspire you to create many sumptuous platters of chilled vegetables.

- Snippets of raw celery, radish, carrot, or spinach can be processed right into some salad dressings (such as Pepper Cheese; see Index) right before serving.
- Save money by using all leftover raw or cooked vegetables. Try placing them in a storage container especially for salads. Empty it out completely every one or at most two days.
- Garlic Oil may be the best way to keep garlic on hand for seasoning. It's one of my favorite hints from Heloise. The oil has the power of fresh garlic without the inconvenience or cost.

  First peel one clove of garlic. An easy method is to place the clove on a flat surface and slam the flat of a knife against

it. The skin bursts enough to peel off easily. Slice the clove in half. Find a small jar with a lid. Place the garlic in it and cover with salad oil. Within a short time you'll have Garlic Oil.* Add it to food just a drop at a time, to taste. The flavor is strong. Used in this way, the clove will keep indefinitely, provided it is kept well covered with oil and refrigerated.

- Prepare your own ginger flavoring by placing peeled fresh ginger root in sherry. Keep it covered and refrigerated, and, like garlic, it will provide a true flavor, to be added drop by drop.
- Using a mortar and pestle is the best way to prepare dried herbs for salads. If you don't have one, release the flavor otherwise locked into the leaves by crushing them before use. Simply cup your left hand to hold the herbs. Rub the herbs with the side of your right hand to crush them.
- My favorite method for drying lettuce comes from Adelle Davis. Designate a new pillowcase as your lettuce dryer. After quickly rinsing off lettuce, transfer it to the case. Go outside. Grasp the ends of the case firmly in one hand and whirl it around until water stops sprinkling out. The method is thorough and fast.

---

*Reprinted, with permission, from "Hints from Heloise," by Heloise.

DRAMATIC CUCUMBER SALAD

Crimson shreds of beet contrast with green-tinged cucumber wedges. The light pink dressing is set off by dill weed flecks. No wonder this salad looks exceptionally impressive.

1 large cucumber, sliced (3 cups)
1 small beet, shredded (¼ cup)
¼ cup celery, chopped medium fine (1 small rib)
1 cup yogurt or sour cream
½ teaspoon dill weed
¼ teaspoon paprika
Dash cumin
1 tablespoon vinegar
2 tablespoons salad oil
Salt to taste

Trim the cucumber. Cut into quarters lengthwise and discard the seeds. Push quarters through the french fry or slicing disc. Set aside in an airtight container.

Steam a small beet with several inches of stem left on it until fork tender. Trim and push through the shredding disc. Measure ¼ cup. Transfer to the airtight container with the cucumber.

Trim celery, process it until medium fine, and measure ¼ cup. Transfer to the container with the cucumber and beet.

Process the yogurt, dill, paprika, cumin, vinegar, and oil until smooth. Pour over the other ingredients. Refrigerate in the container.

For best results, serve the salad within 1 hour. Before turning it into a serving bowl, give it a good stir and add salt to taste.

Yield: 4 servings

REDOUBTABLE RADISHES

Some people find that radishes are always redoubtable—that is, they come on too strong for comfort. This salad makes radishes redoubtable in another meaning of the word— being worthy of respect. No longer crassly formidable, the radishes in this salad have been to finishing school.

1 bunch radishes (about ¾ cup)
2 tablespoons Unadulterated Mayonnaise (see Index)
⅛ teaspoon dill weed
Salt to taste
Lettuce

Trim the radishes. Put the mayonnaise and dill in the workbowl and insert the slicing disc. Push the radishes through.

Remove the disc, stir with a fork, and add salt to taste. Serve over lettuce leaves.

Yield: 2 servings

• Try to get fresh radishes, the kind that come in bunches rather than in plastic bags. Not only do fresh radishes taste better; you can also steam the leaves and eat them along with the salad.

GRATED SPINACH SALAD

Actually, what gets grated is everything gratable but the spinach. The resulting salad does not overpower the eater with its spinachy message. Consequently, its taste does not need to be disguised with the heavy dressing often served with a spinach salad.

1 pound fresh spinach
½ cup minced Parmesan (or from The Cheese Cache—see Index)
1 cup shredded zucchini (1 medium)
2 tablespoons salad oil
1 tablespoon vinegar
Freshly grated black pepper

Trim the spinach. Transfer to a serving bowl.

Pulse, then process 1-inch cubes of cheese until minced. Measure ½ cup and set aside.

Trim the zucchini. Push through the shredding disc and measure 1 cup. *Optional:* bundle the zucchini up in a dish towel and wring out the moisture.

Toss the spinach leaves with the oil. Add all other ingredients and toss again. Serve immediately.

Yield: 4 servings

COLD COLLARD COMBINATION

Enjoy the velvety green richness of collard greens in a salad. The shredded leaves, combined with cooler-tasting accompaniments, may give you a new appreciation for this intense but delicious vegetable.

1 cup shredded cooked collard greens (1 bunch)
½ cup yogurt
1 teaspoon dill weed or dill seed
1 teaspoon salad oil
1 tablespoon lemon juice
Lettuce leaves

Trim collards, cutting off any portions of stem that protrude below the base of each leaf. Steam the greens until tender (judge it by tasting), drain, and chill.

Stack the drained leaves on top of each other and wrap into a roll. Pack this into the feed tube and push through the slicing disc. Measure how much you have and proportion the other ingredients accordingly.

Transfer the collards to a salad bowl or storage jar. Process the yogurt, dill, oil, and lemon juice for 10 seconds. Pour over the collards and toss. Serve at once over the lettuce, or chill and serve.

Yield: 2 servings

SPUNKY CHILLED LENTILS

Crisp vegetable morsels and energetic seasonings don't overcome the lentils in this salad. On the contrary, they bring out the spunk inherent in this wonderful legume.

1½ cups sprouted or cooked lentils
½ cup raw spinach or celery, chopped medium fine
½ cup carrot, minced
2 tablespoons olive oil
1 tablespoon lemon juice
Garlic Oil (see Index)
Salt to taste
Optional: **2 tablespoons toasted wheat germ**
Optional: **⅛ teaspoon cumin**
Lettuce leaves

Should you have sprouted lentils handy, use them either raw or lightly steamed. Otherwise cook lentils, being especially careful to keep their shapes intact. (The boil and bake method is recommended; see Table 4.) Measure 1½ cups and set aside in a mixing bowl.

Trim the spinach. Process until chopped medium fine. Measure ½ cup. Add to the mixing bowl.

Place chunks of raw carrot in the workbowl and mince. Measure ½ cup. Add to the bowl.

Toss these ingredients with the oil, lemon juice, and Garlic Oil, and add salt to taste. If desired, also toss in the optional wheat germ and cumin.

Serve over lettuce leaves.

Yield: 2 main dish servings

MASHED POTATO SALAD

This idea may surprise you. Give it a chance, though, and I think you will find it excellent.

2 medium potatoes (substitute cold leftover potatoes)
½ cup green peas, steamed just tender, or kale, steamed, drained, and minced with the metal blade
½ cup sliced celery (1 small rib)
3 tablespoons salad oil
2 tablespoons vinegar
¼ teaspoon dry or Dijon mustard
⅛ teaspoon salt

Steam the potatoes until fork tender. Prepare the peas or kale. Set aside.

Push celery through the slicing disc and measure ½ cup. Set aside.

Put the oil, vinegar, mustard, and salt into the bottom of the workbowl. Insert the shredding disc. Dry the potatoes, cut into chunks that fit in the feed tube, and gently push through. Remove the disc. Stir with a fork. Turn into a serving dish. Stir in the other ingredients until uniform. Serve immediately or chill (correct seasoning afterward) and serve.

Yield: 4 servings

CELERY JUMBLE

This little salad is delightfully fresh.

2 cups celery pieces (2–3 large stalks)
1 cup diced pepper (1 large red or green pepper)
2 tablespoons sesame oil or 2 tablespoons olive oil + ½ teaspoon chervil + pinch thyme
1 tablespoon lemon juice
Freshly ground black pepper to taste

Cut celery into 1-inch-long pieces and measure 2 cups. Process 3 seconds, 3 times, into a jumble of bite-sized celery pieces.

Use a paring knife to dice red or green pepper (or a combination of both) to yield 1 cup. Place this, along with the celery, in a salad bowl. Toss with the oil and lemon juice. Season to taste with freshly ground black pepper. Serve at once.

Yield: 4 servings

ELEGANT COLD BROCCOLI

To supplement the natural elegance of chilled broccoli, stuff it with a thick, flavorful spread.

1½ cups Spreadable Cheddar Spread, Olives Plus Spread, or Stroganoff Spread (see Index)
2 small broccoli stalks (substitute 1 large stalk)
Lettuce leaves
Optional: olives, walnut halves, sour cream, radish sprouts, watercress leaves

Prepare the spread. (Spread is used rather than dressing because it mounds better.)

Cook the broccoli until fork tender. If you must chop it to fit into the pan, cut so the piece with the flowers on it stays as long as possible. Let the vegetable cool to room temperature or wrap and refrigerate until thoroughly chilled.

Shortly before serving, cut the stalk(s) lengthwise into 2(4) pieces. If you have a short bit of stalk left over, cut it into uniform pieces and process until minced. Use this as a garnish.

Arrange the salads on individual plates or an attractive platter. Crisp lettuce is the base. Add 2 broccoli lengths. Mound ¾ cup spread between them, patting it to be fullest over the flower end and making a sort of broccoli sandwich turned upwards so the filling is visible. Garnish as desired.

Yield: 2 servings

SMILING SUCCOTASH

This is quite a change from the usual succotash. Instead of being dismal and starchy, this salad-style version tastes bright and is high in protein.

- Unlike the traditional succotash, which is usually sauceless, this version has a cottage cheese base. The cheese adds considerable protein value, complementing the amino acids in the limas and corn.

1 cup cooked lima beans, drained
1 cup corn kernels (1 ear)
½ cup large-curd cottage cheese
Pinch salt

1 tablespoon olive oil (substitute salad oil)
1 tablespoon vinegar
½ teaspoon basil
¼ teaspoon oregano
½ cup green pepper, trimmed and cut into pieces (½ large)

Prepare the lima beans. Drain.

If fresh corn is in season, steam 1 ear and scrape off the kernels. Otherwise use frozen corn from a "use what you want at a time" package of individually frozen kernels. Measure 1 cup and then steam until tender.

Put all other ingredients into the workbowl and process 15 seconds. Scrape down and repeat until the mixture is smooth. Sprinkle the limas and corn over the top and pulse once to mix. Turn into a serving dish and enjoy. The salad, refrigerated, keeps well for 24 hours, if necessary.

Yield: 4 servings

SPARKLING POTATO SALAD

Juicy raw green beans can put an extra twinkle into potato salad. The lemony base also contributes to the overall liveliness.

1 cup Pucker Up Spread (see Index)
3 cups potato chunks (4 medium baking potatoes)
1½ cups green beans (¾ pound)
Lemon juice, salt, and freshly ground black pepper to taste

Prepare the spread. Cut baking potatoes into 3 or 4 slices and measure about 3 cups of these chunks. Steam them over boiling water (afterward use the cooking liquid for stock, if you like).

Trim the beans. Cut each one into thirds and measure 1½ cups. If desired, julienne them by packing sideways and pushing through the slicing disc.

With a sharp knife, cut the cooked potatoes into bite-sized pieces. Mix with the spread and beans. Add lemon juice, salt, and pepper to taste. Serve hot or chilled.

Yield: 6 servings

MACARONI AND CHEESE SALAD

Here is a high-protein salad version of a perennial favorite.

Admittedly, mayonnaise is more common in macaroni salads. When you substitute the cottage cheese-based spread, you do more than cut down on the proportion of fat. The protein in the macaroni can be utilized, even if the salad is eaten alone, because the set of amino acids is now complete.

1 cup dried whole wheat macaroni (or 3 cups cooked)
1 cup Spreadable Cheddar Dressing 1 or 2 (see Index)
½–1 cup tomato pieces

Cook the macaroni until al dente. Drain. Prepare the spread. Cut cherry tomatoes in half or salad tomatoes into small pieces, using a sharp knife. Measure ½–1 cup.

Stir together the macaroni and spread. Gently stir in the tomato. Chill in an airtight container. Before serving, correct the seasoning. The salad can be served at once or held several hours.

Yield: 4 main dish servings

BEST EGG SALAD

Why the best? This salad has vivid color, chewy texture, and an offbeat combination of tastes.

½ cup rye or wheat berries
¼ teaspoon caraway seed
1½ cups water
2 cups Avocado Dressing (see Index)
12 eggs
1 cup minced sharp cheddar cheese

Cook the rye with the caraway and water in a covered saucepan until tender. Remove from heat.

Hard-boil the eggs. Peel and chill at least ½ hour. Cut them in half lengthwise (if desired, reserve 2 yolks for garnish). Work with 6 pieces at a time. Place them in the workbowl and pulse until coarsely chopped. Transfer to a mixing bowl. Stir in the cooked berries and dressing.

Prepare Avocado Dressing. Set aside and rinse out the workbowl.

Process the cheese until minced. Measure 1 cup.

Transfer the egg mixture to a serving dish. Garnish with the cheese and also the reserved egg yolks (fluff them by pushing through a dry tea strainer).

Yield: 6 main dish servings

INCREDIBLE SWEET POTATO SALAD

I'll admit that originally this salad was a way of coping with leftover sweet potatoes. Try it, though, and see if you don't agree that the salad is tasty enough to warrant its own especially cooked sweet potatoes.

1 cup cooked sweet potato, cubed
¼ cup Pineapple Cream Dressing, Date Nut Dressing, or Bingo Dressing (see Index)
Lettuce leaves

Prepare the dressing of your choice. Bake or steam enough sweet potato to yield about 1 cup cubed. Refrigerate until thoroughly chilled.

Assemble the salad just before serving. Cut the potato into cubes with a sharp knife. Over a bed of lettuce, alternate layers of potato with dressing.

Yield: 1 serving

COMPOSED CAULIFLOWER BUFFET

Make this festive composed salad the centerpiece at your buffet table. Delicate slices of cauliflower are set off against lettuce; eggs and a bright cheese dressing provide hearty protein.

3 hard-boiled eggs
1 cup sliced cauliflower (3–6 flowerets)
1 cup minced sharp cheddar
1½ cups large-curd cottage cheese
2 tablespoons salad oil
¼ teaspoon dry mustard
⅛ teaspoon cayenne
½ teaspoon chervil, ½ teaspoon savory, or 1
    tablespoon poppy seed
Lettuce
Optional: **fresh parsley, black olives, cherry
    tomatoes, other garnishes of your choice**

Boil and peel the eggs. Dry and cut in half lengthwise. Pulse until coarsely chopped. Set aside.

Steam cauliflower until fork tender. (If you like it raw, so much the easier!) Push the cauliflower through the slicing disc. Remove the most attractive pieces and set them aside. Any "crumbs" can remain in the workbowl, to be incorporated into the dressing.

Insert the metal blade. Mince chunks of cheddar cheese and measure 1 cup. Add the cottage cheese, salad oil, mustard, cayenne, and choice of chervil, savory, or poppy. Process 10 seconds. Scrape down. Repeat until the mixture is uniform.

Assemble on one large platter or four individual serving dishes. Use your imagination to create an arrangement or try the following: Mound the thick dressing in the center of the lettuce-covered platter. Decorate the edges of the platter with cauliflower slices. Arrange the chopped egg on top of the dressing. Garnish with olives and other optional ingredients.

Yield: at least 4 servings

SUMMERTIME SALAD

This salad is colorful, juicy, and fun to eat.

1–1½ cups cooked corn, scraped from 2 ears
2 cups carrot matchsticks (2 large)
1 large green pepper
1 tablespoon olive oil
1 tablespoon salad oil
1 tablespoon cider vinegar
¼ teaspoon basil
¼ teaspoon oregano
Salt and pepper to taste

Steam the corn. Scrape off the kernels and set aside. Wash carrots and push through the french fry disc once or the slicing disc twice. Measure 2 cups.

Trim the green pepper and cut into thin rings.

Toss the carrots, green pepper, oils, vinegar, and herbs together. Add salt and pepper to taste. Lightly stir in the corn.

Yield: 6 servings

UNEXPECTED CARROT RAISIN SALAD

A sweet carrot raisin salad is a little too much for some people or some moods. Here is a tart, lower-caloried version.

2 cups grated carrot (2 medium)
⅓ cup Swiss cheese pieces
3 tablespoons currants or ¼ cup raisins
1 tablespoon vinegar
2 teaspoons salad oil
Salt to taste

Push carrot pieces through the shredding disc and measure 2 cups.

Cut the cheese into tiny chunks with a knife. Toss all ingredients, add salt to taste, and serve at once.

Yield: 2 servings

CURRIED SUMMER CARROTS

Here's another variation on the carrot raisin salad. When you think about it, why should fresh peach be any more unusual than raisin, assuming that you can find it? With the addition of tomato, the colors are superb and the tastes bright and fruity.

Salad

1½ cups grated carrot (1 large)
1 peach
1 tomato

Dressing

1 tablespoon cider vinegar
2 tablespoons tomato juice
1 tablespoon salad oil
¼ teaspoon curry powder
Dash salt
Pinch cinnamon

Push carrot chunks through the shredding disc and measure 1½ cups. Push peach halves or quarters through the slicing disc (skin facing toward the back of the machine, if you've left it on). Cut the tomato into thin wedges with a sharp knife.

Toss salad ingredients with the dressing ingredients. Chill 1 hour and correct seasoning before serving.

Yield: 4 servings

CC SALAD

Thanks to the coconut, this attractive salad gives your teeth a good workout.

½ cup Fresh Grated Coconut, preferably toasted (see Index)
1 cup grated carrot (1 medium)
¾ cup yogurt
Honey to taste
Optional: **golden raisins, fresh pineapple chunks, mango, or papaya**

Prepare the coconut. Push carrot chunks through the shredding disc and measure 1 cup. Stir together with all other ingredients and serve immediately.

Yield: 2 or more servings

CRISPEST COLESLAW

Ah, unsoggy coleslaw.

2 crisp apples, such as McIntosh or Jonathan
3 tablespoons lemon juice
2 cups red cabbage, sliced
2 cups green cabbage, minced
¼ cup salad oil
⅛ teaspoon salt

Trim and quarter the apples. Pack in the feed tube either sideways or upright (choose one) and push through the slicing disc. Transfer to a quart-sized jar or storage container. Shake with the lemon juice.

Push chunks of red cabbage through the slicing disc to measure 2 cups. Transfer to the jar.

Insert the metal blade. Cut cubes of green cabbage and mince. Measure 2 cups.

Shake the jar. Transfer the green cabbage to it. Add the oil and salt and shake again.

Before serving or packing for a picnic, correct the seasoning.

Yield: 6 servings

OLIVE SLAW

This salad could be the hit of your picnic.

1 cup Olives Plus Spread or Dressing (see Index)
3 cups green cabbage, sliced
¾–1 cup corn kernels (1 ear)

Prepare the spread. Push chunks of cabbage through the slicing disc and measure 3 cups. Mix together the cabbage and the spread.

Steam the corn. Scrape off the kernels and gently stir into the salad.

Serve immediately or refrigerate and serve at your convenience.

Yield: 4–6 servings

MINTED CABBAGE SALAD

It's cabbage, all right. But how refreshing and zesty, especially on a hot day or with spicy accompaniments!

3 cups green cabbage, sliced
1 cup cucumber slivers (½ medium)
3 tablespoons salad oil
1 tablespoon cider vinegar
1 teaspoon dried spearmint or peppermint
Salt and pepper to taste
Optional: **2 seedless oranges**

Push chunks of cabbage through the slicing disc and measure 3 cups.

Trim the cucumber. Push chunks of it through the french fry disc or cut into 2-inch lengths and push through the slicing disc.

In a bowl or storage jar, toss cabbage and cucumber together with oil, vinegar, and dried mint. Chill at least 1 hour and add salt and pepper to taste.

If desired, just before serving, peel 2 oranges. Divide them into 2–4 groups of sections and push them through the slicing disc. Mix the orange slivers into the salad.

Yield: 4 or more servings

TIGER'S SLAW

This spicy salad gets attention at picnics and barbecues.

1 cup onion, sliced (1 large)
½ cup salad oil
¼ cup olive oil
1 tablespoon chili powder
8 cups cabbage, minced (1 medium)
¼ cup vinegar
½ teaspoon salt
2 cups adzuki sprouts or cooked, drained
**   kidney beans**

Trim and quarter the onion and push through the slicing disc. In a heavy large skillet, warm the oils and chili powder over medium heat. When the chili starts to release a fragrance, stir in the onion and cook until transparent, stirring occasionally.

Process chunks of cabbage until minced. Measure about 8 cups. (This will take several batches. For efficient chopping, do not overload the workbowl.)

Transfer 7 cups to a large mixing bowl or storage jar. Stir the remaining cabbage into the onion mixture to soak up the oil. Transfer the onion-cabbage mixture to the bowl. Stir in the vinegar and salt.

To prepare this salad for a crowd unaccustomed to sprouts, the raw adzuki taste can be modified by steaming briefly. Gently stir in the raw or steamed sprouts or drained kidney beans.

Chill and correct the seasoning.

Yield: about ½ gallon

Ⓕ THE FP SALAD

A salad a day may work better than apples for keeping the doctor away. Both raw veggies and apples add fiber to our diets and give teeth a workout. However, salads have more potential variety than raw apples; this diversity is necessary for our physical as well as our mental well-being. If you consult charts of food values, you'll find that both raw and cooked vegetables have advantages. For instance, a comparison of raw and cooked tomatoes shows the cooked tomatoes higher in vitamin A and thiamin, while the raw vegetable makes a far better showing in the vitamin B_6 department. With onions, the raw vegetable has a clear nutritional advantage regarding not just vitamin B_6, but protein, iron, calcium, phosphorus, and potassium.

The food processor can help you to achieve dietary diversity in new and impressive ways. Some of these ways were shown in the other recipes in this chapter. I want to conclude with an overview of everyday salad making, which is usually an improvisation, based on the ingredients that are on hand.

Indiscriminate use of the processor could lead to salads of mincemeat. Knowledgeable use, on the other hand, will enable you to create memorable salads of dazzling variety in next to no time at all.

HOW TO MIX AND MATCH

Selecting the components of a salad is a game of contrasts: crisp and soft, whole shapes and cut shapes, crunchy and smooth, thick and thin, raw and cooked, light and dark.

If your improvised salads all tend to be alike, the following design will help you add diversity without producing a kitchen sink hodgepodge. Refer to the lists of ingredients that follow.

1. At least ¾ of the salad should be Whole, Raw Ingredients.
2. If you have more than 3 different ingredients from outside this category, toss the salad with a plain dressing or lemon juice. With 3 or fewer different ingredients, use an interesting dressing, such as the ones in the last chapter.
3. Use at least 1 choice from Munchy Ingredients or Miscellaneous Goodies.
4. Altogether, do not use more than 2 choices from Munchy Ingredient Group A or D or from Marinated Ingredients.

5. Altogether, do not use more than 1 choice from Munchy Ingredient Group B or C.
6. To keep lettuce from wilting, toss the washed, drained leaves with a tablespoon of oil. Then add other salad ingredients, toss in the dressing, and serve at once.

TABLE 2: INGREDIENTS FOR A DAZZLING FP SALAD

Whole, Raw Ingredients—
¾ of the Salad

Lettuce leaves: romaine, red leaf, salad bowl, Boston, and so forth
Spinach
Tender beet greens (use a small amount)
Tender radish greens (use a small amount)
Watercress (use a small amount)
Endive (use a small amount)

My Discoveries:

Munchy Ingredients: Group A—
More Than 2

Prepared with the shredding disc

Grated raw beet
Grated raw carrot
Grated raw broccoli
Grated raw radish
Grated raw jicama

My Discoveries:

Munchy Ingredients: Group B—
More Than 1

Prepared with the slicing disc

Grated raw green or red cabbage
Julienned fresh green or wax beans
Sliced raw or cooked beets
Sliced raw or cooked bok choy
Sliced raw spanish onion
Sliced cucumber
Sliced water chestnut
Sliced cooked broccoli stem
Sliced cooked or raw cauliflower
Sliced raw carrot
Sliced raw celery
Sliced raw turnip
Sliced raw potato
Sliced raw kohlrabi
Sliced raw radish
Sliced raw jicama
Sliced raw or cooked summer squash

My Discoveries:

Munchy Ingredients: Group C—
More Than 1

Prepared with the metal blade

Minced green or red cabbage
Chopped pitted green or black olives
Chopped nuts
Minced stem of cooked artichoke
Chopped hard-boiled egg

My Discoveries:

Marinated Ingredients— More Than 2

Items are cooked until tender, then marinated in 2 parts olive oil, 1 part salad oil, 1–2 parts lemon juice or vinegar. Drain thoroughly before adding to the rest of the salad. For lowfat marinating, simply use lemon juice and herbs.

Artichoke heart
Asparagus
Any legume except split peas or lentils
Green or wax beans
Brussels sprouts
Broccoli
Cauliflower
Sliced or whole mushrooms*
Peeled, cubed eggplant* (or use the french fry disc, if you have one)
Cubed tofu
Rutabaga or turnip (use the french fry or slicing disc to cut before cooking)
Parsnip or carrot (cut into large chunks or pushed through the slicing disc before marinating)

My Discoveries:

Munchy Ingredients: Group D—
More Than 2

Whole items

Tiny beets, cooked
Freshly shelled raw peas
Raw or toasted sunflower seeds
Sprouted beans or seeds
Soy nuts
Cooked brown rice, barley, bulgur, wheat berries, or rye berries

My Discoveries:

Miscellaneous Goodies—
As Few or As Many As Desired

Tomato, cut bite-sized, or whole cherry tomato
Red or green pepper, cut into rings, wedges, slivers, or large sections
Corn kernels, cooked and scraped from the cob
Cubes of cheese
Cubes of tofu (for pressed tofu, see Elegant Vegetable Pie, page 98)
Ripe avocado wedges
Chopped fresh herbs (in moderation)
Cubed cooked squash or sweet potato
Whole olives

My Discoveries:

*These are exceptions to the need for being cooked before marinating. They soak up flavors best when raw.

7 Multitextured Beans and Grains

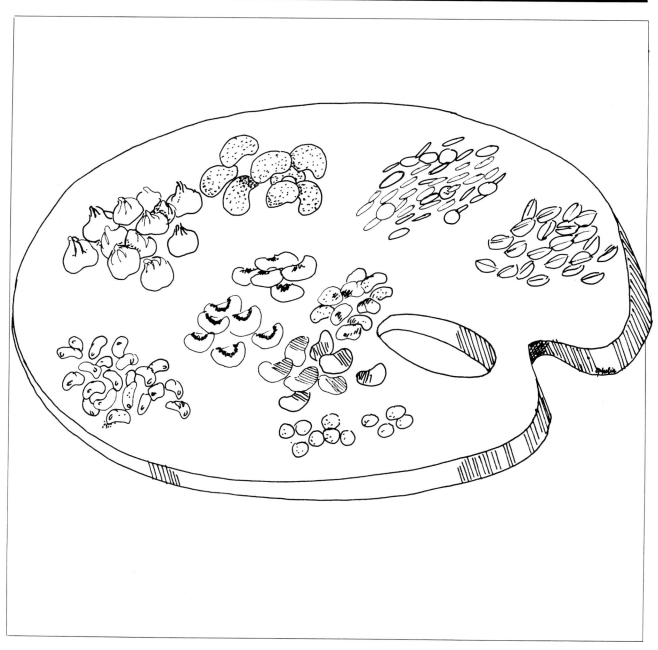

"Winsome as a chick-pea." "As sweet as brown rice." "Kasha tastes good like a buckwheat groat should."

If such phrases are not on everyone's lips, perhaps the main reason is that many of us have never given these foods a chance. To do so, two things are necessary: proper cooking of the natural grain or legume so it can be enjoyed plain, and serving these foods in a variety of special ways. Imagine what people would think of beef if it were served only as jerky!

You may notice that I specified cooking the *natural* grain or legume. Degermed cornmeal and canned cooked split peas are rather limited in their potential, no matter how skillfully used. The texture and flavor, and often most of the nutritive value, have been sacrificed to apparent convenience.

In Table 3 these wonderful foods are arranged in what I call palettes. An artist in the kitchen has these culinary colors available. Don't just dabble with one or two. Why not give them all a chance? They're probably the cheapest foods you can buy. For information on the nutrient density of these foods, see Chapter 15.

Instructions follow for cooking these multitextured marvels.

TABLE 3: PALETTES OF BEANS AND GRAINS

A palette is an arrangement of colors from which a painter can choose in creating works of art. Looking at legumes and grains in this way will help you use them to get just the effect you want when you design original recipes.

A Color Palette of Cooked Beans (Dark to Light)

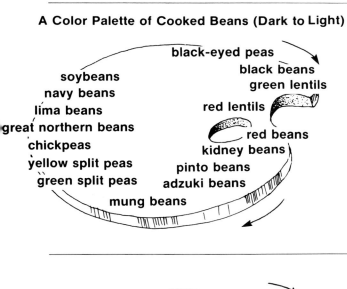

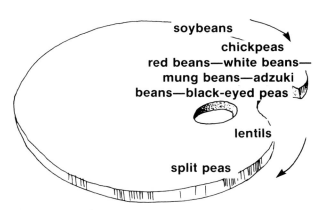

A Texture Palette of Cooked Beans (Dense to Soft)

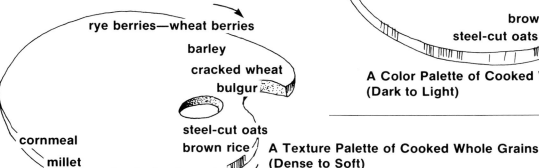

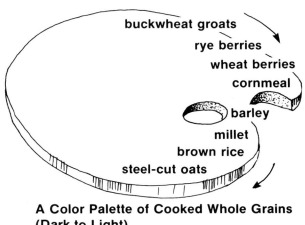

A Color Palette of Cooked Whole Grains (Dark to Light)

A Texture Palette of Cooked Whole Grains (Dense to Soft)

HOW TO COOK NATURAL GRAINS AND BEANS

It's tough at first to understand how something as flimsy as rolled oats could be considered *whole* grains. Actually, *whole* refers to whether or not a grain still contains the germ, not the shape of the cut grain.

To see how important wholeness is, consider barley. Hulled barley is the form sold in health food stores and used in all my recipes. Scotch or pot barley has had a good deal of the protein refined away. Pearl barley has lost even more— 74 percent of its original protein, 97 percent of the fiber, and 88 percent of the minerals.

On the following pages I have given the most precise directions I can so that you can come to share my enthusiasm for the marvelous taste and texture these foods can offer when prepared correctly. Please don't be intimidated by all the details. Information about grain and legume cooking still is not as widespread as it could be. Because many of us are first-generation natural cooks, these details are provided to ensure success.

Grains

General methods for cooking grains are in Table 4; preferred methods are given in Table 5. The *Vital Statistics* that you will need most often have been placed in Appendix II for easy reference. Some additional tips follow.

- The more a grain is processed, the less it needs to be rinsed. Buckwheat groats, bulgur, and cracked wheat do not need rinsing, nor do rolled grains, meals (including cornmeal), or flours.

   To rinse the others, place the amount of grain you plan to cook in a jar and cover with water. Use your hand to stir the grain. Then pour off the water. Repeat until the rinse water is clear. Finally, to avoid throwing off the measurement of water (see Appendix II), drain thoroughly through a sieve.

- Although flours, meals, and rolled grains do not need to be rinsed, they should be tasted periodically for freshness. These foods are different from other forms of grain (or beans), which, when stored for a long time, simply need a longer cooking time and lose the ability to sprout. In contrast, foods such as cornmeal and soy flour turn rancid. All

rancid things taste pretty much alike, so you won't find the characteristic bitterness hard to recognize. Anything with that taste should be discarded.

- Never stir while cooking (except for rolled grains and grains being steamed or cooked breakfast cereal-style). Stirring breaks up the overall pattern of cooking, resulting in a product that is mushy or even inedible.
- Avoid peeking at a grain while it is cooking. When steam escapes from the pot it can slow down the cooking process and throw off the proportion of liquid to grain.
- After cooking, fluff the grain by stirring lightly. If possible, allow the fluffed grain to sit a couple more minutes, covered, before serving. This improves the texture.
- If the grain is not done after the liquid has disappeared, add a little boiling water and continue cooking. Don't stir.
- If the grain burns slightly, you can rescue it by stirring and fluffing. If the grain still looks or tastes too dry, pour in a little water and remove the pan from heat. Let it sit, covered, for a few minutes. Fluff again.
- If the grain is quite burned, remove the good portions layer by layer and turn them into a serving dish. Discard the remaining grain and start soaking the pan immediately.
- To make cleanup after cooking easy, always prepare the cooking pot and lid by oiling lightly.

Bean Basics

Unlike grains, dried beans are all cooked in the same way: simmered in a covered pan for various lengths of time. If you like, slow cookers or the boil and bake method can be used. Pressure cookers are suitable for legumes other than split peas and lentils.

The *Vital Statistics* of times and yields for bean cookery are in Appendix II. Tips follow to give you the benefit of my experience.

- Before cooking beans, always sort through them. Discard discolored or broken beans and any stray pebbles. Rinse thoroughly, as for grains.
- Every cook has heard about soaking beans overnight, as a necessary preparation for cooking, but here are three alternative methods, all of which are better:

TABLE 4: GENERAL METHODS FOR COOKING WHOLE GRAINS

Fluffy Boil

Boil the water in an oiled saucepan. Rinse and drain the grain. As soon as the water boils, add the grain. Stir. When the water returns to a boil, turn the heat down so that the water simmers. Cover and start to time cooking.

***Advantage of Method:** helps preserve grain texture.*

One-Step Boil

Add water and rinsed grain to an oiled saucepan. Cover and bring to a boil (approximate by the sound), then turn heat to a simmer and cook until water is absorbed.

***Advantages of Method:** requires less waiting from the cook and less attention than the fluffy boil.*

Boil and Bake

Oil a covered pan that can be used on a burner as well as in the oven. Once the grain and water boil, as in the one-step boil, transfer the covered pan to a preheated 350° F. oven and continue baking until the grain is tender.

***Advantages of Method:** The cook has more flexibility about timing the grain with the rest of the meal. Once the grain is done it will stay warm for a good half-hour if kept in the same pan. Lentils can also be prepared in this way. The gentle cooking maintains their shape.*

Pressure Cook

Follow instructions from the pressure cooker manufacturer, including which grains are suitable for this method, or see the instructions in The Apartment Vegetarian Cookbook, *Lindsey Miller, Peace Press, 1978, which show you how to pressure cook all beans and grains.*

***Advantages of Method:** quickest overall cooking time; superior texture in finished product.*

Toast and Boil

Pan roast the grain in an oiled skillet with cover. Additional oil for pan roasting is optional (sesame oil is particularly good). Use medium-high heat and stir often to prevent scorching. Meanwhile, bring the measured amount of water to a rolling boil. When the grain is toasted (color darkens somewhat and a delicious odor is given off), pour the water over the grain, cover at once, and turn heat to low, cooking until tender or the water is absorbed.

***Advantages of method:** Deeper flavor, bouncier texture.*

Breakfast Cereal Style

Many grains work well as porridge. When reheating a cooked grain (or preparing raw rolled grains for the first time), add enough additional milk or water to achieve the desired consistency. Cook uncovered in a saucepan. If milk is added, use a double boiler. Either way, stir often. Cook until the grain is heated through and tender.

***Advantages of Method:** When extra liquid is cooked into the cereal, rather than just poured over it in the serving bowl, the porridge stays hotter. It also is easier to control the consistency.*

Steam

Place grain and water (or milk) in the oiled top of a double boiler. Once the water comes to a boil, cover and cook over low heat, stirring occasionally, until tender.

***Advantage of method:** It prevents burning and sticking, especially important with cornmeal or with breakfast cereals cooked in milk.*

TABLE 5: PREFERRED METHODS FOR COOKING SPECIFIC WHOLE GRAINS

Grain	Preferred Methods	Methods to Avoid	General Comments
Barley	Fluffy boil	Breakfast cereal style	
Brown rice	Fluffy boil; pressure cook		
Buckwheat groats (kasha)	Toast and boil	All other methods	Do it right and you'll have tiny fluffy balls of grain—light texture to contrast with the rich earthy flavor. Badly cooked kasha is a hodgepodge of dark undercooked bits and white mush.
Bulgur and cracked wheat	Toast and boil; breakfast cereal style	All other methods	
Cornmeal (polenta)	Steam; breakfast cereal style	All other methods	
Millet	Toast and boil		
Rolled oats, rye, and wheat	Fluffy boil; breakfast cereal style	All other methods	Stir often while cooking.
Rye berries and wheat berries	Fluffy boil; pressure cook	Breakfast cereal style	
Steel-cut oats	Fluffy boil	Pressure cook; toast and boil	

My Discoveries:

1. Sprout whole legumes first (this won't work for split peas or any legumes that have been sprayed). Sprouted beans cook in minutes. They become easier to digest. And the nutritional value improves dramatically. Consider mung beans, the legume most people mean when they talk about bean sprouts. For approximately the same number of calories as cooked, unsprouted mung beans you can ingest 1.1 mg. thiamin instead of .25, 9 mg. of niacin instead of 2.4, 1.3 mg. of riboflavin instead of .2. You'll get about four times the vitamin A, twice the calcium, and double the protein.

2. Quick soak beans by boiling them for 2 minutes in a covered pan. Turn off the heat and let the beans expand for 1 hour. Then cook. Beans soaked in this way have a firmer texture; there is even some evidence that they are less likely to cause gas than beans soaked overnight. Quick-soak beans in the measured amount of water needed to cook them.

3. Throw a few pieces of edible seaweed into the bean pot. Sea vegetables, as they are more properly called, can be purchased at health food stores. Available varieties include hijiki, arame, and kombu. Sea vegetables act as catalysts, enabling you to dispense with soaking. Cooking time is only slightly longer than it would be for

soaked beans. As the sea vegetable cooks, it adds minerals to the beans and subtly enriches the flavor.

- Other people are not enthusiastic about beans at all, and for good reason. Beans give them gas. Luckily you can dispense with the flatulence without giving up the beans.

  According to scientists with the U.S. Department of Agriculture, gas is caused by hard-to-digest elements, most of which can be removed with knowledgeable cooking. After you quick-soak or soak the beans, drain them and substitute new water for cooking. And if someone in your family is especially prone to digestive trouble, increase the amount of cooking water up to 10 times the volume of the beans. It can also help to keep the cooking pot uncovered.

  Split peas and lentils are not suitable for cooking with extra liquid, as discussed later. Fortunately they are the easiest legumes to digest.
- Everyone will find beans most digestible when they have been cooked properly.

  Once you have mastered the basics of bean cookery you can adjust how tender you want beans to be, from just soft to mushy, whole to partly processed. *Just soft* is the bean equivalent of medium rare steak. *Mushy* corresponds to well done. Make your choice according to personal preference, but the extremes of *raw* and *too well done* for beans should be avoided. Burst open, mouth-of-mush beans point to inexpert cooking, just as the tough-skinned, undercooked version signals difficult digestion ahead.
- Soybeans require sufficient cooking for an additional reason. This "meat on a vine" contains an enzyme that inhibits protein digestion—ironic for the legume that is highest in protein. Sufficient cooking will neutralize the enzyme.

  Incidentally, soy sprouts or flour should always be cooked, for the same reason.
- Split peas and lentils need not be soaked before cooking.
- Never add salt to cooking beans until they are thoroughly tender. Otherwise they may never be tender.
- It isn't necessary, as some cooks think, to add oil to produce tender beans. Just cook them long enough.

- If you want to add something to dress up plain cooked beans, try a little vinegar or lemon juice.
- Unlike grains, the flavor of beans is not much affected by cooking in stock rather than water. This makes the bean pot a happy home for the nutritious but strong-tasting water left over from cooking some vegetables (such as spinach). By the same logic, do not waste good-tasting stock on cooking beans—use it afterward, instead, after draining the beans.
- Speaking of stock, excellent stock is yours for free when you add plenty of extra water when you cook soybeans or chick-peas.
- Avoid cooking split peas or lentils in extra liquid. These legumes break down quickly, especially if boiled too hard or too long. (In contrast, soybeans and chick-peas are almost indestructible.) Instead of stock in the form of extra cooking liquid, what you'll get is a pot of soup.
- I repeat, to be digestible, soybeans *must* be cooked tender. That means 5 hours of boiling time in a regular covered saucepan. Don't be discouraged by this; they are worth every minute, due to protein content, versatility, the stock made in the cooking process, and the long keeping time for soybeans if you freeze them.
- Both soybeans and chick-peas freeze well and keep for weeks without loss of texture. (Other whole, cooked beans can be frozen, but I find the results disappointing.)

  To freeze, put partly drained, thoroughly cooked beans in a plastic ice cube tray. Freeze overnight, then transfer to double plastic bags to avoid freezer burn. Close one plastic bag containing bean cubes into a second plastic bag and seal both with a twist.

  Thaw beans at room temperature or under hot tap water. They can always be substituted for freshly cooked beans.
- Stock from the beans can be frozen in the same manner—frozen like ice cubes and transferred to double bags.

PINTO BEAN TRIO

This trio of spreads celebrates the versatility of the all too often stereotyped pinto bean. Use any of these mixtures for satisfying sandwiches or try the suggestions in the recipes.

MEXICAN PINTOS

¾ cup cooked pinto beans, drained
½ cup green pepper pieces (½ large)
1 tablespoon salad oil
1 teaspoon lemon juice
½ teaspoon oregano
¼ teaspoon chili powder
½ cup avocado pulp (½ medium)
Salt and garlic to taste

Process everything but the green pepper and cooked beans until smooth. Pulse in salt and garlic to taste, then the beans and diced green pepper until mixed.

● Stuff Mexican Pintos into raw tomatos. To prepare each tomato, cut a thin slice off the top, scoop out the seeds, and turn the tomato upside down to drain for 15 minutes. Serve as a cold entree.

Yield: 1 cup

SALTY, RICH PINTOS

Yes, this is a salty recipe. I offer it without apology. Satisfying an occasional craving for salt (or sugar) does not wreak havoc on health. Long-term damage is caused by frequent doses.

2 tablespoons peanut butter
2 tablespoons soy sauce
2 tablespoons lemon juice
1 cup cooked pintos, drained

Process everything but the cooked beans until smooth. Scrape down as necessary. Pulse in the beans until the mixture is uniform.

● Stuff Salty, Rich Pintos into green peppers. Serve cold or warmed in a preheated 350° F. oven. Before baking, oil a loaf pan well and fit in the peppers so that they prop each other up.

Yield: 1 cup

SWEET AND SOUR PINTOS

1 cup cooked pinto beans, drained
1 tablespoon honey
5 drops Liquid Smoke
1 tablespoon salad oil
¼ cup carrot chunks, cooked or raw
⅛ teaspoon dry mustard
2 teaspoons vinegar
Salt and ginger to taste

Process everything but the cooked beans until uniform. Scrape down as needed. Pulse in salt and ginger to taste. Pulse in the pintos until the mixture is uniform.

● Stuff Sweet and Sour Pintos into avocado halves. They become sweet, sour, and impressive.

Yield: 1 cup

BEAN SPECIALTIES
BLONDE BEANS

1 cup navy beans + 2⅓ cups water, or 2½ cups
   cooked navy beans
Stock, as needed
⅛ teaspoon marjoram
⅛ teaspoon rosemary
1 tablespoon olive oil
⅛ teaspoon salt
⅛ teaspoon black pepper
Optional: lemon slices and parsley sprigs

Quick-soak the beans and simmer until tender along with the marjoram and rosemary. Drain, reserving liquid if desired. (If leftover cooked beans are used, warm the herbs in the olive oil.)
Process smooth ½ cup of the cooked beans, ¼ cup liquid left over from cooking them or other mild stock, and all other ingredients.
Stir this mixture into the beans. Serve steaming hot.
Optional: garnish with sliced lemon and sprigs of parsley.

Yield: 5 servings

SUNNY SPLIT PEAS

When hot, this is invigorating. Cold and processed smooth, it makes a high-protein dip.

1 cup yellow split peas
2½–3 cups water
1 cup Spreadable Cheddar Spread (see Index)
Optional: **whole grain Bread Crumbs (see Index) or croutons**

Cook the split peas in the water until tender (check after 1 hour). Prepare the spread. Process the split peas and spread until uniform.

Transfer to a saucepan and cook, stirring often, over medium heat. Serve as soon as it is hot—do not let it come to a boil.

If desired, garnish with whole grain Bread Crumbs (see Index) or croutons.

Yield: 4 main dish servings

FAVORITE SOYBEANS

Soybeans have a chameleonlike ability to change their appearance to blend in with the environment. This recipe makes good use of that trait. If you like the taste of butter and the feel of spices warming your mouth, this soybean dish may become one of your favorites.

1½ cups cooked soybeans
1 cup carrot matchsticks (1 medium)
2 tablespoons clarified butter (substitute 2 tablespoons butter + 1 teaspoon oil)
½ teaspoon mustard seed
½ teaspoon ground coriander
¼–½ teaspoon cayenne
½ teaspoon turmeric
2 tablespoons soy stock or water
Salt to taste

Drain the soybeans.

Trim the carrot. Pack sideways and push through the french fry disc. Otherwise push through the slicing disc. Measure 1 cup.

In a heavy saucepan or skillet with cover, melt the clarified butter over medium heat. Add the mustard, coriander, and cayenne. When the mustard seed starts to sizzle, stir in the carrots, soybeans, turmeric, and stock. Cover.

Every couple of minutes, shake the saucepan, holding the cover down with one hand and grasping the pan handle with the other. This way you keep the food from sticking and scorching without letting liquid evaporate. Taste after 5 minutes. When it is done to your liking, add salt and serve.

Yield: 4 servings

PINEAPPLE CHILI BEAN BAKE

Pinto beans go so well with chili seasoning that the association becomes almost automatic. Unfortunately, such dishes can have a dismal sameness—and a mouth-burning pungency. Try this for a mild-flavored alternative. (For hotter tastes, see recipe for El Chili sauce, soup, and casserole.)

1⅓ cups pinto beans
⅓ cup long-grain brown rice (substitute short- or medium-grain)
4 cups unsalted stock or water
Optional: **pinch dried seaweed (hijiki or arame)**
2 cups jack or other mild cheese, shredded
1 cup carrot circles (1 medium)
1½ cups fresh pineapple, cubed, along with the juice gained from cutting it, or 1 15-ounce can of pineapple chunks, canned in unsweetened juice
1 teaspoon chili powder
¼ teaspoon dry mustard
½ teaspoon salt

Preheat oven to 350° F.

Cook the pintos and rice in the stock in a covered saucepan. If a little hijiki or arame is available, it is not necessary to quick-soak before cooking.

Push chunks of cheese through the shredding disc and measure 2 cups. Set aside.

Trim fresh carrot. Push through the slicing disc and measure 1 cup. Set aside.

Insert the metal blade. Process the pineapple juice, spices, and salt into ½ cup of the cooked pinto mixture. Stir this sauce into the cooked beans and rice, the pineapple chunks, and the sliced carrots. Oil an 8″ × 8″ × 2″ casserole or other broad-shaped 2-quart baking dish. Transfer the mixture to the baking dish and top with the cheese. Bake until the cheese is bubbly (check after 20 minutes). Serve hot.

Yield: 6 main dish servings

AUTUMN ALMOND CASSEROLE

When almonds and squash have been freshly harvested they are at their peak of flavor. Autumn is the best season to warm up this hearty stew, though it makes good eating any time of the year.

½ **cup chick-peas**
½ **cup red beans (substitute kidney or pinto beans)**
½ **cup rye berries**
6 **cups water**
Optional: **2 tablespoons dried seaweed**
1 **bay leaf**
¼ **cup Almond Butter (see Index)**
1 **cup winter squash, cubed**
1½ **cups brussels sprouts**
¼ **teaspoon salt**
¼ **teaspoon black pepper**
2 **tablespoons whole wheat flour**
⅛ **teaspoon sage**
¼ **teaspoon ground ginger**
1 **tablespoon lemon juice**

In a large covered pan, cook together the chick-peas, red beans, rye berries, water, bay leaf, and optional seaweed. If seaweed is not available, quick-soak. Simmer until the beans are tender (check after 3 hours).

Meanwhile, prepare almond butter, if you don't already have some on hand.

Steam squash until barely tender and measure 1 cup cubed meat. Wash and trim the brussels sprouts. Cut upright, to produce look-alike halves.

Transfer about 1 cup liquid from the cooked beans to the workbowl. Add the almond butter, salt, pepper, flour, sage, and ginger. Process until smooth. Scrape down and reprocess as necessary.

Transfer the mixture to a large saucepan. Bring to a boil over medium-high heat, stirring constantly. Simmer 5 minutes. As needed, thin with additional liquid from the bean pot. Pour into the bean pot along with the cooked squash and cut brussels sprouts. Cook, uncovered, until the brussels sprouts are fork tender. Remove the bay leaf and stir in the lemon juice. Correct seasoning and serve hot. Confidence Biscuits (see Index) are an excellent accompaniment.

Yield: 6 main dish servings

PEPPER BEAN STEW

Three different peppery tastes contrast with the soothing blandness of three different beans. When serving this dish to children, omit the cayenne.

Like any stew, Pepper Bean Stew is saucy. Serve it along with Flexible Cornbread (see Index) or some other delectable dunker.

½ **cup lentils**
1 **cup baby limas**
1 **cup navy beans**
6½ **cups water**
1 **large bunch watercress (substitute parsley)**
¼ **teaspoon salt**
¼ **cup tahini**
⅛ **teaspoon black pepper**
⅛ **teaspoon cayenne**
½ **teaspoon ground ginger**

Rinse and sort through the legumes, discarding any that are broken or shriveled. Quick-soak in the water, then simmer until done (check after 2 hours). Cook at a simmer to maintain the shapes of the beans. Check periodically to make sure that no extra water is needed. Your goal is to produce beans cooked as dry as possible but not burned.

When the beans are tender, process watercress leaves and tender stems to produce 1–2 cups chopped greenery. Sort through this to remove any lengths of unchopped stem. Set aside.

Scoop 1 cup beans from the pot and process them along with all remaining ingredients. Return the chunky tan sauce to the stew pot, add the watercress, and stir gently. Serve bubbling hot.

Yield: 6 main dish servings

CURRIED CHICK-PEAS

Genuine Indian cooking doesn't reek of the seasoning we call curry powder. A curry can be mild and subtly complex, like this dish. Serve it over a steaming layer of rice or millet. Yogurt makes a good accompaniment.

½ cup cooked chick-peas
2 cups carrot pieces (2 medium)
2 cups yellow squash slices (1 large)
½ cup stock, preferably from the chick-peas (substitute milk)
½ teaspoon salt
2 tablespoons clarified butter (substitute butter)
½ teaspoon ground coriander
½ teaspoon ground cardamom
1 cup additional stock (or milk)
2 tablespoons chick-pea flour or whole wheat flour
2 tablespoons raisins

Preheat oven to 350° F.
Prepare the chick-peas. Drain.
Trim carrots and push through the french fry or slicing disc. Measure 2 cups. Set aside.
Push chunks of yellow squash through the slicing disc and measure 2 cups. Set aside.
Insert the metal blade. Process the ½ cup stock, salt, and chick-peas until uniform, scraping down as necessary.
In a large skillet, melt the butter over medium heat. Stir in the coriander and cardamom. Once the spices release their fragrance (if you have a cold, allow 2–3 minutes), stir in the chick-pea mixture, remaining stock, flour, and raisins. Remove from heat without waiting for the gravy to thicken. Stir it into the carrots and squash. Oil a 1½-quart baking dish with cover. Transfer the mixture to the casserole and cover.
Bake until the carrots are tender (check after 20 minutes).

Yield: 4 servings

LIMA WIGGLE

This creation is both delicious and whimsical. The smoky smoothness of gouda contrasts with tarragon-tinted limas and noodles. Bold bursts of peanut ensure that this dish is authentically non-Italian.

2 cups cooked lima beans or 1 cup limas + 2½ cups water
1 cup whole wheat pasta, preferably in the form of elbow macaroni
3 tablespoons butter
3 tablespoons whole wheat flour

2 cups milk
½ teaspoon tarragon
½ teaspoon black pepper
⅛ teaspoon salt
½ cup peanuts
1 7- or 8-ounce gouda cheese

Preheat oven to 350° F.
If cooked limas are not available, quick-soak limas in the water and cook until tender.
Cook the pasta al dente and drain.
Make a cream sauce, using butter, flour, and milk (see recipe for Flexible Cream Sauce). Stir in the tarragon, pepper, and salt. Mix with the pasta.
If you are fortunate enough to start off with raw peanuts, roast them by spreading them out on a baking sheet in a preheated 300° F. oven. Check by sampling, starting after 20 minutes. Let peanuts cool to room temperature.
Pulse peanuts in a dry machine until coarsely chopped. Stir into the pasta mixture.
Push chunks of cheese through the shredding disc.
Transfer the cooked, drained limas to the pasta mixture. Correct the seasoning. Pour it out into an oiled 2-quart casserole and top with the cheese. Bake until the Wiggle is bubbly (check after 15 minutes).

Yield: 6 main dish servings

ORIENTAL LENTILS

This hearty dish has a dusky-spiced flavor.

1 cup lentils
3½ cups stock or water
¼ teaspoon minced fresh ginger or ½ teaspoon ground ginger
½ cup sliced mushrooms (substitute salted, drained eggplant pieces)
¼ cup minced onion (1 small)
1 tablespoon sesame oil (substitute salad oil)
Soy sauce to taste
Garlic Oil (see Index) to taste
Optional: mushroom slices

Cook together in a covered saucepan the lentils, stock or water, and ginger. Trim mushrooms, push through the slicing disc, and measure ½ cup. Set aside.

Trim onion and process until minced. Measure ¼ cup. Sauté in the oil until transparent. Remove from heat.

When the lentils are tender, transfer ¾ of them to the workbowl and process with the onions and oil until smooth. Return this mixture to the pot of lentils. Add the mushroom or eggplant, soy sauce, and Garlic Oil to taste.

Heat at moderate temperature in a covered saucepan or casserole, until the vegetables are done.

If desired, garnish with sautéed mushroom slices.

Note: To create a rich soup rather than a casserole, process all but 1 cup cooked lentils. Then add the mushroom, soy sauce, and Garlic Oil and proceed with the rest of the recipe.

Yield: 4 servings

GOLDEN CABBAGE

The golden, spicy sauce for this cabbage dish is replete with crunchy, delicate pieces of cabbage and onion.

1 cup yellow split peas + 2½ cups water, or 2¼ cups cooked split peas
2 small onions, sliced (2 cups)
2 tablespoons clarified butter, 2 tablespoons Butter for the Table (see Index), or 3 tablespoons butter + 1 teaspoon salad oil
¼ teaspoon cayenne
1½ teaspoons ground ginger
5 cups green cabbage, sliced
¼ cup stock or water
½ teaspoon salt
⅓ cup Freshly Shredded Coconut (see Index) (can come straight from freezer)
2 teaspoons lemon juice

Cook the split peas in the water until tender.
Push chunks of peeled onion through the french fry or slicing disc. Measure about 2 cups.

In a large skillet with cover, melt the butter over medium heat. Add the cayenne and ginger, then the onions. Cook until the onions turn transparent, stirring as needed.

Trim the cabbage and push wedges through the slicing disc. Measure 5 cups. Set aside.

Process smooth the cooked peas, coconut, and salt. Do this in 2 batches to avoid having the machine overflow.

Stir this mixture into the onions. Stir in the cabbage. Cover.

Cook until the cabbage is tender (check after 7 minutes). During this time, stir occasionally to keep the sauce from sticking. Add more water if necessary. Just before serving, stir in the lemon juice.

Yield: 4 servings

GRAIN SPECIALTIES
KASHA SUPREME

This dish is as sumptuous as kasha can be, but it's easy on the cook's schedule.

2 cups cooked buckweat groats or ½ cup raw groats + 1 cup boiling water + dash salt
⅓ cup brazil nuts, hazelnuts, or walnuts
4 tablespoons butter

Cook the buckwheat groats (see Table 5, page 56). Fluff with a fork.

Process the nuts in a dry machine until chopped medium fine. In a large skillet, melt the butter over medium heat. Stir in the nuts. Cook, watching carefully. The instant the butter turns light brown, stir in the kasha. Continue to stir until the grain is heated through. Turn into a serving dish and serve hot.

Yield: 4 servings

CARROTY KASHA

Make a cheerful, hearty dish out of buckwheat groats.

1½ cups carrot chunks (2 medium)
Optional: ½ cup minced onion (2 medium)
1½ tablespoons clarified butter (substitute 2 tablespoons butter + 1 teaspoon salad oil)
½ teaspoon ground ginger
⅛ teaspoon cayenne
¾ cup buckwheat groats

1/8 teaspoon salt
2 cups boiling water
2 tablespoons golden or dark raisins
Optional: soy sauce

Trim carrots and push through the french fry disc or process chunks until coarsely chopped. Measure 1½ cups. Set 2 cups water to boil.

If onion is desired, process chunks until minced and measure ½ cup.

In a heavy skillet or saucepan with cover, heat the clarified butter over medium temperature. Stir in the ginger and cayenne. After 1 minute, stir in the kasha and salt. Turn heat to medium high. Stir constantly. After 1 minute, stir in the carrot and optional onion. After 2–3 minutes, add the raisins, pour in the boiling water, and cover. Turn the heat to low and cook until all water is absorbed (check after 10 minutes). If desired, serve with soy sauce.

Yield: 4 servings

JEWELED RICE

A simple vegetable like broccoli can add a sumptuous touch to rice. The secret here lies partly in the tiny green morsels (minced broccoli stalk), partly in the seasoning.

²⁄₃ **cup short-grain brown rice + 2 cups soy
    stock, or 2 cups cooked brown rice**
1 **cup broccoli, chopped medium fine (1 large
    stalk; flowers not used)**
3 **tablespoons clarified butter or butter**
1 **teaspoon dill weed**
1/8 **teaspoon salt**
1 **tablespoon lemon juice**
Optional: **lemon slices**

Cook the rice in the stock.

Wash a large stalk of broccoli. Trim the flowers away, for use elsewhere. Cut off any discolored portions of stem. Starting with the bottom of the stalk, cut 2-inch lengths and place them in the workbowl. Process several lengths at a time until chopped medium fine. Measure 1 cup.

Melt the butter in a large, heavy skillet, over medium heat. Add the broccoli and dill. Stir frequently. After 2 minutes, stir in the rice and salt.

Either heat through, stirring occasionally, and serve at once or transfer to a covered baking dish and warm for 15 minutes at 350° F. before serving. In either case, taste to make sure the broccoli is done to your taste. Otherwise, cook longer, adding more stock if necessary.

Right before serving, stir in the lemon juice. If desired, garnish with lemon slices.

Yield: 4 servings

BURGERS WITH BEANS AND GRAINS

The rest of this chapter is devoted to burgers, a very useful topic. Patties, balls, sausages, and so forth can become the focal point of your dinner—an unmistakable main dish and a special favorite with children.

In theory, any bean or grain can become a burger. In practice, cooked beans and grains vary widely in moisture content and tenderness. Yet the right balance of wet to dry is critical: too moist and burgers fall apart, too dry and they crack. Once you get a feel for making them, however, you can easily tell where adjustments are needed before you bake. It often helps to boldly overcook the bean or grain to be used in the burger, which makes it mushier and stickier. Properly cooked leftovers can easily be reheated in water to get to this point. For Sticky Brown Rice Burgers, extra long cooking is essential.

What do you use for flavor and protein in a meatless burger? The four following recipes are based respectively on rice, chick-peas, kidney beans, and lentils. Use these recipes as a point of departure for your own creations.

STICKY BROWN RICE BURGERS

This burger has a chewy texture and pleasant (but unobtrusive) flavor.

1 **cup cooked short-grain brown rice, lightly
    salted, sticky**
1/3 **cup walnuts**
1 **egg**
1/3 **cup cheddar cheese, minced**
1/3 **cup rutabaga or carrot, minced**
1 **tablespoon olive oil**
1/8 **teaspoon sage**

Preheat oven to broil.

Prepare the rice and cool to room temperature.

Process the nuts in a dry machine until chopped medium fine. Set aside in a mixing bowl. Beat in the egg.

Process the cheese until minced. Add to the mixing bowl.

Process chunks of peeled, raw rutabaga until minced. Measure packed. Heat the oil in a heavy skillet over medium-high heat. Add the rutabaga, stirring occasionally, until the vegetable softens (about 5 minutes). Then, quickly and gently, stir in the rice to soak up any oil left over in the skillet. Transfer the mixture to the bowl.

Stir in the sage. Shape the mixture into patties and place on a very well-oiled baking sheet. (For easy, uniform shaping, pack the mixture into a ⅛-cup measure. Turn it out on the baking sheet and flatten it into a circle by tapping down with the palm of your hand.)

Broil 6 to 8 inches from the heat source. After 5 minutes, the burger bottoms should be somewhat browned. Gently turn them over with a spatula and cook 2 minutes longer. Serve sizzling hot.

Yield: 10 patties

CHICK-PEA SAUSAGE

These sausages are crisp on the outside, chewy on the inside, spicy through and through. Serve them hot or cold, plain or in casseroles, or on Pizza (see Index).

1 cup cooked chick-peas
1 cup potato pieces (1 medium baking potato)
½ cup stock or water
¼ cup olive oil
½ teaspoon salt
3 tablespoons brewer's or torula yeast
1¼ teaspoons sage
¼ teaspoon cayenne
¼ teaspoon ground ginger

Preheat oven to 350° F.

Cook the chick-peas until tender, if you don't already have some on hand.

Prepare the potato by cooking it until almost tender—a fork goes through it but with some resistance. You will need enough potato for pieces of it to fill a 1-cup measure. Refrigerate the cooked potato for ½ hour or overnight.

Process the chick-peas for 30 seconds. Add all ingredients except the potato and process 10 seconds. Scrape down and reprocess. Repeat until the mixture is smooth. Transfer to a mixing bowl.

Push the chilled potato through the shredding disc. Stir it vigorously into the other ingredients with a fork.

Pack the mixture into a ¼-cup measure. Then roll it into a sausage shape. Generously oil a baking dish with cover. Place the sausages on the bottom of the baking dish. Do not layer the sausages. Cover and bake 25 minutes. Turn with a metal spatula, re-cover the pan, and bake until the bottoms brown (check after 25 minutes).

Yield: 9 large sausages

BEANBALLS

We like to eat these with whole wheat spaghetti and Pizza Sauce (see Index). They are not as sturdy as meatballs but will hold their shape with reasonably careful handling.

2 cups cooked kidney beans (substitute pinto or red beans)
1 medium potato, cooked (1 cup shredded)
1 teaspoon salad oil
½ teaspoon black pepper
⅓-½ cup sunflower seeds
***Optional:* 6 teaspoons Liquid Smoke**
Salt to taste
Garlic Oil (see Index) to taste
Salad oil
Cornmeal

Preheat oven to 400° F.

Cook kidney beans if you don't already have some on hand. Drain.

Bake or steam a potato that will fill about 1 cup. Refrigerate ½ hour or overnight.

In a large, heavy skillet, warm the oil, pepper, and seeds. Stir often, over medium heat, and remove from heat as soon as the seeds brown.

Insert the shredding disc. Push the unpeeled potato through. Replace the shredding disc with the metal blade. Add the kidney beans, the seed mixture, and the Liquid Smoke. Pulse 2 or 3 times, adding salt and Garlic Oil to taste. The mixture should be moist enough to stick when pressed together. If necessary, add a little stock or oil.

One heaping tablespoon at a time, roll the bean mixture between your palms to form balls. Dunk in a shallow cup of oil, then roll in a shallow plate of cornmeal until thoroughly coated.

Bake on a generously oiled cookie sheet until browned on the bottom (check after 7 minutes). Serve hot.

Yield: 20 beanballs

LITTLE MAXES

Sesame seed bun? Pickles? Unnecessary. Tomato sauce, though, is a definite asset to this dish.

1　**cup cooked lentils**
¼　**cup walnuts**
¼　**cup chopped onion (1 medium)**
2　**tablespoons salad oil**
½　**teaspoon coriander**
3　**tablespoons whole wheat flour**

1　**cup stock or water**
1　**cup diced green pepper (1 large)**
⅛　**teaspoon salt**
¼　**teaspoon ground cumin**
¼　**cup rolled oats or rye**
1　**egg, lightly beaten**
Optional: **additional walnut halves**

Preheat oven to 400° F.

Cook lentils until very soft. Drain and measure 1 cup. Transfer to a large mixing bowl.

Pulse the nuts in a dry machine until chopped medium fine. Transfer to the mixing bowl.

Trim onion. Process until chopped medium fine. Sauté in a large skillet with the oil and coriander.

Once the onion turns transparent, stir in the flour. After 2 minutes (stirring often), add the stock in a thin stream. Once the liquid is stirred in, bring the mixture to a boil and simmer 2 minutes. Transfer to the mixing bowl.

Trim the green pepper and dice with a sharp knife. Transfer to the mixing bowl with the salt, cumin, rolled oats, and lightly beaten egg. Stir ingredients together until well mixed.

Drop the batter by ⅛-cup measures into generously oiled muffin compartments in 2 tins or onto 2 generously oiled baking sheets. If desired, press half a walnut meat into the center of each Little Max. Bake until the bottoms brown (check after 12 minutes).

Yield: about 20

8 | Vegetables with Vitality

TABLE 6: VEGETABLE COOKERY

Bake Whole

Many vegetables are delicious when baked whole: summer and winter squash, potato, and sweet potato are my favorites. Wash the vegetable and dry it. Oil either the skin of the vegetable(s) or the surface of the baking dish. It's important to prick several holes in the skin to act as steam valves. Place the vegetable in a pan in a moderate oven. Large roasted vegetables can be carved at the table and served with a sauce. Small whole vegetables make tidy servings. In addition to deepened flavor (compared to steaming), many vegetables develop a chewier crust.

Cut and Bake

Almost every vegetable can be baked in a covered casserole after being cut if it is in a sauce of some kind. The amount and kind of preparation before baking varies—recipes help you get a feel for how to treat individual vegetables.

Steam

This is the quick, nutritious way to prepare vegetables. Use it whenever an old-fashioned recipe calls for boiling (which squanders water-soluble vitamins—see Appendix I).

To steam, use a collapsible stainless steel steamer in a saucepan or kettle with a tight-fitting lid. Bring 2 to 4 inches of water to a boil. Add whole or cut vegetables, put on the cover, and let the water simmer until the vegetables are done.

Since flavors of vegetables remain distinct during steaming, a whole meal's worth of vegetables can be cooked together in one pot. The art of packing a steamer with foods that require various cooking times must be developed with plenty of practice.

Microwave Preparation

Follow manufacturer's instructions, which include different amounts of water to be used according to the type of vegetable.

Pressure Cook

Pressure cookers can be used whenever a recipe calls for steaming. The freshness of flavor is unsurpassed.

Waterless Cooking

For another variation on steaming, place a few tablespoons of water in a pan with a tight cover. When it boils, add sliced vegetables, cover, and after a couple of minutes turn the heat to low.

Since vegetables basically stew in their own juice until cooked, peeking should be kept to a minimum. This method works best with moist vegetables, such as zucchini. Essential to the success of this method is a tight-fitting lid. Pans especially designed for waterless cooking can be purchased.

Stir Fry

The processor is invaluable for this quick-cooking method. Use the slicing disc to prepare most vegetables. Pieces will be thin for greatest crispness; in addition, a great deal of time will be saved.

Stir-fried food is more digestible than deep-fried (not recommended for this reason).

Start with a dry wok or dutch oven. Warm it over high heat until water dropped on the surface sizzles. Distribute a thin layer of oil over the bottom of the pan. If desired, garlic and ginger root can be added at this point. Next, vegetables should be added in order of cooking time needed. Throwing in a handful at a time keeps the cooking heat relatively constant. Stir and cook until vegetables are tender. A bit more oil might be necessary if the vegetables start to stick, and keep stirring.

Braise

This is a versatile method, less oily than stir frying. Heat a small amount of oil in a large skillet or pan with cover until water dropped on the surface sizzles. Stir and fry the vegetable until it starts to brown, then add enough stock or water to barely cover the surface.

Immediately cover the pan and reduce the heat to low. If all the water has been absorbed but the vegetables are not yet tender, add a little water, recover, and continue to cook.

Sauté

This method of pan frying is especially useful for browning onions. Over medium-high heat, warm a small amount of oil or clarified butter in a skillet. When water dropped on the surface sizzles, add the vegetables and stir as needed until browned.

Broil

Unless considerable care is taken, the result of broiling is a charred outside and a raw inside. However, broiling is useful in preparing eggplant. The broiling method on page 82 gives you the effect of sautéed eggplant, but lets you control the amount of oil. That's important with eggplant, which can soak up moisture better than a blotter.

What do you consider to be the best thing about fresh vegetables: the colors? the shapes? the nutrients? the textures? the flavors?

The best part of all may be the vitality. Like freshly cut flowers, healthy vegetables can be kept alive for days. Compare that to meat. Or dried legumes and grains. (Unless you sprout these, the germ of life remains dormant.) Enjoyable though grains, beans, and meat can be, they are inanimate.

By comparison, fresh vegetables burgeon with life. For that reason, it is especially challenging to cook with these plants in versatile ways. This chapter explores the many ways to enjoy the life within vegetables. When vegetables are cooked by a variety of methods, simple and complex, with all sorts of seasonings, their vitality shines out more clearly.

This chapter starts with a table of basic cooking methods for vegetables and a few tips on cookware. (Supplement this by reading the in-depth information on cookware and nutrient conservation in Appendix I.)

Recipes for vegetables follow. They range from quick to elaborate (not necessarily in that sequence—the artichoke recipe is the most complex of them all). You will not find every vegetable represented in this chapter; check the Index for many other vegetable recipes. Few of the vegetables here are exotic. I've chosen them with an eye to convenience and moderate cost, but, as you'll discover, they do not taste commonplace. The processor brings out nuances of taste and texture which will delight long-time vegetable lovers. If you aren't a lover of vegetables yet, this chapter will help you discover each one's characteristic excellence.

ARTIPOPPY CASSEROLE

Artichoke sauce is one of the most remarkable things you can make with a food processor. If you've had artichokes at a meal, you may have noticed how their aftertaste imparts sweetness to everything else you eat. In the form of a sauce, it has the same effect, working as a taste catalyst.

Sauce

1 large artichoke
2 cups water
1 tablespoon vinegar
2 tablespoons lemon juice
⅛ teaspoon salt
1 tablespoon olive oil
Green food coloring

Vegetables

1 cup parsnip slices (substitute carrot slices) (1 medium)
½ cup carrot slices (1 small)
2 tablespoons clarified butter, or 2 tablespoons butter + 1 teaspoon oil
2 teaspoons poppy seeds
1 medium yellow squash (1 cup chopped)
1 medium green squash (1 cup chopped)

Wash a large, fresh artichoke. Trim off only the darkened portion of the stem. You want to use as much stem length as possible. Cook until tender in water with the vinegar added.

Push trimmed parsnip and carrot through the slicing disc. Measure the needed amount. Melt the butter over medium heat. Add the poppy seeds. After 1 minute, stir in the vegetables and heat until crisp tender—not wilted. Stir as needed. Set aside.

Prepare the summer squash for steaming. Cut it only as necessary to fit into the pan. While it cooks, prepare the artichoke pulp for the sauce. Remove the squash from the heat once it is steamed tender.

Make sure the artichoke is so well cooked that the leaves peel off without resistance. If the vegetable is too hot to handle comfortably, plunge it into cold water. Remove all leaves. Discard the tough outermost ones. Carefully spoon out the heart and discard all the thistles (the choke). Put the stem and heart into the workbowl, outfitted with the metal blade. Now set to work on the leaves.

With a sturdy spoon, scrape the soft flesh from the underside of each leaf. Altogether, the artichoke should yield 1 cup of flesh from leaves, stem, and heart combined; the entire process should take only 10 minutes.

Process this with the lemon juice, salt, and olive oil. With the motor running, pour a stream of stock or water through the feed tube, just enough to create a smooth mixture (approximately ¼ cup, but the amount will vary). Scrape down as needed. The purpose of food coloring is to improve the hue of the puree from an uninspiring brownish green to an olive green. Easy does it. Process in a minimal amount, a drop at a time.

Cut the cooked summer squash into attractive small wedges. Add to the carrot mixture, along with the sauce. Heat the mixture to boiling, either baked in an oiled covered casserole at 350° F. or in a saucepan. If you use the saucepan, stir it often; should the mixture stick, add a little more water. Serve piping hot.

Optional: garnish with a few reserved attractive artichoke leaves.

Yield: 4 servings

FRESH FRENCH BEANS

My mother used to make a casserole like this and I loved it. Her recipe called for canned soup, frozen french cut beans, and canned fried onions. This version is made with all fresh ingredients and tastes three times as good— when Mom cooks it, nine times as good.

5 tablespoons butter
4 tablespoons whole wheat flour
⅛ teaspoon salt
2 cups milk
¼ teaspoon sage
¼ teaspoon tarragon
¼ cup Grape Nuts cereal or whole grain Bread Crumbs (see Index)
¼ cup toasted wheat germ
¼ teaspoon salt
1½-2 cups onion, sliced (2 medium)
2 teaspoons salad oil, more if needed
2 cups julienned green beans

Preheat oven to 350° F. Oil a 2-quart baking dish with cover.

Make a cream sauce (see Index for Flexible Cream Sauce recipe), using butter, flour, salt, milk, sage, and tarragon.

Prepare the topping. If Grape Nuts are not available, process bread into bread crumbs. Pulse the cereal or crumbs together with the wheat germ and salt. Set aside.

Trim and quarter onions. Push through the slicing disc and measure 1½-2 cups slices. Sauté in the oil, stirring occasionally. Add more oil if needed to prevent sticking. When the onions are transparent or lightly browned (as you prefer), remove from heat.

Rinse out the workbowl and insert the slicing disc. Trim the beans and pack sideways into the feed tube. Push through and measure about 2 cups.

Stir the beans into the sauce. Transfer to the baking dish. Top with the onions. Last, add the wheat germ mixture. Bake until heated through (check after 30 minutes).

Yield: 6 main dish servings

CALIFORNIA CABBAGE

This mellow cabbage casserole can make a warming winter supper. Just add a steamy hot grain plus some fresh fruit for dessert.

7 cups green cabbage, sliced
2½ cups milk
¼ cup whole wheat flour
¼ teaspoon nutmeg
Dash salt
1-2 cups sliced sunchoke or kohlrabi
Zesty Spread (see Index) or salad oil
Salt to taste
½ medium avocado
1 tablespoon lemon juice

Preheat oven to 350° F.

Trim a cabbage and push chunks through the slicing disc. Measure 7 cups. Lightly oil the top of a double boiler (to keep the milk from sticking). Heat the cabbage in the milk, covered. (If no double boiler is available, use an oiled saucepan. Since scorching of the milk is more likely this way, watch it carefully. You also may take the precaution of diluting the milk, by substituting up to 1 cup water for milk.)

When the cabbage is barely tender, remove it with a slotted spoon and set aside. Stir in the flour, nutmeg, and salt. Bring to a boil, then simmer 2 minutes, uncovered, stirring often. Remove from heat.

Rinse out the workbowl and use the slicing disc again. Trim the sunchokes. Push through and measure 1-2 cups of slices. Sauté in a minimum of Zesty Spread until crisply cooked. Add salt to taste.

Cut the avocado into wedges. Dip in lemon juice.

To assemble, stir the cabbage into the sauce. Pour two-thirds of this mixture into an oiled 2-quart baking dish with a broad shape. Layer with avocado wedges. Cover with the remaining mixture. Top with sunchoke.

Bake until heated through (check after 15 minutes).

Yield: 6 main dish servings

MINTED CARROTS

Carrots braised in peppermint tea— refreshing!

2 teaspoons peppermint or spearmint tea
½ cup boiling water
6 cups carrot pieces (3 large)
1 tablespoon clarified butter or Butter for the Table (see Index), more if needed
Dash salt
Optional: **fresh mint leaves**

Steep the tea in boiling water for at least 5 minutes. Strain.

Trim carrots, pack sideways into the feed tube, and push through the french fry or slicing disc. Measure 6 cups.

In a saucepan with cover, melt the butter over medium heat. Stir in the carrots and cook, stirring often, for 2 minutes. Add more butter if needed to prevent sticking. Pour in the tea and salt. Cover.

Simmer until the liquid is absorbed. Serve hot or cold. Garnish with fresh mint leaves, if available.

Yield: 6 servings

CARROT CINCH

Although this rice casserole is a cinch to prepare, we find that the flavors are subtly delicious.

⅔ cup short-grain brown rice + 2 cups water, or 2 cups cooked brown rice
2 tablespoons clarified butter or butter

1½ teaspoons poppy seeds
1 cup grated carrot (1 medium)
¼ cup stock or milk
Salt to taste

Prepare the cooked rice.

In a large skillet, melt the clarified butter over medium heat. Add the poppy seeds and warm for a few minutes.

Push trimmed carrot through the shredding disc and measure 1 cup. Stir the carrot into the butter. Stir in the rice, then the stock. Add salt to taste.

If possible, serve as soon as the rice is steaming hot. This way the carrot still will retain some crispness.

Yield: 4 servings

SHIMMERING CARROTS

Carrots are set off by an unthickened sauce so flavorful that the taste shimmers.

½ cup stock, preferably from soybeans
2 teaspoons soy sauce
Fresh or ground ginger
Garlic
½ cup cashews (substitute walnuts)
2 cups carrot slices (2 large)

In a saucepan with cover, heat the stock and soy sauce. Add a whisper of ginger and garlic in any form you like.

Meanwhile, pulse the cashews in a dry machine until chopped medium fine. Set aside.

Trim fresh carrots. Pack sideways into the feed tube and push through the slicing disc. Measure 2 cups.

Add carrot and cashew to the boiling liquid. Cover and simmer until the carrots are done to your taste.

Yield: 4 servings

CAULIFLOWER STEAKS

Hearty and instantly definable as a main dish, these well-decorated cutlets are just the thing to serve with a saucy vegetable, a grain, and an amply dressed salad.

1 **medium cauliflower**
1 **cup minced cheddar or gouda cheese**
½ **cup stuffed olives, pitted black or green olives, or pecans or walnuts**
½ **cup chopped parsley**
1 **teaspoon dill weed**
2 **tablespoons lemon juice**
Black pepper

Preheat oven to 350° F.

Wash and quarter the cauliflower. Pare away the central core and discolored leaves. Do not discard the connective portions between the flowerets or the healthy-looking leaves. Steam over boiling water until barely tender.

Meanwhile, chop chunks of cheese with the metal blade and measure 1 cup. Set aside in a mixing bowl.

Pulse the olives or nuts until chopped medium fine. Add to the bowl.

Process fresh parsley until chopped fine. Measure ½ cup. Transfer to the bowl. Stir in the dill weed and lemon juice.

Place the cooked cauliflower in 4 individual oiled casseroles or 1 large oiled casserole with a broad shape. Sprinkle with pepper. Use your hands to distribute the multicolored mixture over the vegetable. Bake, uncovered, until the cheese melts (check after 10 minutes). Serve at once.

Yield: 4 main dish servings

REFRIED GREENS

You've heard of refried beans but did you know you can also refry greens? In both instances, refrying is a useful technique for recycling leftover food—and the processor's efficiency is indispensable.

1 **bunch collards, kale, turnip greens, or mustard greens**
2–3 **teaspoons olive oil or butter (substitute salad oil)**
Salt and pepper to taste

Steam whole greens or used cooked leftovers. Dry with a paper towel or press into a colander to drain thoroughly. Process a handful of leaves at a time until minced. Incidentally, often tender stems can be used as well as leaves.

Stir-fry the minced greens in the oil until steaming hot. Season to taste.

Yield: 2 servings

- For refried beans, use any cooked, drained legume. Process smooth. Stir-fry, season, and serve. Shredded cheddar cheese can be added for the final few minutes of cooking.

DOWN HOME GREENS

Some of the simplest foods can be mighty tasty. If you take a closer look at what makes this entree so satisfying, you'll notice fine contrasting textures, easily achieved with the processor.

1 **cup navy beans**
3 **cups water**
4 **cups shredded sharp cheddar cheese**
2 **cups finely chopped onion (2–3 medium)**
2 **cups finely chopped collards (1 bunch)**
2 **tablespoons clarified butter or butter**
Salt and freshly ground pepper

Cook the beans in the water until tender. While beans are cooking, push wedges of cheese through the shredding disc and measure 4 cups. Set aside.

Also while beans are cooking, trim and quarter onions. Process until finely chopped. Measure 2 cups. Add to the cooking beans. Rinse out the workbowl.

Wash the greens and discard any yellow or unappetizing leaves. Trim only the tough ends of the stems. Steam until tender. Cut the greens (both leaves and stems) into 4-inch lengths and process until chopped medium fine. Measure 2 cups.

Once the beans are tender, and shortly before serving, add the collards to the pot with beans and onions. Turn heat to medium high. Stir in butter, then salt and pepper to taste. When ingredients are boiling hard, reduce heat to low. When a sample of greens tastes done, stir in the cheese. Serve immediately.

Yield: 4 main dish servings

KOHLRABI FOR ARTISTS

This visually striking dish also happens to be surprisingly spicy. It's sure to win everyone's attention, whether you serve it as part of a simple soup-and-casserole lunch, or include it in an elaborate menu.

½ cup cracked wheat + 1 cup stock, or about 1 cup cooked cracked wheat
3 tablespoons Zesty Spread (see Index)
1–2 kohlrabi roots (substitute 1 broccoli stalk, stem only)
Cauliflower
⅛ teaspoon cumin
Dash salt
⅛ cup grated radishes (4 medium)

Prepare the cracked wheat by the toast and boil method, using the stock. Meanwhile, process Zesty Spread, if you don't already have some on hand. When all the liquid is absorbed by the wheat (check after 14 minutes), remove it from heat, fluff with a fork, and let it stand.

Peel the kohlrabi with a paring knife. Cut into chunks that fit into the feed tube. Push through the french fry or slicing disc. Measure and set aside.

Push enough cauliflowerets through the slicing disc so that you can measure a combined cauliflower-and-kohlrabi volume of 2 cups. Sauté the vegetables in the Zesty Spread in a large skillet. When they are tender, stir in the cumin and salt, then the cracked wheat. Stir quite often as you warm them together.

Just before serving, trim fresh radishes and push through the shredding disc. Measure about 2 tablespoons. Turn the wheat mixture into a serving dish. Layer the radish on top. Serve at once.

Yield: 4 servings

DUXELLES (MUSHROOMS WITH SHALLOTS)

Duxelles *is a classic of French cookery and a marvelous household staple. I like to transfer each ¼ cup to a tightly sealed plastic bag. One of the bags goes into the refrigerator, where it is* accessible for steamed vegetables, bean dishes, and improvised spreads. Refrigerated duxelles keep for a week, while the frozen, well-sealed bags keep indefinitely.

½ pound fresh mushrooms (3 cups)
⅓ cup shallots, scallion bulbs, or onion
2 tablespoons butter

Trim mushrooms. Pulse until minced. To avoid producing a mush, check between every couple of pulses, scraping down every time you check. Also, work with only 1 cup of mushrooms at a time.

Wring out the mushrooms by bundling in a dish towel and squeezing vigorously. (You can squeeze the mushrooms over a bowl to collect the strong-flavored juice and add it to your container of stock.)

Set aside the mushrooms.

Measure chunks of trimmed shallot and process until finely chopped. Measure ⅓ cup.

Melt the butter in a large, heavy skillet over medium heat. Add the shallots, stirring occasionally. When they turn transparent, add the mushrooms. Continue to stir occasionally. When the mixture cooks into a paste, with a deep earthy aroma, it is ready.

Yield: at least ½ cup

POTATO MASHTERPIECE

This is a high-protein, slightly exotic version of a perennial favorite.

- Did you know that potatoes contain protein? The potato in this recipe contributes about 5 grams. Of course, the amino acids must be balanced for that protein to be utilized. The time-honored custom of serving meat with potatoes works, but so does cottage cheese or milk.

1 medium turnip
1 large or 2 small potatoes
¼ cup large-curd cottage cheese
1 tablespoon salad oil
Dash salt
Milk
Optional: chives or green onion tops

Pare turnip, trim potato, and steam both until very tender. Process the cottage cheese, oil, and salt until smooth. Scrape down the workbowl. Repeat as needed. Leaving this mixture in the workbowl, insert the shredding disc.

Towel dry the potato(es) and turnip and push them through. Remove the disc. Gently stir all ingredients with a fork.

Transfer the mixture to a serving dish. If a lighter consistency is desired, stir in more milk by the tablespoon, until you achieve the right degree of fluffiness.

The serving dish may be garnished with snippets of chive or scallion top.

Yield: 3–4 servings

RUTABAGA RAGOUT

Are all those wonderful morsels, pale pink and temptingly sweet in a spicy background, really rutabaga?

½ **cup onion, minced (1 large)**
2–2½ **cups rutabaga pieces (½ medium)**
2 **tablespoons olive oil**
¼ **teaspoon black pepper**
¾ **cup carrot circles (1 large)**
¾ **cup green pepper cubes (1 small)**
¼ **teaspoon dill weed**
Dash salt
¼ **cup stock or water**

Trim onion and process until minced. Measure ½ cup. Set aside. Rinse the workbowl.

Pare the rutabaga and cut it into pieces that fit into the feed tube. Push through the french fry or slicing disc and measure 2–2½ cups.

In a dutch oven or large skillet with cover, heat the olive oil and pepper over medium heat. When the pepper releases a fragrance, stir in the onion and cook until the onion becomes transparent. Add the rutabaga, then turn up the heat to medium high. Cook 5 minutes, stirring occasionally.

Meanwhile, push carrots through the slicing disc and measure ¾ cup. Cut ¼-inch cubes of green pepper with a paring knife.

Give the rutabaga a good stir, adding the dill weed and salt. Sprinkle the carrots on top, then the green pepper. Pour on the stock and cover the pan. Turn the heat to medium. Heat until the green pepper darkens and the rutabaga turns transparent.

Yield: 4 servings

SUMPTUOUS SQUASH CASSEROLE

Ever get stuck with a tasteless wonder when you thought you were buying a squash? There's still hope.

1 **large acorn squash, baked or steamed until fork tender (substitute the flesh from other winter squash, up to about 2 cups per recipe)**
1 **cup cooked, drained chick-peas or great northern beans**
2 **tablespoons hazelnuts, brazil nuts, or walnuts**
Maple syrup, brown sugar, or honey
Pinch salt
3 **tablespoons stock or water (amount will vary)**

Preheat oven to 350° F.

Prepare the squash and chick-peas, if you don't already have some on hand.

Process the nuts in a dry machine until chopped fine. Set aside.

Remove the skin and seeds from the cooked squash and spoon the flesh into the workbowl. Process 10 seconds. Select 2 of the 3 sweetener options. Add 1 tablespoon of each and a pinch of salt. Process 10 seconds. Scrape down. Taste. Continue in this way until desired sweetness is reached. Then process in stock by the tablespoon until you reach a smooth consistency. Pulse in the beans.

Turn the mixture into an oiled loaf pan. Sprinkle with the nuts. Bake until heated through (check after 10 minutes). (*Note:* you may double the recipe and it still will fit into the loaf pan.)

Yield: 4 servings

SWEET POTATOES WITH CRANBERRIES

Here is a way to bring out the best in sweet potatoes and cranberries. We serve it every Thanksgiving.

5 cups sliced sweet potatoes (3–4 large
   potatoes)
⅓ cup honey
⅓ cup orange juice
4 tablespoons frozen butter, cut into 4 pieces
Dash salt
2 cups fresh or frozen cranberries

Preheat oven to 350° F.
   Scrub sweet potatoes, cut into chunks, and push through the slicing disc. Measure 5 cups. Set aside.
   Rinse the workbowl and insert the metal blade. Process the honey, juice, butter, and salt until uniform.
   Wash and sort through the cranberries.
   Oil a 1½-quart baking dish with cover.
   To Assemble:
      Layer 1: half the potatoes
      Layer 2: a third of the honey mixture
      Layer 3: the cranberries
      Layer 4: the rest of the potatoes
      Layer 5: the rest of the honey mixture
   Bake until the potatoes are fork tender (check after 1 hour).

Yield: 6 servings

JUICY TURNIPS

Cooked by this method, turnips acquire an almost fruity taste.

1 medium turnip (about 2 cups pieces)
1 medium green pepper, cut into matchstick
   slices (¾ cup)
1–2 tablespoons sesame oil (substitute salad oil!)

Mostly, this requires cutting, and the processor can do the hardest part for you. Peel the turnip and cut it into wedges that fit into the feed tube. Push through the french fry or slicing disc to yield about 2 cups turnip pieces.

Trim the green pepper and cut into thin matchstick slices.
   Stir-fry turnip and green pepper in the oil. Serve at once.

Yield: 4 servings

F FLEXIBLE RATATOUILLE

This ratatouille has several enjoyable features. As eaters we appreciate its lack of oiliness and the way the sauce holds together (no need to chase vitamin-laden juices around the plate). The optional added tahini may be unorthodox, but it tastes wonderful.

From the cook's standpoint, too, this dish has definite advantages. You can vary the proportion of vegetables according to your preference and your on-hand ingredients. And of course, thanks to the processor, preparation time is amazingly short.

Stock or tomato juice
Oregano or basil
Garlic Oil (see Index)
Green squash, yellow squash, onion, celery, ripe
   tomato
Mung or alfalfa sprouts
Green pepper
Optional: **eggplant**
Tahini or olive oil

Preheat oven to 350° F.
   Oil a dutch oven or covered casserole with a 3-quart capacity. Pour in enough stock or juice to cover the bottom 2 inches of the casserole. For each serving you plan to produce, put in ¼ teaspoon oregano or basil and 1 or 2 drops of Garlic Oil, if desired.
   Use the slicing disc to cut pieces of green squash, yellow squash, onion, and celery. Cut tomato pieces with a sharp knife, setting aside enough attractive slices to cover the top of the casserole, to be added later as a garnish.
   Place these vegetables in the casserole, with the onions on the bottom (other vegetables in any order). Cover and bake for 1 hour. If you will be using eggplant, salt and weight it to remove any bitterness (see box).

For the next step, you need a large bowl as well as the processor, fitted with the metal blade. Remove the casserole from the oven and start to measure. Transfer 2 cups ratatouille into the large bowl and ½ cup into the processor. Repeat until all the casserole has been transferred. Note how much you add to the processor and for every ½ cup vegetables, add 2 tablespoons tahini or olive oil (choose one for the entire dish). Process until smooth.

You have now produced the sauce for the ratatouille. Correct the seasoning.

Prepare items for the final baking: cut pieces of green pepper with a sharp knife; rinse off the salted eggplant.

Replace the cooked vegetables in the casserole. Place green pepper and eggplant near the bottom of the casserole, so they can cook first as the dish warms. Distribute any bean sprouts among the cooked vegetables. Pour the sauce on top and finish with a layer of tomato pieces.

Bake 15 minutes to enhance the flavors or, if the dish is being reheated, until bubbling hot.

Yield: 4–8 servings

ZUCCHINI LACE

This delicately textured dish takes minutes to prepare with a processor. Try it with an Italian-style meal.

**¼ cup grated Parmesan, imported Swiss, or
  other suitable cheese
1 cup shredded zucchini, packed (1 large)
½ teaspoon basil
2 teaspoons olive oil**
Optional: **1 egg**

Cut small chunks of cheese and process until minced. Measure ¼ cup. Or use cheese from The Cheese Cache (see Index). Set aside.

Insert the shredding disc. Trim zucchini, push through, and measure 1 cup packed gratings. Squeeze out excess moisture by wrapping the pieces in a cloth dish towel and wringing.

Sprinkle the basil over the zucchini.

Heat the olive oil in a heavy skillet or griddle over medium or medium-high heat. Once drops of water sizzle in the pan, distribute the zucchini into 4 patties. Press down with a metal spatula as they cook. When the bottom starts to brown, gently flip each patty over and top with the cheese. Once the cheese melts, serve at once.

Be forewarned that the zucchini lace must be handled very gently to keep the patty shapes. If you think you'll have trouble, beat an egg into the zucchini and basil before putting it on the skillet. The eggless version, however, has a flavor that, to my taste, makes it worth developing the art of careful turning.

Yield: 4 servings

9 | Sauces, Soups, and Casseroles

Sauces can make your reputation as a fine cook. They also can become one of the greatest convenience foods in your kitchen.

A well-prepared, well-chosen sauce turns plain food into something special.

First, sauce creates a contrast and thus conveys a feeling of completeness. Think of creamed onions or rice topped with chili sauce. Sometimes the sauce lingers pleasantly in the background. Sometimes it leaps into the forefront. Either way, it serves to set up a more sophisticated way to appreciate food. When a sauce is well seasoned, the complexity of flavor wakes up the eater and reminds him or her to taste further.

No wonder fine cooks depend on sauces. They make food more tempting, easier to savor. Table 7 will help you appreciate how many types of sauce you can easily make from natural ingredients. You may wish to complete the table by adding the names of additional sauces or by listing your favorite uses for each one.

The idea behind this chapter is to show how a sampling of sauces can be used as convenience foods. This aspect of using sauces should not be overlooked, especially when a food processor is available. The processor can be much more than an emergency gadget for sauces (something to smooth out lumps when a sauce hasn't been stirred enough). The processor actually enables you to transform textures and flavors with push-button ease, or to assemble supplementary ingredients quickly. That is why, with skill, you can metamorphose any sauce worth its name into the basis of a soup or casserole.

Why not prepare a large batch of sauce? Serve some today and use the rest tomorrow, not as a leftover but to start an entirely different dish.

TABLE 7: A REPERTOIRE OF SAUCES

All sauces named can be found in this book. Sauces from this chapter are listed in italic type. Sauces used elsewhere in this book have the name of the recipe listed after the sauce name in parentheses.

Sauces are classified by the base, more precisely by what I consider the primary taste. Tomatoes and tofu have been singled out to head their own categories because the sauces they make are so distinctive.

Milk Sauces
Flexible Cream
Creme du Jardin

Milk Product Sauces
Delectable Cheese
Tangy Curry

Nut Sauces
Walnut
Cashew *(Nut Butters)*
Almond *(Nut Butters)*
Peanut *(Nut Butters)*
Autumn Almond *(Autumn Almond Casserole)*
Shimmering *(Shimmering Carrots)*

Vegetable Sauces
Simply Carrot
Avocado Cream
Ratatouille *(Flexible Ratatouille)*

Tomato Sauces
Oomphy Tomato (with 5 variations)
El Chili
Pizza *(The Pizza Principle)*

Fruit Sauces
Sweet and Sour
Lemon *(Lemon Vegetable Showcase)*

Bean Sauces
Amazing Green
Herbed Navy Bean Sauce *(Blonde Beans)*
Pineapple Pinto Sauce *(Pineapple Chilibean Bake)*
Pepper Bean *(Pepper Bean Stew)*
Curried Chickpea *(Chickpea Stew)*
Ginger Lentil *(Oriental Lentils)*
Coconut *(Golden Cabbage)*

Tofu Sauces
Mustard *(Mustard Butter)*

Grain Sauces
Brown Barley *(Celestial Chestnut Casserole)*

Butter Sauces
Lemon Dill *(Jeweled Rice)*
Jane Freiman's Reheatable Hollandaise

JANE FREIMAN'S PROCESSOR HOLLANDAISE*

Jane Salzfass Freiman's discovery is a real food processor marvel. Since it's the best hollandaise recipe I've ever seen, I'm delighted to list it here for you to sample.

The clarified butter may be prepared well in advance and stored in an airtight container in the refrigerator, but it takes only minutes to make.

2 large egg yolks, at room temperature
2 tablespoons warm water
Generous pinch salt
¾ cup hot clarified butter (180° F.)
Freshly ground white pepper
1 teaspoon fresh lemon juice, or more to taste
2 dashes Tabasco sauce

Insert the metal knife blade. Place egg yolks, warm water, and salt in container. Process until frothy, at least 1 minute. With machine running, pour hot clarified butter through food chute within 30 seconds. Process 5 seconds after all butter is added.

Add pepper, lemon juice, and Tabasco. Process to mix 5 seconds, then adjust seasonings to taste. Sauce is ready to serve. If desired, cover with lid (be sure pusher is inserted in food chute) and sauce will stay warm about 15 minutes; process 5 seconds before serving.

Or transfer sauce to a small heavy-duty saucepan and place plastic wrap touching the top. Set aside at room temperature as long as 2 hours (do not refrigerate). To reheat, remove plastic, place saucepan over low heat and whisk vigorously until sauce is hot to the touch—it will thicken slightly. (*Note:* A small amount of hot water may be added to restore light consistency. Do not allow sauce to approach a simmer.)

Yield: 1¼ cups or 4–5 servings

---

*Reprinted with permission from *The Art of Food Processor Cooking*, by Jane Salzfass Freiman, copyright © 1980, Contemporary Books.

F T FLEXIBLE CREAM SAUCE

When you enjoy the taste of this most versatile of sauces, don't limit yourself to wheat flour. Each variety has a unique character. Table 8 lists six good choices in order of the increasing density of flavor they bring to cream sauce.

2 tablespoons butter
1 flour unit
1 cup milk
Salt and pepper to taste

TABLE 8: FLEXIBLE CREAM SAUCE THICKENERS

Each listing equals one unit

3 tablespoons oat flour
2 tablespoons brown rice flour
3 tablespoons barley flour
3 tablespoons whole wheat flour
3 tablespoons chickpea flour
6 teaspoons buckwheat flour +
2 tablespoons whole wheat flour

Use a heavy saucepan and medium heat to melt the butter and then stir in the flour unit. Heat 2–3 minutes to bring out the best taste in the flour. Stir in about ¼ of the milk (a wire whisk is recommended). Stir constantly until it thickens. Should any flour appear to be sticking to the saucepan, use a sturdy spoon to get it back into circulation. Pour in the remaining milk and stir occasionally. Let the sauce come to a boil and simmer for 1 minute.

Yield: 1 cup

FLEXIBLE CREAM SOUP

You won't believe the sweetness of this gentle pink soup until you taste it.

1 cup Flexible Cream Sauce (see preceding recipe)
½ cup sliced beets (3 small)
***Optional:* ¼ cup sliced onion, salad oil**
½ cup milk

Prepare the sauce. Steam the beets with several inches of stem attached. Trim and peel. Push through the french fry or slicing disc and measure ½ cup.

If you wish to add onion, push enough through the slicing disc to measure ¼ cup. Sauté it in a very thin layer of oil until transparent.

Stir together all ingredients. Serve hot.

Yield: 2 servings

FLEXIBLE CREAM CASSEROLE

Creamed greens appeal to almost everyone, no matter how much the individual eater likes vegetables. The secret of making this casserole most appetizing is to keep the sauce creamy by draining the cooked greens thoroughly.

1 cup Flexible Cream Sauce (see Index)
⅛ teaspoon nutmeg
1½ pounds fresh spinach or 1 large bunch collard greens or 1 medium bunch Swiss chard
1 cup alfalfa sprouts, packed
Optional: **replace ¼ cup of the alfalfa sprouts with radish sprouts or fenugreek sprouts**
2 tablespoons flax seeds or toasted sesame seeds

Prepare the sauce; stir in the nutmeg. Trim the greens. Cook spinach in a covered saucepan, using only the water that clings to the leaves. Steam collards or chard.

Thoroughly drain the greens when tender. One method is to press them into a colander with the back of a large spoon. Put a handful of cooked spinach or collards into the workbowl at a time and process until minced. With chard, separate the leaves from the stalks. Push the stalks through the slicing disc and coarsely chop the leaves with the metal blade.

Drain the chopped greens and stems again. Measure. If you have more than 1–1½ cups, decrease the amount of sprouts accordingly. Stir the greens and sprouts into the sauce. Or turn the mixture into a covered casserole and keep warm in a moderate oven.

Just before serving, sprinkle flax seeds over the top.

Yield: 4 servings

□ CREME DU JARDIN SAUCE

Do I have the time to manage a garden? Frankly, no. Would I settle for some fresh parsley? Sure, as far as this sauce is concerned. That's enough to supply the exuberant taste of freshly grown herbs. No matter how you get your fresh parsley, use some for this.

2 tablespoons butter
2 tablespoons whole wheat flour
1 cup milk
⅛ teaspoon peppermint or tarragon
⅛ teaspoon black pepper
Dash salt
¼ cup parsley, minced

Melt the butter over medium heat. Stir in the flour and cook 2–3 minutes. Stir in ¼ cup of the milk, the peppermint, pepper, and salt. Stir constantly until it thickens. Pour in the remaining milk and stir occasionally; meanwhile, trim parsley and process until minced. Measure ¼ cup. Add it to the sauce as soon as the sauce comes to a boil. Stir and let it simmer 1 minute longer.

Yield: about 1 cup

CREME DU JARDIN SOUP

1 cup Crème du Jardin Sauce (see preceding recipe)
1 cup cooked lentils
1 cup milk
½ teaspoon salt
2 tablespoons frozen lemon juice

Stir the first 4 ingredients together over medium heat. Bring to a boil. Just before serving, stir in the lemon juice.

Yield: 3–4 servings

CREME DU JARDIN CASSEROLE

An unusual, sprightly version of macaroni and cheese.

3 cups Crème du Jardin Sauce (see recipe)
1 cup whole wheat pasta (noodles, shells, or tubes)
2 cups shredded sharp cheddar
Optional: **¼ cup of the cheese could be from The Cheese Cache (see Index) or minced Parmesan**

Preheat oven to 375° F. Prepare the sauce. Cook the pasta in water until almost al dente. Drain. Stir into the sauce. Place the mixture in an oiled 2-quart baking dish.

With a dry machine, process chunks of cheese and measure 2 cups. Distribute over the top.

Bake until the cheese is bubbly (check after 20 minutes).

Yield: 8 main dish servings

⊤ DELECTABLE CHEESE SAUCE

Freshly grated cheese plays a starring role in this memorable sauce. The food processor makes cheese grating easy, of course.

Another treat for the cook: at the end of this recipe it's fun to watch how quickly the tiny flakes of cheese melt into the sauce. The result is luxuriously thick, a superb accompaniment to almost any grain, bean, or vegetable.

2 tablespoons butter
2 tablespoons whole wheat flour
1 cup milk
¼ cup Parmesan cheese, minced
½ cup sharp cheddar cheese, minced

Melt the butter in a saucepan over medium heat. Stir the flour in with a wire whisk and cook for 2–3 minutes to eliminate any raw flour taste in the finished sauce.

Slowly add the milk. As it heats, prepare both kinds of cheese by processing chunks in a dry machine. Stir the milk occasionally.

Once the ingredients thicken and start to boil, whisk in the cheese quickly. Remove the sauce from heat and, if possible, serve at once.

Yield: 1½ cups

DELECTABLE CHEESE SOUP

Here's an elegant soup you won't want to reserve just for company.

½ cup cooked navy beans + ¾ cup extra cooking liquid or stock
¾ cup Delectable Cheese Sauce (see preceding recipe)
½ teaspoon olive oil
⅛ teaspoon tarragon
Salt to taste

Prepare the beans, if you don't have some on hand. Make the sauce.

Process the sauce, oil, tarragon, and bean stock until smooth. Heat them in a saucepan along with the cooked beans. Stir gently and add salt to taste. Once the soup starts to boil, remove from heat and serve.

Yield: 2 servings

DELECTABLE CHEESE CASSEROLE

Cheesy grain plus a hearty vegetable: it's a wonderful theme for variations. Try substituting any cooked grain.

2 cups cooked millet
1½ cups Delectable Cheese Sauce (see recipe)
3 cups broccoli pieces (1 large stalk)

Preheat oven to 350° F. To prepare millet just for the casserole, use ½ cup millet and 1½ cups water. Using the fluffy boil method, it will cook in about 35 minutes.

Prepare the sauce.

Trim broccoli. Steam the stalk whole until the middle is fork tender. Cut off the flowers and chop the stalk into bite-sized pieces by placing 2-inch lengths of stalk in the workbowl and pulsing until coarsely chopped. Measure 3 cups cooked flowers and chopped pieces.

In a mixing bowl, combine all ingredients. Turn into an oiled 1½-quart baking dish with a lid. Cover. Heat until steaming (check after 15 minutes).

Yield: 4 main dish servings

⊤ TANGY CURRY SAUCE

Here's an inexpensive sauce that adds sparkle to almost any grain, bean, or vegetable.

¼ **cup minced onion**
3 **tablespoons clarified butter, or 2½ tablespoons butter + 1 teaspoon salad oil**
2 **tablespoons chick-pea flour or whole wheat flour**
⅛ **teaspoon salt**
½ **cup soy stock or apple cider**
1½ **teaspoons curry powder**
1 **cup buttermilk**

Trim onion and process until minced. Measure ¼ cup. Sauté in the clarified butter until transparent. Stir in the flour and salt, stirring constantly over medium heat for 2 minutes. Stir in the stock and curry powder. Allow the sauce to come to a boil and simmer for 2 minutes longer, still stirring.

Stir in the buttermilk. Take care not to curdle it by allowing the sauce to boil. If this precaution is taken, the sauce may be served successfully hot or chilled.

Yield: 1½ cups

TANGY CURRY SOUP

Squash soup made special with a touch of curry.

1½ **cups cooked winter squash**

1½ **cups Tangy Curry Sauce (see preceding recipe)**
½ **cup stock (substitute water)**
Optional: **slices of ripe banana**

Steam the squash and measure 1½ cups flesh.

Prepare the sauce. Process together with the squash, scraping down after 10-second processings. When the mixture is smooth, transfer to a saucepan along with the stock. Heat until almost boiling.

Optional: garnish each serving with some banana slices, cut at an angle to give oval rather than round pieces.

Yield: 3 servings

TANGY CURRY CASSEROLE

Sweet and soothing.

1 **cup Tangy Curry Sauce (see Index)**
½ **cup Fresh Grated Coconut (see Index)**
1 **cup yellow split peas**
2 **cups apple cider**
½ **cup stock or water**
2 **cups green cabbage, minced**
½ **teaspoon turmeric**

Preheat oven to 350° F. Prepare the sauce. Prepare the coconut or start to defrost what you already have.

Cook the split peas, cider, and stock. Check occasionally to make sure there is enough liquid in the covered pot. Aim for the driest possible consistency of cooked peas without burning.

Process chunks of cabbage and measure 2 cups.

Stir together the cooked peas, cabbage, and turmeric. Transfer to an oiled 2-quart casserole. Pour on the sauce. Top with coconut. Bake until heated through (check after 30 minutes).

Yield: 6 main dish servings

⊤ WALNUT SAUCE

Nut-based sauces, though delicious, are an acquired taste. Accordingly, an alternative version is given, based on milk and only enriched with nuts.

¼ cup walnuts
3 tablespoons tahini or butter
3 tablespoons whole wheat flour
1½ cups soy stock or water mixed with 2 tablespoons tahini (if you use tahini) or 1½ cups milk (if you use butter)
Dash salt

Pan roast the nuts. Pulse in a dry machine to chop medium fine.

Warm the tahini over medium heat. Stir in the flour. After 2 minutes, stir in the liquid and salt. Bring the mixture to a boil and simmer for a few minutes, stirring occasionally. Stir the nuts into the thickened sauce.

The immediate yield is 1 generous cup of very thick sauce. Thin it with more liquid according to what you are saucing.

Try these proportions:
For moist steamed vegetables, such as zucchini: 3 parts sauce to 1 part liquid
For firmer steamed vegetables, such as broccoli: 2 parts sauce to 1 part liquid
For drained, cooked legumes, such as pinto beans: 1 part sauce to 1 part liquid
For use in the following recipes for soups and casseroles, do not dilute.

WALNUT SOUP

A celery soup, mild and pleasing.

1 cup Walnut Sauce (see preceding recipe)
1 cup soy stock or water mixed with 2 teaspoons tahini, or 1 cup milk (as in recipe for Walnut Sauce)
1 cup sliced celery (2 large ribs)
2 teaspoons salad oil or butter
⅛ teaspoon sage

Prepare the sauce. Stir in the liquid.

Push celery through the slicing disc and measure 1 cup. Sauté in the oil. Stir in the sauce. Add the sage and bring to a boil. Correct the seasoning and serve hot.

Yield: 2 servings

WALNUT CASSEROLE

A luscious, unusual eggplant dish without tomato sauce or pasta.

2 cups cooked chick-peas, drained
1 large eggplant
Salad oil
1 recipe Walnut Sauce (see recipe)
1½ cups soy stock or water mixed with 2 tablespoons tahini, or 1½ cups milk (as in recipe for Walnut Sauce)
⅛ teaspoon salt
½ teaspoon basil
¼ teaspoon black pepper
1½ cups whole grain bread crumbs (3 slices of bread)
2 tablespoons salad oil
2 tablespoons stock or water
¼ cup brewer's yeast
⅛ teaspoon cumin

Cook fresh chick-peas or start to defrost those you've already prepared.

Cut the stem off the eggplant. Cut a lengthwise slice ½ inch thick. Turn the eggplant onto a cutting board cut side down and cut the rest of the eggplant into ½-inch-thick slices. Salt and weight, as described on page 75. Allow the eggplant to rest at least ½ hour.

Rinse off the eggplant and dry it. Turn on the broiler. Place salad oil in a bowl. Bring a baking sheet within easy reach. Cut each slice of eggplant into 2-inch rectangles. Coat them with oil—either brush both sides or quickly dip the eggplant into the oil. Transfer the eggplant to the baking sheet. Repeat until all the eggplant is on the sheet—pile on no more than 1 layer at a time. Broil until lightly browned on top (for eggplant 9 inches from the heat source, check after 8 minutes).

In preparation for the casserole, preheat the oven to 350° F. Oil a 2-quart casserole.

Prepare the Walnut Sauce. Stir in the liquid, salt, basil, and pepper.

Prepare the topping. Process whole grain bread with a dry machine and measure 1½ cups crumbs. Add the oil, stock, yeast, and cumin. Pulse just enough to mix.

To Assemble
Layer 1: 1 cup sauce
Layer 2: the drained chick-peas
Layer 3: half the topping
Layer 4: the broiled eggplant
Layer 5: the rest of the topping
Layer 6: the rest of the sauce

Bake until bubbly (check after 30 minutes). Serve hot.

Yield: 6 main dish servings

⊤ AVOCADO CREAM SAUCE

This is basically liquid avocado, excellent over most grains or pasta. If you're adventurous, it also goes well with steamed greens, such as collards. (To offset the bitterness of the greens, you may choose to process a teaspoon of brown sugar into the sauce before stirring it into well-drained greens.)

1 tablespoon butter
3 tablespoons whole wheat flour
1 cup milk
¼ cup cold soy stock or milk
1 teaspoon lemon juice
½ cup ripe avocado pulp (½ medium)
⅛ teaspoon salt

In a heavy saucepan, melt the butter and stir in the flour over medium heat. Cook the flour for 2–3 minutes, stirring often, and slowly pour the milk in. If the flour starts to stick to the bottom of the pan, pour the milk in before 2 minutes are up.

Allow the sauce to come to a full boil, stirring often. Remove from heat. Stir in the cold liquid.

Process all remaining ingredients together until uniform, scraping down as needed. Process in the cooked mixture. Either serve the lukewarm sauce immediately or heat it before using. Take care not to bring the sauce to a full boil. (Avocado curdles at hot temperatures.)

Yield: 1¾ cups

AVOCADO CREAM SOUP

Tasty bits of onion, olive, and melted cheese greet the tongue, making this an attention-getting appetizer.

1 cup Avocado Cream Sauce (see preceding recipe)
1 cup stock or water
⅛ teaspoon ginger
Dash cayenne
½ cup minced imported Swiss cheese
¼ cup black olives, pitted
¼ cup onion, minced (1 small)
Salt and pepper to taste

Prepare the sauce. Rinse and dry the workbowl. Start to heat the stock in a saucepan with cover, along with the ginger and cayenne.

Process chunks of cheese until minced. Measure ½ cup and set aside.

Pulse the olives until coarsely chopped. Set aside with the cheese. Process onion until minced. Measure ¼ cup and transfer to the saucepan. After the mixture boils, let it simmer, covered, until the onion softens.

Stir in all other ingredients. Serve the soup right before it comes to a boil.

Yield: 2–3 servings

AVOCADO CASSEROLE

We have been conditioned to view the avocado as a high status luxury. But today avocados can be quite inexpensive. In a casserole like this one, we see the avocado in an unpretentious role in a hearty dish.

• How many people have been scared away from avocados due to rumors of high fat content? In actuality, avocados offer much more than fat. A 1-pound avocado does provide 389 calories—equivalent to a little over 3 tablespoons of salad oil. Even good-quality, cold-pressed oil lacks vitamins, minerals, and protein. That makes the avocado look pretty good, with its notable quantities of B vitamins, iron, potassium, phosphorus, vitamin A, and protein.

2 cups cooked barley (substitute rice, wheat berries, or rye berries)
1¾ cups Avocado Cream Sauce (see Index)
¼ teaspoon dill weed
1 cup cheddar, minced
1 cup green beans
1 cup carrot, coarsely chopped (1 large)

Preheat oven to 350° F.

Prepare the barley, if you don't already have some on hand. Prepare the sauce and stir the dill weed into it.

Pulse chunks of cheese until minced. Measure 1 cup. Set aside.

Trim green beans and measure 1 cup. Cut each bean into 2 or 3 pieces. Start to steam them in a collapsible stainless steel steamer.

Trim a carrot and cut it into inch-long pieces. Pulse until coarsely chopped. Measure 1 cup. Transfer to the vegetable steamer (on top of the cooking beans).

When the beans and carrots are barely tender, remove from heat. Stir them into the barley. Stir in the cheese. Transfer this mixture to an oiled 2-quart baking dish or an oiled 8″ × 8″ × 2″ dish. Pour the sauce on top.

Bake until the dish is heated through (check after 20 minutes).

Yield: 6 main dish servings

⊤ SIMPLY CARROT SAUCE

Many recipes with cooked carrots emphasize their considerable sweetness. This can be done, and done well, but it certainly should not be the only way to make a fuss out of them. Their honest taste as simply carrots is appealing, too.

1 cup carrot, shredded, packed (1 large)
⅛ teaspoon salt
¼ teaspoon basil
1 tablespoon clarified butter (substitute butter)
A few gratings black pepper
2 tablespoons whole wheat flour

Push chunks of carrot through the shredding disc and pack into the measure for 1 cup. Steam it over a minimum of water until very soft. Reserve this "vitamin water." Add to it enough water to make 1 cup liquid. Process this, along with the salt, basil, and cooked carrots, for 60 seconds.

Warm the clarified butter and pepper over medium heat. Stir in the flour. After 2–3 minutes, slowly stir in the carrot mixture. Bring to a boil and simmer, uncovered, 5 minutes longer.

If a smoother texture is desired, process again.

Yield: about 1½ cups

SIMPLY CARROT SOUP

Aromatic sunshine, even during the winter, thanks to its zesty seasonings and cheering yellow color.

1⅓ cups chick-peas + 5 cups water, or 3½ cups cooked chick-peas + 2⅓ cups stock
1½ cups Simply Carrot Sauce (see preceding recipe)
1 tablespoon vinegar
¼ teaspoon anise
¼ teaspoon ginger
2 tablespoons butter
Salt and pepper to taste

Cook the chick-peas in the water. Once they are tender, you may process all or part of them until smooth, depending on how chewy or smooth you want the texture of the soup to be.

Stir in the other ingredients. Serve the soup hot.

Yield: 6 servings

SIMPLY CARROT CASSEROLE

Zucchini is baked extra tender on the inside, crisp on the outside, for an unusual combination of textures.

3 cups Simply Carrot Sauce (see recipe)
2 medium zucchini (approximately)
Olive oil (substitute salad oil)
⅓ cup grated Parmesan or brick cheese or cheese from The Cheese Cache (see Index)
Optional: **whole wheat spaghetti**
Optional: **walnut halves**

Preheat oven to 425° F. Oil a shallow 1½-quart baking dish.

Prepare the sauce and pour it into the baking dish. Trim the zucchini. Dry thoroughly and slice in half lengthwise. Rub the skin of each long piece with oil. Place pieces in the baking dish cut side down. The amount of zucchini you use is actually fairly flexible; just do not crowd it into the baking dish or try to squeeze in more than one layer.

Baking time varies with the size of the zucchini. For zucchini with a 1½-inch diameter, check after 25 minutes. Test with a fork for crisp skin outside, extra soft vegetable inside.

While zucchini are cooking, mince cheese and measure. Right before serving, sprinkle it over the zucchini and sauce. If desired, you may serve the casserole over cooked pasta and garnish servings with roasted walnuts.

Yield: at least 4 servings

⊞⊤ OOMPHY TOMATO SAUCE

This richly textured sauce is rich in protein too. For extra enjoyment, experiment using the sauce in a flexible way (see Table 9, page 86).

1 **small onion, minced**
1 **clove garlic**
2 **tablespoons olive oil, or more if needed**
1 **cup unsalted soy nuts or cooked drained**
  soybeans
1 **can tomato paste (6 ounces)**
1 **quart tomato juice**
1 **cup stock, preferably soy stock (substitute**
  water)
1 **bay leaf**
¼ **teaspoon rosemary**
1 **teaspoon thyme**
1 **teaspoon basil**
⅛ **teaspoon salt**
½ **teaspoon black pepper**

Start off with a dutch oven, if you can. Otherwise start off with a large skillet and switch to a large pot when you add the tomato paste.

Trim the onion and garlic and process until minced. Sauté in the oil until transparent.

Push soy nuts or soybeans through the

shredding disc and stir into the onions. Heat 3 minutes, stirring often. (Why the use of soy nuts? As an instant convenience food and for sturdier texture than regular boiled soybeans.)

Stir in the other sauce ingredients. Simmer, uncovered, for 30 minutes. After it cools, refrigerate or freeze the sauce.

Yield: 6 cups

EXTRA OOMPH FOR TOMATO SAUCE

This is your chance to add variety to homemade tomato sauce. The additions in Table 9 are based on using 1 cup of Oomphy Tomato Sauce at a time. This is a simple way to calculate how much to add to however much sauce you happen to need at a given time.

Also, this way of varying the sauce is ideal for a small household. You can freeze the sauce in 1-cup batches, heat it up plain or with a choice for extra oomph, and have enough for 2 servings.

𝔼 OOMPHY TOMATO SOUP

Turn the sauce into a free-form minestrone with your choice of additions.

Possible additions

pasta	peas
barley	corn
wheat berries	celery
rye berries	cabbage
cubed potato	pinto beans
summer squash	kidney beans
green beans	navy beans
wax beans	great northern beans
broccoli	chick-peas
cauliflower	

To keep items from overcooking, cook each one separately until the desired degree of tenderness is reached. Bring the sauce to a boil and stir in additions at the last moment. The exception is pasta, which may be added raw during the last 10–15 minutes of cooking. The starch in the pasta helps thicken the soup.

Should the soup become too thick for your liking, you can always dilute it with stock or water.

TABLE 9: EXTRA OOMPH FOR TOMATO SAUCE

Ingredient	Amount	How to Add It	What It Contributes
Mushrooms, chopped with metal blade	⅓ cup	After onions are transparent, add and then sauté until brown. If needed, add a small amount of extra stock to prevent sticking.	A meatier taste. More protein and B vitamins.
Duxelles (see recipe)	¼ cup	Stir into the cooked sauce.	A meatier taste. More protein and B vitamins.
Spinach, fresh leaves washed and dried	Pack into a 2-tablespoon measure.	Process into the cooked sauce with the metal blade. You will see little green flecks in the sauce. Return to heat until the spinach cooks, imparting a deeper color to the sauce.	A meatier color and taste.
Peanut Butter (see recipe)	2 tablespoons	Process into the cooked sauce with the metal blade. This addition is particularly recommended for using the sauce in a casserole.	It helps give the sauce the "hard to stop eating" properties of peanut butter. The color of the sauce is altered from red to salmon, which is why this version is recommended for a casserole.
Sunflower Meal (see recipe)	2 tablespoons, packed	Stir into the cooked sauce.	Adds brightness to the flavor, chewiness to the texture. Like peanut butter, it complements the protein in the sauce.
Brewer's Yeast plus Toasted Wheat Germ	1 tablespoon 2 tablespoons	Stir into the sauce right before serving.	A slightly darker flavor; a somewhat denser texture; a lot more B vitamins.

My Discoveries:

OOMPHY TOMATO CASSEROLE

Who doesn't enjoy lasagne?

2 cups Oomphy Tomato Sauce (see recipe)
Whole wheat lasagne flats (about 8 ounces)
3 cups sliced zucchini (3 medium)
1 cup minced Parmesan
2½ cups grated mozzarella
2 tablespoons parsley
2 cups ricotta cheese
¼ teaspoon black pepper
¼ teaspoon marjoram
1 egg
2 tablespoons salad oil

Preheat oven to 375° F.
Prepare or thaw the sauce.
Calculate how much lasagne to cook. The most accurate method I know when you are using a dish for the first time is to stack dry pasta in the dish you will use for cooking. Allow enough for 3 layers.
Cook the pasta according to package directions. If there are no package directions, cook it until almost al dente; break off 2 or 3 pieces from an extra flat to cook and use for taste testing. Drain the cooked pasta and lay it flat.
Trim zucchini and push through the slicing disc. Measure about 3 cups. Steam it tender and towel dry.
Put the mozzarella in the freezer to chill before grating.
Process the Parmesan until minced. Measure and set aside.
Push the mozzarella through the shredding disc. Measure 2½ cups and set aside. Process fresh parsley until minced. Measure. Return to the workbowl, adding all remaining ingredients, and process until smooth. This is the "parsley mixture."
Oil a lasagne dish with at least a 2½-quart capacity.

To Assemble
   Layer 1: lasagne
   Layer 2: the parsley mixture
   Layer 3: lasagne
   Layer 4: the zucchini, each piece sprinkled
            with some of the Parmesan
   Layer 5: lasagne
   Layer 6: the sauce
   Layer 7: the mozzarella

Bake until heated through and the cheese is bubbly (check after 30 minutes).

Yield: 8 main dish servings

⊤ EL CHILI SAUCE

Here is a hearty, high-protein sauce that is also vegetarian.

1 cup cooked soybeans
½ cup cooked pinto or kidney beans (substitute soybeans)
1 cup peeled tomatoes (3-4 medium) or 1 1-pound can
½ cup onion pieces (1 medium)
2 tablespoons olive oil (substitute salad oil)
1 tablespoon chili powder
1 6-ounce can tomato paste
1 teaspoon oregano
½ cup soy stock or tomato juice (substitute water)
1-2 teaspoons fresh green chili pepper
1 tablespoon vinegar
Salt to taste
Brown food coloring

Cook soybeans, or thaw frozen ones, and drain. Set aside.
Cook pintos. Measure ½ cup. Drain and set aside separately.
Prepare the tomatoes. To remove the skins of ripe tomatoes, bring water to a rolling boil. Plunge in the tomatoes. Lift them out after 15 seconds and pare. If good fresh tomatoes are not available, don't feel bad about using canned Chop the tomatoes coarsely with a knife and add to the bowl with the pintos.
Trim fresh onion and push through the french fry or slicing disc. Measure ½ cup. In a dutch oven or large skillet, sauté in the oil. After the onions start to cook, stir in the chili powder.
Rinse out the workbowl. Push the soybeans through the shredding disc. With the soybeans still in the workbowl, insert the metal blade. Process in the tomato paste and oregano for 10 seconds. Scrape down. Add stock. Process for 10 seconds and scrape down repeatedly until smooth.
Trim the chili pepper. Cut 1 or 2 teaspoons (remember, this kind of pepper heats up as it

cooks), and process into the mixture for 10 seconds.

When the onions are tender, stir in the processed mixture, the tomatoes, pintos, and vinegar. Bring to a boil and simmer, uncovered, 10 minutes. Add salt to taste. Stir in food coloring to deepen the red hue of the sauce.

Yield: 2¾ cups

EL CHILI SOUP

Invigorating!

1 cup El Chili Sauce (see preceding recipe)
1 cup soy stock or tomato juice
1 tablespoon olive oil
¼ teaspoon cumin
Salt to taste
¼ cup shredded jack or brick cheese
¼ cup avocado pieces (¼ medium avocado)

Prepare the sauce. Bring it to a boil, stirring in the stock, oil, and cumin. Simmer and add salt to taste.

Meanwhile, push cheese through the shredding disc and measure ¼ cup. Cut or spoon the avocado section into small pieces, equivalent to ¼ cup.

Divide the liquid between 2 serving bowls. Top each with ½ the cheese, then ½ the avocado.

Yield: 2 servings

EL CHILI CASSEROLE

These stuffed green peppers are a chili lover's delight.

1 batch El Chili Sauce (see recipe)
1½ cups cooked brown rice
2 large, well-shaped green peppers
1 cup shredded mozzarella
¼ cup pitted green olives
¼ teaspoon basil

Preheat oven to 350° F.
Prepare the sauce. Cook the rice. Trim the peppers and cut in half lengthwise. Select a casserole dish shaped to hold them quite snugly and oil it.

Push chunks of chilled cheese through the shredding disc and measure 1 cup. Set aside.

Rinse out the workbowl and insert the metal blade. Pulse the olives until coarsely chopped. Stir into the cooked rice, along with the basil.

Place the rice mixture at the bottom of the casserole. Stuff the peppers, alternating layers of sauce, cheese, and sauce. Set the peppers atop the rice.

Bake uncovered until the peppers are tender (check after 30 minutes).

Yield: 4 main dish servings

⊤ SWEET AND SOUR SAUCE

Here's a tasty rice topper with loads of pineapple.

2 tablespoons vinegar
2 tablespoons soy sauce
2 tablespoons molasses (substitute honey or brown sugar)
2 tablespoons cornstarch
½ cup pineapple juice
1 tablespoon salad oil
½ teaspoon mustard seed (substitute dry mustard)
Ginger to taste
Garlic to taste
1½ cups pineapple chunks (or less, to taste)

Process the first 5 ingredients until smooth. For the pineapple juice, you have a choice. You can drain the liquid from a 15-ounce can of pineapple chunks canned in unsweetened pineapple juice. Or, if you are fortunate enough to be using fresh pineapple, get your flavored liquid this way: soak the pineapple chunks in ½ cup water for 15 minutes. Drain the pineapple and reserve the liquid.

Warm the oil, mustard seed, garlic, and ginger. When the spices release a scent (mustard seed will actually sizzle) add the liquid mixture and the pineapple chunks. Bring the sauce to a boil, stirring often. Remove from heat immediately. Serve hot.

Yield: about 2 cups

SWEET AND SOUR SOUP

A colorful appearance makes this soup especially festive.

1 cup Sweet and Sour Sauce (see preceding recipe)
1 cup green beans or broccoli
1 cup soy stock
1 cup cubed tofu, drained

Prepare the sauce. Trim the beans and process until minced. Measure 1 cup. Boil them in the stock until tender. Gently stir in the sauce and tofu, with the heat turned to medium. Bring back to a boil and serve at once.

Yield: 4 servings

SWEET AND SOUR CASSEROLE

The crunchy texture of this casserole contrasts well with cooked grains.

2 cups Sweet and Sour Sauce (see recipe)
3 cups carrot matchsticks (3 medium)
8 ounces water chestnuts, fresh or canned (1 cup)

Preheat oven to 350° F.
Prepare the sauce.
Pack pieces of carrot sideways into the feed tube and push through the french fry disc. Or push carrot through the slicing disc. Measure 3 cups carrot matchsticks.

Transfer carrots to an oiled 1½-quart baking dish with cover. Pack peeled water chestnuts into the feed tube and push through the slicing disc. Add to the carrots. Pour the sauce on top of the other ingredients. Bake until the carrots are tender (check after 30 minutes).

Yield: 4 servings

⊡ AMAZING GREEN SAUCE

We're used to thinking of parsley as a throw-away garnish, but the large amount used here adds a notable vivid flavor. Parsley, by the way,

also adds B vitamins, iron, calcium, potassium, and protein.

1 cup green split peas
2½ cups water
½ cup chopped parsley (1 bunch)
½ cup minced onion (1 large)
1 tablespoon olive oil
⅛ teaspoon salt
¼ teaspoon marjoram

Cook the split peas and water in a covered saucepan until tender. Trim and process parsley until minced. Measure ½ cup. Set aside.

Trim onion and process until minced. Measure ½ cup. Sauté in the oil until transparent.

Stir the cooked onions into the split peas. Add all other ingredients. Bring to a boil and serve. Thin with water as desired.

Yield: at least 2½ cups

AMAZING GREEN SOUP

This is a quick vegetable soup: colorful, satisfying, and distinctive.

1 cup Amazing Green Sauce (see preceding recipe)
1 tablespoon tahini or almond butter (substitute salad oil)
¼ cup stock or water
½ cup carrot pieces (1 medium)
½ cup corn kernels or yellow squash slices
1 cup water
Optional: **croutons from Daily Bread (see Index)**

Prepare the sauce. Process smooth with the tahini and stock. Transfer to a saucepan.

Trim fresh carrot and push through the french fry or slicing disc. Measure ½ cup.

Measure ½ cup corn, frozen or to be scraped from a steamed cob, or push yellow squash through the slicing disc.

Steam the vegetables until tender. Add enough liquid to the water left over from steaming to give 1 cup liquid. Stir this and the vegetables into the sauce. Bring to a boil.

Serve hot. If desired, garnish with croutons.

Yield: 2 large servings

AMAZING GREEN CASSEROLE

A chewy casserole with considerable delicacy of flavor.

1 batch Amazing Green Sauce (see recipe)
½ **cup short-grain brown rice**
½ **cup barley**
2½ cups water
2 cups grated brick or other mild cheese
8 ounces mushrooms (2½–3 cups sliced)
3 tablespoons butter
½ **cup water**

Preheat oven to 350° F.
Prepare the sauce. Cook rice, barley, and water together.
Push chunks of cheese through the shredding disc and measure 2 cups. Set aside.

Trim mushrooms. Pack sideways and push through the slicing disc. Sauté in butter until browned.
Insert the metal blade. Process sauce and ½ cup water together until almost smooth. (Do this in 2 batches to avoid overloading the machine.)
Oil a 2-quart baking dish.

To Assemble
  Layer 1: the grain mixture
  Layer 2: the mushrooms
  Layer 3: the cheese
  Layer 4: the sauce

Bake until heated through (check after 15 minutes).

Yield: 8 main dish servings

10 | Entrees for Cooks and Bakers

Why do desserts have such intense appeal? One possible reason is the attitude of those who bake them. Some of the world's most talented home chefs save their skill for dessert. The rest of the meal merely serves as a prelude. Artistry and enthusiasm are lavished on the goodies.

Yet that same artistic flair can be applied to main course dishes, hence the theme of this chapter. Here you will find the most elegant entrees in the book, the real company showpieces. You also will find some maverick main dishes: finger foods children will love.

Simple or sophisticated, these recipes are all considered Entrees for Cooks and Bakers since each dish employs both skills: the precision of baking and the spontaneity that exemplifies cooking.

Most people have a preference for either cooking or baking. Bakers are often people who like to play by the rules. They have the patience to measure. They are thorough enough to follow a recipe just as written, step by step, and wait for the perfect finished product. Cooks, on the other hand, tend to be strong on spontaneity. They'd just as soon approximate as measure, and when they nibble they feel it has a constructive purpose. Which part of a recipe do cooks follow to the letter? "Correct the seasoning," because that is their chance to be creative.

These entrees are expressly offered to please both types of personalities. Bakers can look forward to the perfect way the processor mixes toppings or batters in a trice, and the technique required for artistic assembly of many of these entrees can challenge a baker's skill. Meanwhile, the flexible nature of these entrees will let a cook show off a discriminating palate and knack for combining flavors.

Cook or baker, you can't lose. Approach these entrees from your favorite angle. Just don't be surprised if along the way you develop a liking for the other culinary art. Whether you instinctively prefer to bake or cook, there's no reason you can't become an expert at both. Practice helps, and so does the processor.

PIZZA WITH A SMILE

When photographers try to evoke a beaming expression, they often ask you to say "Cheese."

"Pizza" might prove more effective. It summons up visions not only of cheese, but of tomato sauce, Italian seasonings, and other savory goodies. "Pizza" does more than make you smile; it can start your mouth watering.

Food processor pizzas are very easy to make. Whether you choose a yeast dough or a pastry crust, mixing time is kept to a minimum. Preparation of vegetable extras and cheese can be done in seconds. With such an efficient kitchen helper, pizza assembly becomes effortless and creative. So if you're the one who's expected to do the cooking when others say "Pizza," you can afford to smile.

Three different types of pizza are given in the following pages: Crusty Italian Pizza, Italian Pizza Pie, and Freestyle Pizza.

⊡ CRUSTY ITALIAN PIZZA

People tell me this is the best pizza they've ever tasted, and they are invariably surprised when they find out how simple it is to make. All it takes is a loaf of bread (made up when I did the week's baking), a knockout sauce made with 3 ingredients, and whatever good optional ingredients happen to be around the kitchen. Fresh, high-quality food is used; that probably has a lot to do with this pizza's success. Still, it costs a fraction of what you would pay for pizza from a restaurant.

THE CRUST

Dough for 1 loaf of Daily Bread (see Index) or any other plain yeasted bread
Pizza Sauce (below) or 1–2 cups of another tomato sauce of your choice
Grated mozzarella cheese
Pizza Trimmings (see Table 10)

Prepare a loaf of Daily Bread dough. Let it rise to double its size once.

Knead the dough 2–3 minutes. Roll out on a floured board, with a floured rolling pin, according to the shape and thickness you desire. For a thin, crisp crust, shape dough to fill an entire 10½″ × 15″ baking sheet. For a thick,

TABLE 10: PIZZA TRIMMINGS

Select as many or as few of the following as you like.

Broiled eggplant (see recipe for Walnut Casserole)
Chickpea Sausage (see recipe)
Cubes of tofu, pressed (see recipe for Elegant Vegetable Pie), plain, or sautéed in oil with soy sauce
Pine nuts
Sautéed or broiled summer squash
Steamed or sautéed sliced onion
Steamed green or wax beans
Sautéed red or green pepper slices
Avocado wedges (see recipe for Black-Eyed Pie)
Artichoke hearts, cubed
Corn kernels, cooked and scraped off the cob
Sliced hard-boiled eggs
Steamed cauliflower
Steamed broccoli
Sautéed mushroom slices
Duxelles (see recipe)
Sprouted mung beans
Black olives

My Discoveries:

chewy crust, partially fill the baking sheet. Or you might use 1 or more round baking pans made especially for pizza, two or three 8-inch square baking dishes, or whatever you like. The crust will not rise appreciably in baking, so you can roll it out exactly as thick as you want the final product to be.

Before you place the rolled-out dough in the pan, be sure the pan is oiled. Then gently transfer the dough to the pan. Trim it around the sides of the pan so that you can fold over the dough to form a little rim. This rectangular (or circular) rim adds to the appearance of the pizza; it also keeps ingredients from spilling out.

Partially bake the crust. Bake it until cooked, but not necessarily browned. Obviously baking time varies with the dough, its thickness, and baking pan material. Using a 400° F. oven, check first after 7 minutes. Tap the dough; if you hear a hollow sound, the dough is cooked.

Remove the crust from the oven and seal by brushing lightly with olive oil. It is best to assemble and bake the pizza within 30 minutes. Turn the oven to 350° F.

THE SAUCE

You won't believe how good it tastes until you try it.

8 tablespoons butter (1 stick)
1 6-ounce can tomato paste
¾ cup stock or water
Salt and pepper to taste

Melt the butter in a saucepan over medium heat. Stir in the tomato paste. After the mixture boils, add enough stock to achieve a good spreading consistency. Add salt and pepper to taste.

For nutritional balance, when this sauce is used I like to go easy on oily options. Before choosing avocado, black olive, broiled eggplant, and so forth, I'd use a lowfat sauce such as Oomphy Tomato (see Index).

Yield: 1¾ cups

Note: This sauce does appear to have a high proportion of fat, but the average serving contains just two teaspoons.

THE CHEESE

Put 10 ounces or more fresh mozzarella in the freezer for 5 minutes. Then cut it into chunks and push through the shredding disc. Measure 2–3 cups.

To Assemble
Spread the partially baked crust with sauce.
Top with cheese and trimmings.

Return the pan to the 350° F. oven until the cheese is bubbly (check after 10 minutes). Serve immediately. Cut into slices and scoop from the baking pan with a metal spatula.

Yield: 12 main dish servings

Ⓔ ITALIAN PIZZA PIE

Here's a somewhat more sophisticated pizza, thanks to the pastry crust and the switch in the usual order of ingredients. (Remember when you assemble it: cheese first, then sauce.)

Flexible Pastry or Tender Crackers (see Index)
1 cup Oomphy Tomato Sauce (see Index) or other tomato sauce of your choice
1½ cups shredded mozzarella
⅓ cup minced Parmesan
Pizza Trimmings (see Table 10)

Preheat oven to 350° F.
Choose an 8- or 9-inch round or square baking pan. When you roll out the pastry dough and fit it into this pan, bring the edges up only ½–¾ inch from the base, to form a little rim. Prick generously with a fork and bake until cooked but not browned.
Prepare the sauce, cheese, and trimmings.

To Assemble
   Layer 1: mozzarella cheese
   Layer 2: sauce
   Layer 3: any trimmings
   Layer 4: the Parmesan

Bake until heated through (check after 15 minutes). Serve at once.

Yield: 6 main dish servings

Ⓔ FREESTYLE PIZZA

Put together just about any good-tasting combination of sauced food on hot crust to create other pizza-like entrees. Whimsical creations are especially welcome at a pizza party, where guests can sample slices from many different varieties of pizza.

Crust (see Crusty Italian Pizza, or other bread recipes in Chapter 11)
Any tasty sauce, not necessarily tomato (try Chili, Brown Barley, Delectable Cheese, or Crème du Jardin—see Index)
Pizza Trimmings (see Table 10)
***Optional:* shredded cheese or tofu cubes sautéed in oil and soy sauce**

Assemble as in the following example.

VEGAN'S PIZZA

Crust

Whole wheat Tender Crackers (see Index)

Sauce

Walnut Sauce (2 batches, thinned with ⅔ cup soy stock) (see Index)

Trimming Options

1 cup cherry tomatoes, stemmed and halved
1½ cups cooked, drained chick-peas
2 green peppers, trimmed and cut into thin rings
1 cup Duxelles (see Index)

Prepare the crust and partially bake as in Crusty Italian Pizza in this chapter.

To Assemble
Spread the sauce on the partly baked crust. Arrange the green pepper rings to mark 8 large servings for the thin-crust pizza. Cut leftover rings into tiny cubes and arrange decoratively. Pat Duxelles into each green pepper ring. Place tomato halves cut side down on top of the Duxelles. Arrange chick-peas and remaining tomato halves decoratively.

Bake at 350° F. until sauce is bubbly (check after 10 minutes) and serve hot.

HOW TO LOAF

Loafing is an invaluable skill for vegetarian cooks. I define *loafing* as putting together a certain type of casserole, which is baked in a loaf pan and served as an unmistakable main dish.
Meatloaf isn't the only such loaf by any means. Three different types of meatless loaf follow.

Ⓔ THE CREAMY LOAF

Whatever combination of beans, nuts, and vegetables you select for this loaf, the overall effect will be creamy. The extra cream sauce served with the entree enhances the effect of luxuriousness.

2 cups Flexible Cream Sauce (see Index)
3 cups cooked beans: kidney, soy, navy, lima, pinto, or chick-pea (either alone or in combination)
½ cup nut meats: walnut, hazelnut, pecan, cashew, or blanched almond (either alone or in combination)
1 cup coarse bread crumbs (from 2 slices whole grain bread)
1 cup sliced cooked vegetable: cauliflower, broccoli, summer squash, winter squash, sweet potato, or carrot
Optional: ¼ cup mushroom or celery, 2 tablespoons onion or parsley + butter when needed to sauté them
1 egg
½ teaspoon sage or tarragon
Optional: 2 tablespoons brewer's or torula yeast
Salt to taste

Preheat oven to 375° F.
Prepare the sauce. Set aside 1 cup for use when serving the loaf. Cool the other cup of sauce to room temperature.
Prepare the beans, unless leftovers are available.
Pan roast the nuts. Process in a dry machine until minced. Set aside.
Process whole grain bread and measure 1 cup coarse crumbs. Set aside in a large mixing bowl.
Steam a vegetable until barely tender (or use leftovers). Cut into bite-sized pieces. Transfer to the mixing bowl.
If the mushrooms or other optional ingredients are to be used, process until minced and measure. Sauté mushrooms or onion. Celery or parsley should be used raw. Transfer to the mixing bowl.
Process the sauce, egg, herb, and optional yeast until smooth. Stir into the mixing bowl. When ingredients are mixed thoroughly, add salt to taste. Transfer to an oiled 8½″ × 4½″ × 2½″ loaf pan. Top with the nuts.
Bake until a tester comes out clean (check after 50 minutes).
Either serve immediately or reheat and serve. Or chill, slice, and serve. In any case, heat the remaining cup of sauce and serve it along with the loaf as a gravy.

Yield: 6 main dish servings

THE CRUNCHY LOAF

Here you have a denser loaf, with a chewy, savory quality.

1¾ cups cooked grain: barley, wheat berries, rye berries, or brown rice
½ cup cooked beans: chick-peas, lima, or soy
1 cup shredded mild cheese, such as muenster or brick
½ cup sunflower seeds, cashews, walnuts, or hazelnuts
1½ cups vegetable: broccoli, cauliflower, yellow squash, green squash, green pepper, carrot, or onion
Oil as needed
1 egg
1 tablespoon brewer's or torula yeast
½ teaspoon sage
⅛ teaspoon salt
2 tablespoons whole wheat flour

Preheat oven to 375° F.
Cook enough grain and beans for the recipe or use leftovers.
Push cheese through the shredding disc and measure 1 cup.
Roast the seeds or nuts in a heavy saucepan. (See box on page 31.) Cashews, walnuts, or hazelnuts should be chopped coarsely afterward. Pulse with a dry machine. Transfer to a mixing bowl.
Chop broccoli, cauliflower, squash, or carrot with the metal blade. These vegetables may be used raw or cooked. Green pepper should be cut with a knife into small pieces. Onion should be prepared by trimming, pushing through the french fry or slicing disc, measuring, and then sautéing in oil until transparent or browned.
Measure a total of 1½ cups vegetable pieces (For crispness, raw vegetables may be sautéed.) Transfer them to the mixing bowl.
Place in the workbowl the egg, yeast, sage, and salt (omit the salt if grain, bean, or vegetable has been salted heavily). Process 10 seconds. Distribute 1 cup of the grain and the flour evenly over the mixture. Pulse a few times, just to mix. Stir into the ingredients in the mixing bowl. Add the drained beans.
Oil an 8½″ × 4½″ × 2½″ loaf pan.

To Assemble
Layer 1: the mixture
Layer 2: the remaining ¾ cup grain
Layer 3: the shredded cheese

Bake until cheese is bubbly (check after 30 minutes). Avoid overcooking. A crunchy texture loses its appeal if it gets dried out!

Yield: 6 main dish servings

⊞ THE LOAF FOR COMPANY

This loaf is very rich, so I wouldn't recommend serving it for everyday occasions. That's one reason I call it the Loaf for Company. The second reason involves the kind of company. When three-meat-meals-a-day guests sit down to your dinner table, how can you satisfy them with a vegetarian meal? This loaf is designed to please even that kind of company.

2 cups cooked grain: barley, buckwheat groats, bulgur, or brown rice
1½ cups cooked beans: lentils, adzukis, black, pinto, or kidney
1 cup mushroom slices
2 tablespoons butter + 1 teaspoon salad oil
⅛ teaspoon black pepper
Salt to taste
½ pound fresh spinach
½ cup minced onion (1 large)
1 teaspoon salad oil, or more if needed
Salt to taste
1 cup dairy sour cream
½ cup large-curd cottage cheese
½ teaspoon paprika

Since this loaf takes longer to prepare than most casseroles, turn on the oven to 375° F. about halfway through the recipe.

Cook enough grain and beans for the recipe or use leftovers.

The Grain Mixture

Trim mushrooms. Pack sideways and push through the slicing disc. Measure 1 cup. Saute in the butter and oil, along with the pepper. Pulse the mushrooms and cooked grain until barely mixed. Pulse in salt to taste. Transfer to an oiled 8½″ × 4½″ × 2½″ loaf pan. Rinse the workbowl and metal blade.

The Bean Mixture

Wash the spinach. Trim off the ends of stems, but do not discard the rest of the stems, unless wilted. Cut them into 1-inch pieces. Cook leaves and stems in a covered saucepan, using just the water that clings to the spinach. When tender, drain thoroughly. Pulse a few times until coarsely chopped. Drain again. Transfer to a large mixing bowl along with the drained beans.

Trim onion and process until minced. Measure ½ cup. Sauté in 1 teaspoon oil. Add the tender onion to the spinach and beans. Stir lightly to preserve the shape of the beans. Add salt to taste. Set aside.

The Dairy Mixture

Process the sour cream, cottage cheese, and paprika until smooth.

To Assemble

Layer 1: all the grain mixture
Layer 2: ¼ cup of the dairy mixture
Layer 3: all the bean mixture
Layer 4: the rest of the dairy mixture

Bake until the loaf is bubbly around the edges of the creamy topping (check after 30 minutes). Serve hot.

Yield: 6 main dish servings

MAIN DISH PIES

Here are pies to divert even the most resolute dessert-first eaters.

CREAMY BROCCOLI PIE

Here is a quichelike creation where the egg taste is understated. One unusual feature of this broccoli pie is the cream cheese base; another distinctive aspect is the use of thin-sliced broccoli stalk.

1 8- or 9-inch piecrust, partially baked and cooled to room temperature (see Index for Flexible Pastry)
2 large broccoli stalks

Optional: ½ cup minced Parmesan
Optional: **1 tablespoon minced parsley**
Optional: **1 tablespoon minced onion**
1 cup large-curd cottage cheese
4 ounces cream cheese
2 eggs
¼ teaspoon nutmeg
¼ teaspoon tarragon
Dash salt
2 tablespoons arrowroot

Prepare the pastry. Steam the broccoli stalks until the stems are barely tender. Meanwhile, prepare the optional Parmesan, parsley, and onion, setting the vegetables and cheese aside separately.

Roll out and partially bake the piecrust (approximately 10 minutes at 400° F.—baked but not brown).

Push broccoli stem through the slicing disc and measure about 2 cups. Insert the metal blade. Mince broccoli flowerets and measure about 1 cup—enough to bring the total amount of broccoli to 3 cups. Set aside.

Process the cottage cheese, cream cheese, eggs, nutmeg, tarragon, salt, and arrowroot for 10 seconds. Scrape down. Repeat until smooth. Process in the optional parsley and onion. Stir this mixture into the broccoli.

Transfer to the piecrust. Sprinkle with the optional Parmesan. Bake at 375° F. until the filling is almost set; it will look solid but not dried out (check after 30 minutes). Let the pie rest 10 minutes at room temperature and serve. Chilled or room-temperature leftovers are also delicious.

Yield: 6 main dish servings

FEATHERED BROCCOLI QUICHE

Here's a more conventional quiche, quickly put together with the processor. The "feathered" broccoli lightens up the custardy texture.

1 8- or 9-inch pastry shell, partially baked (recommended: Flexible Pastry with whole wheat pastry flour and lemon options; see Index)
1 cup cooked broccoli, mostly flowerets
1 cup shredded imported Swiss cheese
Optional: **2 tablespoons minced Parmesan**
3 eggs
1 cup half and half, or 1 cup whole milk + 2 tablespoons noninstant powdered milk (substitute 1 cup whole milk)
¼ teaspoon marjoram
Dash cayenne
Optional: **2 tablespoons butter**

Preheat oven to 400° F.

Prepare an 8- or 9-inch pastry shell (see Flexible Pastry recipe) and partially bake. Let it cool.

Steam a stalk of broccoli until the flowerets are barely tender. Place them in the workbowl and process 15 seconds. Transfer to a measuring cup. If necessary, chop a few inches of stalk. Work your way down the stalk until you have ¾–1 cup finely chopped broccoli. Set aside.

Push chunks of cheese through the shredding disc and measure 1 cup. Set aside.

If Parmesan is available, process chunks of it until minced. Measure 2 tablespoons. Set aside separately.

Process the eggs for 15 seconds. Add the half and half, marjoram, and cayenne. Pulse twice. Add the shredded Swiss and pulse twice. Add the broccoli and pulse once. Turn into the pastry shell. If Parmesan is available, sprinkle it over the top. If desired, dot with butter.

Bake for 10 minutes, then turn the heat down to 325° F. and continue baking 20 minutes longer. The quiche need not be firm to be done, since it will gain firmness as it stands. Let it stand for 10 minutes before serving.

Note: To preserve the texture of the quiche, keep it out at room temperature. It will be better off that way, for up to 12 hours, than if you refrigerate it, risking sogginess.

Yield: 6 main dish servings

BLACK-EYED PIE

Served with a hearty green salad, this dish will make your dinner. It's an unusual pastryless pie, layered with two spicy fillings, ripe avocado, and a melted cheese topping.

1 cup black-eyed peas
2½ cups water
1 cup cooked brown rice
1 medium onion, coarsely chopped (¾–1 cup)
¼ teaspoon black pepper
2 tablespoons salad oil
½ cup sliced celery (½ large rib)
⅓ cup stock or water, or more if needed
½ teaspoon oregano
1½ cups grated mozzarella cheese
⅛ teaspoon salt
½ large avocado or 1 small avocado
2 tablespoons vinegar
¼ teaspoon cumin
¼ teaspoon coriander

Preheat oven to 350° F.

Cook the peas and water together in a covered saucepan. Do not overcook to the point of mushiness (easy to do with this particular legume).

If no cooked rice is available, you're probably better off by cooking a cup of it and saving the remaining 2 cups as leftovers. However, if you wish, ⅓ cup short-grain rice can be cooked with 1 cup water.

Trim and quarter the onion. Process until coarsely chopped. Although the amount of onion is quite flexible in this dish, be sure not to use more than a cupful. Rinse out the workbowl.

Sauté the onion along with the pepper in the oil until the onion is transparent.

Meanwhile, push celery through the slicing disc. Measure ½ cup.

When the onion is transparent, stir in the celery. Remove the skillet with the onion from heat. Pour in the stock. Stir and taste the vegetables. They'll still have a lot of crunch left. Should a softer texture be more to your liking, simmer the mixture, covered, until you have it.

Stir in the rice, oregano, and salt. The mixture should be fairly moist. Otherwise stir in stock by the tablespoon until it is.

Push chunks of chilled mozzarella through the shredding disc. Measure 1½ cups.

Cut the avocado in half lengthwise. Grasping one half in each hand, rotate your hands until the halves separate. The half with the pit still in it will be the more convenient one to store for further use because it has fewer exposed surfaces. Rub them with a few drops of lemon juice, wrap in plastic, and refrigerate.

Turn the avocado cut side down on a cutting board. Cut semicircular wedges by slicing crosswise. Just before you assemble the pie, pull off the peel that covers each semicircle.

Rinse the cooked black-eyed peas in water and drain. Gently stir in the vinegar, cumin, and coriander.

Oil a 9-inch pie pan or a 2-quart casserole with a broad shape.

To Assemble
Layer 1: the rice mixture—pat it into the pie pan as though it were a graham cracker crust
Layer 2: half the black-eyed peas
Layer 3: the avocado wedges
Layer 4: the rest of the black-eyed peas
Layer 5: the mozzarella

Heat until the cheese is bubbly (check after 20 minutes).

Note: If you let the pie sit for 15 minutes before serving, it will have less of a tendency to fall apart when you are serving it. Because of the tendency to crumble, however, this entree should not be chosen for a very formal occasion.

Yield: 6 main dish servings

ELEGANT VEGETABLE PIE

A delicate, custardlike filling, scented with herbs and olive oil, is the basis of this exquisite main dish. It contains no dairy products or eggs, which will be no surprise if you are familiar with the versatility of tofu.

1 pound firm tofu (if available in various textures. To firm tofu, see box.), drained (about 2 cups packed)

1 **batch Flexible Pastry (see Index) or other
    pastry for an 8- or 9-inch crust**
Optional: **1 artichoke heart, diced**
2 **cups sliced yellow squash (1 large)**
1 **cup diced green pepper (1 large)**
3 **medium tomatoes, fresh and peeled or
    canned and drained**
¼ **cup olive oil**
1½ **teaspoons lemon juice or vinegar**
1½ **teaspoons water**
½ **teaspoon basil**
¼ **teaspoon marjoram**
¼ **teaspoon cumin**
⅛ **teaspoon salt**
A few grinds of black pepper
Optional: **2 tablespoons parsley leaves, loosely
    packed**
2 **tablespoons arrowroot**

Preheat oven to 400° F.

For best texture in the finished product, firm the tofu before using, even if you were able to buy the firm-textured variety. If this is not done, a small amount of liquid will puddle at the bottom of the pie, which will be particularly noticeable in leftovers.

To Firm Tofu

Rinse off the cake of tofu. Pat it dry and wrap in a dry dish towel. Set this on a plate and refrigerate 2–8 hours.

If a fresh artichoke is available, boil it until tender and set aside the heart.

Trim the yellow squash. Either cut it in half lengthwise or cut across the width in sections that will fit into the feed tube. Push through the slicing disc. Measure 2 cups. Transfer to a large mixing bowl. Rinse the workbowl and insert the metal blade.

Trim green pepper and dice into small pieces with a sharp knife. Transfer to the mixing bowl.

Peel the tomatoes, if fresh. Cut them into small pieces. Measure about ¾ cup. Transfer to the mixing bowl.

Cut the artichoke heart into small pieces. Transfer to the mixing bowl.

Process for 10 seconds the tofu, oil, lemon juice, water, basil, marjoram, cumin, salt, black pepper, and optional parsley. Scrape down and

repeat until the mixture is smooth. Pulse in the arrowroot.

Gently stir this mixture into the vegetables in the bowl, until all the vegetables are coated. Transfer to an oiled 8- or 9-inch pie pan. (The amount of filling is generous.) Once the sides of the pan are filled, heap up the rest of the filling in the center of the dish.

Roll out the top crust. Place it over the filling. Flute edges and prick generously with a fork.

Bake for 50 minutes. Serve at once. Leftovers can be reheated in a 350° F. oven.

Yield: 8 main dish servings

CASSEROLES

Each entree exemplifies the kind of complexity and finesse one would customarily associate with an exquisite dessert.

LIMA CRUNCH

This cashew crusted casserole covers the range of types of crunches. Its textures are especially accentuated because the spicy dish is not bound together with a thick sauce or eggs.

The Filling
1 **cup cooked barley, drained**
2 **cups cooked lima beans, drained**
1 **cup onion slices (2 medium)**
1 **tablespoon salad oil**
Dash cayenne
½ **cup stock (substitute water)**
½ **cup celery slices (½ large rib)**
1–1⅓ **cups tomato pieces**
1 **teaspoon basil**
⅛ **teaspoon salt**
5 **drops Liquid Smoke**
1 **tablespoon vinegar**

The Topping
½ **cup raw or roasted cashews**
¼ **cup toasted wheat germ**
Dash salt
Optional: **⅛ teaspoon coriander**
⅛ **teaspoon black pepper**
2 **tablespoons salad oil**

Preheat oven to 400° F.

Prepare the barley and limas. If leftovers are not available, quick-soak together 1 cup baby limas, ½ cup barley, and 3½ cups water. After an hour, cook until tender over moderate heat. Drain.

Prepare the topping. With a dry machine pulse the cashews until they are coarsely chopped. Add the other topping ingredients. Pulse until barely mixed. Set aside.

Rinse the workbowl and insert the slicing disc. Push through trimmed onion and measure 1 cup. In a heavy skillet with cover, heat the oil over medium-high heat. Use a metal spatula to distribute the oil evenly. Add the sliced onion and the cayenne. Heat 2–3 minutes, stirring often. Pour in the stock and cover the pan.

Push celery through the slicing disc and measure ½ cup. Add it to the onions; cover and reduce the heat to medium. Continue cooking until the onions are tender.

With a sharp knife, cut cherry tomatoes in half or salad tomatoes into bite-sized pieces. Measure 1–1⅓ cups. Stir the basil, salt, Liquid Smoke, and vinegar into the onion mixture, then gently stir in the tomatoes. Turn this mixture into an oiled 8″ × 8″ × 2″ baking dish or other 2-quart casserole with a broad shape. Take the topping mixture a handful at a time; crumble it between your fingers as you distribute it evenly over the top of the dish.

Bake until the top starts to brown and ingredients are heated through (check after 15 minutes). (If chilled leftovers were used, heating time must be increased and the baking dish should be covered once the topping has browned.)

Serve immediately, so that the casserole does not dry out. If you have leftovers, reheat in a saucepan, adding enough stock or water to keep the ingredients moist.

Yield: 6 main dish servings

CELESTIAL CHESTNUT CASSEROLE

Prepare this dish for your most discriminating guests. The delicate flavors of fresh chestnut, brown barley sauce, and brussels sprout are unforgettable.

1 cup long-grain brown rice
2¼ cups water
1 cup peeled chestnuts (about ½ pound in the shell)
1½ cups brussels sprouts
3 tablespoons butter
3 tablespoons barley flour (substitute whole wheat flour)
1 cup soy stock or other mild stock
Salt and pepper to taste

Cook the rice in the water, using the fluffy boil method.

Peel the chestnuts as described in the box.

To Peel Chestnuts

Cut a large X in the shell of each chestnut. Meanwhile, boil a large amount of water. Set the cut chestnuts in a saucepan and pour in enough boiling water to cover them by an inch or more. Let the chestnuts soak for 10 minutes. Then remove a few at a time, paring off the shell and brown skin. Set the peeled nut meats aside.

Steam the peeled chestnuts until tender. Steam the trimmed brussels sprouts barely tender. In both cases, take care not to overcook.

To prepare the sauce, use a large skillet and medium-high heat. Warm the butter and barley flour until they brown *lightly,* stirring constantly. Immediately stir in the stock. (If you must substitute whole wheat flour, don't try to roast it in this way. Brown the butter, then stir in the flour. After 2 minutes, stir in the stock.) Stir in salt and pepper to taste. Bring the mixture to a boil, then simmer 5 minutes longer.

Pulse the nuts until chopped medium fine. Stir into the sauce.

Push the chestnuts through the slicing disc.

Cut the brussels sprouts in half.

Stir both into the sauce, with the heat again at medium. Correct the seasoning. Put the freshly cooked rice into a serving dish and top it with the sauce mixture. Top this with the nuts.

Yield: 6 main dish servings

LEMON VEGETABLE SHOWCASE

This delightful showcase for green vegetables works on the principle of the pudding cake. The popover-style batter, rather than popping up, dunks itself down into the lemon-flavored sauce.

6–7 cups cooked green vegetables, such as zucchini, green beans, or broccoli (choose a single vegetable, or a combination)
2 tablespoons lemon juice
2 tablespoons arrowroot
¼ teaspoon marjoram
¼ teaspoon salt
4 tablespoons butter
Yellow food coloring
2 eggs
1 cup whole milk, or 1 cup lowfat milk + 1 tablespoon salad oil
⅛ teaspoon salt
½ cup whole wheat flour
¼ cup wheat germ
¼ cup oat flour, whole wheat pastry flour, or unbleached white flour
1 tablespoon salad oil

Preheat oven to 450° F.

The Filling
You will need 6–7 cups cooked green vegetables, sliced as delicately as possible. For maximum nutrition, steam vegetables whole, or as nearly whole as possible, letting them cool and then processing. Cooked zucchini can be pushed through the slicing disc, or better yet, a thin slicing disc, if you have one. Green beans can be frenched by packing sideways and pushing through the slicing disc. Broccoli stem also slices nicely. Although broccoli flowerets could be used, for the best texture of this dish it is better to use only thin-sliced stem.

Reserve the water over which the vegetables are steamed (later referred to as "vitamin water").

Measure the vegetables and transfer to an oiled 8″ × 8″ × 2″ baking dish.

The Sauce
Rinse out the workbowl. Insert the metal blade. Process 2 cups vitamin water with the lemon juice, arrowroot, marjoram, and salt. Melt the butter over medium heat in a saucepan. Stir in the mixture and enough food coloring to turn it light yellow. Stir constantly until the sauce becomes transparent and starts to bubble. Remove from heat and pour it into the baking dish. Stir gently to ensure that some of the sauce covers the bottom of the dish.

The Topping
Rinse out the workbowl. Process the eggs, milk, and salt for 3 seconds. Distribute the remaining ingredients over the top. Process 10 seconds. Scrape down and process 5 seconds longer.

Pour this batter over the vegetables and sauce. Smooth it even with the back of a large spoon. After baking 15 minutes, turn the heat down to 350° F. Bake an additional 20 minutes. Serve at once.

Yield: 6 main dish servings

CAULIFLOWER WALTZ

2 cups whole grain Bread Crumbs (see index) (4 slices of bread)
2 ounces blue cheese, cut into 4 pieces
1½ cups minced sharp cheddar
2 tablespoons butter
3 tablespoons whole wheat flour
1¾ cups milk
½ cup milk
2 cups cauliflower slices
3 large eggs
⅛ teaspoon cumin

Preheat oven to 350° F.

Process bread and measure 2 cups coarse bread crumbs. Add the blue cheese and pulse until uniform. Set aside in a large mixing bowl.

Process cheddar chunks until minced. Measure 1½ cups. Set aside in a separate bowl.

Make a cream sauce with the butter, flour, and 1¾ cups milk (for detailed instructions, see recipe for Flexible Cream Sauce). When the sauce thickens, remove it from heat.

Meanwhile, insert the slicing disc and push through cauliflower flowerets. Measure 2 cups. Simmer in the ½ cup milk until barely tender. Let it cool. Remove this cauliflower mixture from heat.

Replace the metal blade. Process the eggs for 30 seconds. Pour in the cooled cream sauce. Add the cumin. Process until smooth.

In the large mixing bowl, lightly stir together the bread crumb mixture, cream sauce, cauliflower, and milk. Transfer to an oiled 8- or 9-inch square casserole. Top with the cheddar. Bake until the cheese is bubbly (check after 20 minutes).

Yield: 6 main dish servings

SWISS PEA CASSEROLE

Here is a truly distinctive and elegant combination of flavors.

1 cup yellow or green split peas
3 cups water
½ teaspoon cardamom
½ teaspoon coriander
⅛ teaspoon salt
1 cup minced imported Swiss cheese
2 cups yellow or green squash slices (2 medium)
¼ cup large-curd cottage cheese
2 tablespoons salad oil
1 cup green pepper pieces (1 large)

Preheat oven to 350° F.

In a covered saucepan, cook together the split peas, water, cardamom, and coriander. When the legumes are tender, stir in the salt.

Mince the cheese and measure 1 cup. Set aside.

Trim the squash. Push chunks through the slicing disc and measure 2 cups. Set aside. Rinse the workbowl.

Process the cottage cheese, oil, green pepper, and minced cheese until uniform, scraping down as needed.

Oil 4 individual covered casseroles or 1 covered casserole with a 1½-quart capacity.

To Assemble
Layer 1: enough of the split pea mixture to cover the bottom of the pan(s) with a ½-inch layer
Layer 2: half the summer squash
Layer 3: half the cottage cheese mixture
Layer 4: the rest of the split pea mixture
Layer 5: the rest of the summer squash
Layer 6: the rest of the cottage cheese mixture

Bake until heated through (check after 20 minutes). Serve hot.

Yield: 4 main dish servings

Note: If you wish to double the recipe for a large gathering, you may be able to purchase both colors of squash and split peas. Of course, yellow and green peas must be cooked separately before layering into the casserole in order to preserve the different colors.

▣ CONFIDENCE CASSEROLE

Confidence Casserole is more than a recipe for a main dish; it's a new way of looking at what it takes to put together a main dish. This dish is comprised of three basic elements: the crust, the base, and the featured ingredients, plus, if desired, a flavor or texture accent. Each component (except the crust) can be varied to create a countless variety of unique Confidence Casseroles. Use Table 11 as your guide; it is provided as a framework within which you can improvise with reliable results.

Use your common sense, your taste, and your imagination for this casserole. Then you can serve it weekly for a year without repeating yourself once. My favorite Confidence Casserole so far has an Oomphy Tomato Sauce (see Index) base, broccoli and tofu as featured ingredients, Duxelles (see Index) as a flavor accent.

Confidence base (see Table 11)
Featured ingredient(s) (see Table 11)
***Optional:* flavor or texture accent (see Table 11)**

Confidence Crust

1 cup Confidence (see Index)
1 egg
½ cup milk, peppermint tea, or apple cider
2 tablespoons corn oil (substitute salad oil)

Preheat oven to 425° F.

Prepare the base. Correct seasoning as desired. Prepare the featured ingredient(s). Stir together with base. Transfer half the mixture to an oiled 8- or 9-inch square pan.

If a flavor or texture accent is used, add it here, in an evenly distributed layer. Put the remainder of the mixture into the baking dish.

To prepare Confidence Crust, process the egg 10 seconds. Pulse in the milk and oil. Distribute the Confidence mix over the top and process 5 seconds. Scrape down. Repeat until the mixture is smooth. It should have the consistency of pancake batter. Pulse in more liquid if necessary.

Pour crust mixture over the top of the other ingredients in the baking dish and smooth with the back of the spoon. Bake until the crust is firm (check after 25 minutes). Serve hot.

Yield: at least 6 main dish servings

TABLE 11: A YEAR'S WORTH OF CONFIDENCE CASSEROLES

Confidence Base—Choose 1 of the Following:

2 cups any sauce or gravy
1½ cups cooked legumes + ½ cup stock or tomato juice + seasonings
2 cups thick, flavorful soup
(Seasonings will vary with desired effect.)

My Discoveries:

Featured Ingredient—Choose A, B, C, or D:

A. *Total of 4 cups of bite-sized pieces of cooked, drained vegetable (the food processor speeds up preparation). Use any combination of the following ingredients, which you think go together well and are compatible with the base and optional accent. Although you may combine as many vegetables as you wish, in most cases it is best to use only 1 or 2.*

beet
broccoli
brussels sprout
carrot
chard
corn kernels
green beans
green cabbage
kale
mustard greens
parsnip
red cabbage
rutabaga
spinach
summer squash
turnip
turnip greens
wax beans

B. *Use 3 cups of the above vegetables + 1 cup cooked, drained:*

black beans
black-eyed peas
chickpeas
great northern beans
kidney beans
lima beans
pinto beans
red beans
soybeans

C. *Use 3 cups of the above vegetables + 1 cup:*

cubed tofu
adzuki bean sprouts
lentil sprouts
mung bean sprouts
soy sprouts

My Discoveries:

Flavor or Texture Accent— May Choose 1 of the Following:

Raw or cooked ingredients:

⅓ cup sliced or minced celery*
½ cup minced onion*
½ cup green peas
½ cup sliced or chopped mushrooms*

Cooked vegetable, cooled and cut into ½-inch cubes:

½ cup winter squash
½ cup sweet potato
½ cup baking potato

Miscellaneous ingredients:

½ cup Duxelles (see recipe)*
½ cup chopped nuts
½ cup sunflower seeds, roasted or sprouted
½ cup sesame seeds, roasted or sprouted
⅓ cup Sunflower Meal (see recipe)*
½ cup water chestnuts, sliced*
½ cup bite-sized pieces of red or green pepper
1 cup shredded mild cheese, such as jack*
½ cup olives

My Discoveries:

---

*Use the food processor to speed up preparation.

COOKIES AND CHEESECAKE

Even these favorites can be modified to serve as sensible, nutritious fare.

CHICK CHIP BARS

Try these maverick entrees for Sunday brunch or on a picnic. They are delightful as finger food.

¾ **cup cooked chick-peas**
1 **cup whole wheat pastry flour, or ½ cup whole wheat flour + ¼ cup toasted wheat germ + ¼ cup barley flour or unbleached white flour**
1 **teaspoon baking powder**
⅛ **teaspoon salt**
½ **teaspoon ground coriander**
⅓ **cup butter (substitute margarine)**
1 **egg**
2 **tablespoons milk**
⅓ **cup hazelnuts (substitute roasted peanuts)**

Preheat oven to 375° F.
Prepare the chick-peas and drain well. Processor sift the flour(s), baking powder, salt, and coriander. Set aside.
Process the butter and egg for 10 seconds. Scrape down. Add the milk. Process 10 seconds. Repeat until the mixture is smooth (or uniform, if you are substituting margarine). Distribute the flour mixture evenly over the liquids and pulse until barely mixed.
Distribute the nuts and chick-peas over this mixture. Pulse twice.
Transfer to an oiled 8″ × 8″ × 2″ baking dish. Bake until a tester inserted in the center comes out clean (check after 40 minutes).
After the mixture has cooled for 10 minutes, cut it into bars and place on the rack for further cooling.

Yield: 9 main dish servings

CHEESE CAKE SQUARES

If possible, serve these main dish bars fresh from the oven, while the cheese is still temptingly gooey. Cold, the bars have a soft chewy texture, which is also delicious.

2 **tablespoons butter**
1¼ **cups whole wheat flour**
1 **teaspoon baking powder**
1 **cup shredded sharp cheddar**
1 **egg**
1 **cup milk**
⅛ **teaspoon black pepper**
Optional: **1 teaspoon chervil**
¼ **cup rolled oats or rye**

Preheat oven to 350° F. Oil an 8-inch square pan. Place the butter in the oiled pan and set it in the oven for a few minutes to melt.
Processor sift the flour and baking powder. Set aside.
Push chunks of cheese through the shredding disc and measure 1 cup. Set aside. Remove the butter from the oven to cool slightly.
Process the egg, milk, pepper, and optional chervil for 15 seconds. Pour in the melted butter and process 5 seconds. Add the flour mixture and cheese. Pulse until barely mixed.
Sprinkle ½ the oats evenly over the bottom of the pan. Pour in the batter. Smooth with the back of a spoon. Sprinkle the remaining oats evenly over the top. Bake until the surface springs back to the touch (check after 20 minutes). If possible, cut into bars and serve at once.

Yield: 9 main dish servings

11 | Almost-Instant Whole Grain Baking

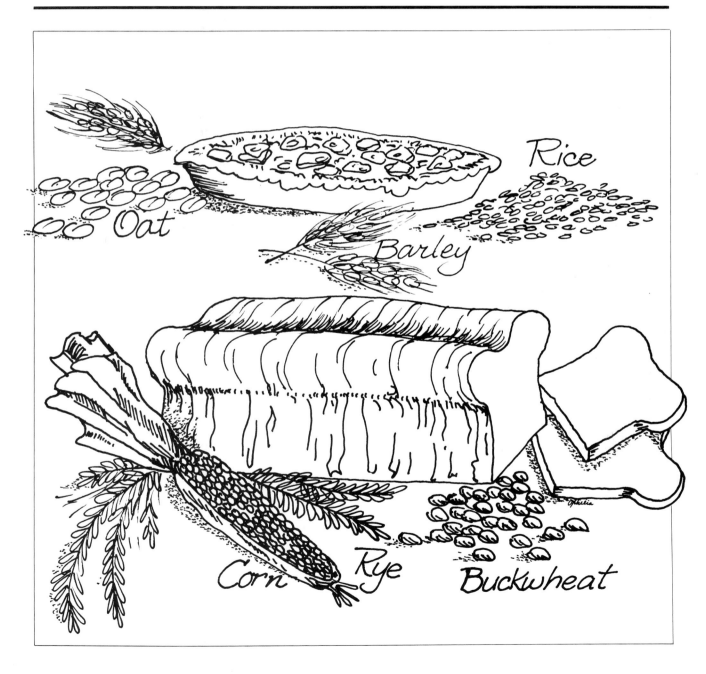

One of the most exciting discoveries you can make about natural food is *flour*—not the lifeless wheat extract many people consider synonymous with flour, but a variety of whole grain products.

Get ready for some delectable flavors. Have you ever sampled the nutty flavor of roasted rice flour? Have you tickled your palate with cornmeal? Unlike the degermed imposter, fresh whole cornmeal has an invigorating bright sweetness.

You probably wouldn't dream of eating only one type of vegetable or one type of fruit. Well, the stuff you can use for papier mâché isn't the only flour.

A newcomer to whole grain baking could spend years improvising with Confidence (see Chapter 5) in all its various uses. To graduate to other flours is another big step—equally fascinating. As far as I'm concerned, complete knowledge about flours is a prerequisite to true gourmet baking. Without different flours to add variety, bakers largely add interest by escalating the amounts of sugar and fat used. In contrast, the recipes in this chapter depend on the unique excellence of different flours.

With the processor, these recipes are incredibly convenient. Imagine a yeast bread you can put together in 15 minutes of active time, or pastry impeccably mixed in seconds.

It's fortunate that these whole grain recipes are so easy to make. They're so good that even health food haters sing their praises. Aside from tempting tastes, this chapter contains simple, flexible recipes to coax you into baking often. You will find you can serve corn bread in a dozen different variations, or fine tune the flavor of piecrust to harmonize with the filling, without being limited by inconvenient procedures. These recipes won't clutter up your kitchen with spattered batters or sticky dishes.

So I invite you to spend the few minutes it takes to bake from scratch. The rewards are great: subtle new flavors, more dietary diversity, a savings in cost over products of lesser quality. And don't forget a side benefit free for every home baker: *that wonderful fragrance!*

THE LESSER-KNOWN FLOURS

Rye, most commonly used of the nonwheat flours, tastes excellent in both its light and dark varieties. The flavor is deeper than that of wheat. Using about ¼ cup in a bread recipe suffices to bring this flavor through. Rye also teams up well with cornmeal and, of course, caraway seed.

Barley and *brown rice* flours taste superb when pan roasted and added to baked goods in place of part of the wheat flour (up to ¼ of it). For extra flavor, add a little sesame oil to the skillet when roasting these flours. The same goes for *chestnut flour, chick-pea flour,* and *sweet brown rice flour,* though generally these flours are harder to find and more costly: roasting just before use in a recipe brings out the flavor dramatically. And usually a 25-percent addition to a recipe is plenty.

High-protein *oat flour* has a delicate flavor and adds flakiness when used in Flexible Pastry (see Index). For other baking uses, I find rolled oats preferable to oat flour. (The rolled forms of oats, rye, and wheat are all delicious but have special properties quite different from flour when used for baking. To avoid preparing the kind of baking experiment you have to throw away instead of eat, learn to use rolled grains by following recipes before you improvise on your own.)

Small amounts of *buckwheat flour* make for hearty breads, muffins, and pancakes. A small percentage (10 percent) is enough to impart the characteristic flavor. Beware of using larger amounts. The result can be very heavy—or very satisfying, depending on your taste. Crackers and muffins can be made with buckwheat flour exclusively (see Tender Crackers recipe)—unconventional but tasty. For a wonderfully fresh buckwheat flour with a delightfully coarse texture, process your own from buckwheat groats. Place 1 to 2 cups groats in the workbowl and process for 2 minutes.

Natural *cornmeal* is an utter delight: golden, sweet, chewy. I'm partial to it. Wheat flour can lighten it; so can eggs and buttermilk. For yeast breads, do not use more than 1 cup per loaf, or you risk producing an excessively crumbly loaf.

Millet flour lacks the superb texture of the unground grain. Even worse, its baked products have a disconcerting tendency to fall apart. Frankly, the only really good use I've found for millet flour is Flexible Brownies (see Index).

With a processor you can lightly crack whole millet (see Speckled Bread recipe). Try that for more versatile bread and muffin baking.

Even more than chick-pea flour, *soy flour* boosts protein content enormously when added to whole grain doughs—it balances the amino acids in grains. Used in small amounts (no more than ¼ cup per loaf), it can help breads rise higher and delay staleness. Soy flour can also be used as an egg replacer (see page 153).

In general, though, the best way to employ soybeans in baking is to use beans you have already cooked, rather than to purchase dried soy flour. To do this, while mixing the liquid ingredients of a recipe, process in well-drained soybeans. As happens when preparing the soybean-based spreads in Chapter 6, a spectacular transformation occurs, in which the beans turn from tan to white and become thickly creamy in texture. By processing home-cooked, frozen, thawed beans, you are using the least expensive high-protein food that money can buy (see Chapter 15). You also are likely to be using a fresher food than store-bought soy flour.

In addition to baking, all the flours mentioned here make superb breakfast cereal. Why not give yourself a hot breakfast without either wheat or oats? Base a porridge on rye, brown rice flour, or cornmeal. Add a small amount of buckwheat, barley, chick-pea, or soy flour, or processed soybeans, dried fruit, or cinnamon. Stir in leftover grains for a contrasting texture— or chopped nuts. (For more detailed instructions, see Table 4, page 55.) Top the morning masterpiece with yogurt, milk, tahini, or butter and salt.

⒡ FLEXIBLE WHOLE GRAIN PASTRY

Pies always make a meal special. Unfortunately, unless you are careful, pies can add a lot of fat to your diet.

The recipe for multipurpose pastry that follows is for 1-crust batches. Because of the fat content, I don't recommend baking a 2-crust pie under any circumstances.

Open-faced pies are a delight. If you're worried about the filling drying out, a paper bag can help. See the method used in making Honey Pie (see Index).

Or try a deep dish pie with a top crust only, such as Elegant Vegetable Pie (see Index). Lightly oil the pie pan before filling it.

The quantity of pastry is sufficient for a 10-inch pie pan. Any leftover dough can be used for Pastry Scrap Cookies (see Index).

1 flour option (see Table 12)
Dash salt
3 tablespoons cold butter, cut into 3 pieces
2 tablespoons cold corn oil (substitute salad oil)
1 choice of additional liquid (see Table 12)

Processor sift the flour option and salt. Add the butter and oil and process for 10 seconds. Scrape down the workbowl and process 10 seconds longer.

Pour 3 tablespoons of additional liquid over the mixture, distributing it fairly evenly. Process 5 seconds. Let the machine come to a stop. Reprocess for 5 seconds. If the dough does not form a ball (start to clump together), sprinkle in another tablespoon of liquid. If a ball still does not form, repeat 5-second processings, adding a teaspoon of cold water each time.

Gather the dough into a compact shape, including crumbs of flour in the machine. (Occasionally at this point you will discover that the dough still is really too dry to hold together. Process it 5 seconds longer with another teaspoon of cold water and reshape.)

Wrap the dough airtight in plastic and chill ½ hour. If longer chilling is more convenient, let the dough sit out at room temperature afterward until pliable, for perhaps 30 minutes.

Heat the oven to 400° F. Lightly oil a 10-inch pie pan.

Roll out the dough between 2 sheets of wax paper or on a pastry cloth. Flour this bottom surface, the top of the dough, and (if you do not use wax paper) the rolling pin. Use a light flour: barley, oat, or unbleached white.

Roll from the center outward. Stretch the dough as thinly and evenly as possible. Work quickly to preserve the pastry texture.

Transfer the dough, without pulling it, into the pie pan. Trim off the edges, tuck them under, and flute to form a rim. Prick the bottom and sides of the crust generously with a fork.

To prevent sogginess, a crust should be at

TABLE 12: FINESSE WITH FLEXIBLE PASTRY

Flour Options	*What They Contribute*
1½ cups whole wheat pastry flour	lightest of the whole grain pastries
1¼ cups whole wheat flour + ¼ cup wheat germ (raw or toasted)	a chewy crumb
1 cup whole wheat flour + ½ cup barley flour (raw or roasted)	delicately delicious
1 cup whole wheat flour + ¼ cup oat flour	flaky, crumbly

My Discoveries:

Additional Liquids	*What They Contribute*
3–4 tablespoons cold water	standard pastry texture
1 teaspoon molasses or blackstrap molasses stirred into 3–4 tablespoons cold water	richer flavor and color, suitable for sweet and savory pies alike
½ teaspoon vanilla extract and 1 teaspoon cinnamon stirred into 3–4 tablespoons cold water	a delightful start for a dessert pie
1 tablespoon lemon juice stirred into 2–3 tablespoons cold water	an overall quality of crispness
3–4 tablespoons peppermint tea, brewed strong, strained thoroughly, and chilled	brightens a dessert pie
3–4 tablespoons apple cider	enhances the sweetness of natural flours
3–4 tablespoons cold milk	extra rich and crumbly

My Discoveries:

least partially baked. The exception is when a filling is quite dry and requires considerable baking (see recipe for Honey Pie).

When done sufficiently, a partially baked crust will appear baked rather than raw, but will still not be brown. Ten minutes should do it. A fully baked crust will be lightly browned. Check after 12 minutes.

Remember to let pastry cool sufficiently before filling. A filling cooler than the crust may cause it to crack.

Most of all, remember that pie making is an acquired art. Don't let yourself get discouraged. It takes practice to produce pastry that looks professional, but homemade-looking pies can taste just as delicious.

TENDER CRACKERS

This dough for light whole grain crackers can also be used as pastry.

¼ teaspoon lecithin granules
2 tablespoons boiling water
1½ cups whole wheat pastry flour or buckwheat flour (Note that these produce very different products. Buckwheat flour crackers are heavier than crackers made with whole wheat.)
Dash salt
¼ teaspoon baking soda
3 tablespoons corn oil (substitute other salad oil)

2 tablespoons cold water for whole wheat; ¼ cup cold water for buckwheat
More cold water as needed

Put the lecithin into a small cup and pour in the boiling water. Let it soften at least 10 minutes.

Processor sift the flour, salt, and baking soda. Set aside.

Turn the lecithin and water into the workbowl. Add the oil and process 60 seconds. Add the flour mixture and 2 tablespoons or ¼ cup water, as appropriate. Process 5 seconds.

Scrape down. Repeat until the dough starts to whirl around in a mass, adding 1 tablespoon water each time you process.

For crackers, preheat the oven to 350° F. and oil 1 or 2 baking sheets. Roll out the dough, using plenty of flour, as thin as possible without tearing it. Cut into rectangles or another shape of your choice. Transfer to a baking sheet. Bake until a sample cracker tastes crisp (check after 12 minutes for wheat, 15 minutes for buckwheat).

Yield varies greatly, depending on how the dough is rolled and cut. Dough rolled into an 8″ × 13″ rectangle yields about 100 1-inch square crackers.

To use the dough for pastry, press it into a 10-inch pie pan, prick, and bake until partially baked or fully baked (see recipe for Flexible Pastry). Allow extra baking time for buckwheat.

DAILY BREAD

Even if you find kneading therapeutic, give yourself the benefit of processor dough mixing. You'll save on time and cleanup.

The following recipe for whole wheat bread has a carob accent for subtly enriched flavor.

1½ teaspoons granular baker's yeast
1 tablespoon honey, brown sugar, or blackstrap molasses
½ cup very warm water
3 cups whole wheat flour
1 tablespoon carob flour
¼ teaspoon salt
¾ cup cool water

Insert the metal blade. Place the first three ingredients in the workbowl. When the yeast turns frothy (about 15 minutes), add the other ingredients. Run the processor until a dough forms out of the separate ingredients (about 3 minutes).

The reason for using cool water is that the internal temperature of the processor during kneading increases so much that otherwise the yeast may be killed. If you intend only to mix in the machine, and not knead, you should substitute lukewarm water for cool.

To processor knead, run the machine an additional 60 seconds.

Let the dough rise double (about 40 minutes). Punch it down. Shape it into a loaf. Let it rise in an oiled loaf pan (8½″ × 4½″ × 2½″) until the dough doubles again. Bake on the middle rack (6 to 8 inches from the heat source) of a 400° F. oven. To check for doneness, tap the top of the bread after 40 minutes. If you hear a hollow-sounding tap, the bread is probably done. Remove the bread from the pan; tap it on the bottom. If this tap, too, sounds hollow, the bread is done. If not, return the loaf to the pan and the oven. Check again after five minutes.

Once you get accustomed to the procedure for this recipe, you will be able to prepare bread using just 15 minutes of active time per loaf.

Yield: 1 loaf

- To prepare more than one loaf at a time, place the first 3 ingredients for each loaf in separate bowls. After you proof the yeast (the yeast mixture turns frothy) for the processor loaf, continue to mix and knead that batch of dough. Set it to rise and transfer the ingredients in the bowl to the workbowl. Mix and knead it and set it to rise. Repeat for each loaf in the batch.
- An easy test to determine if dough has doubled is to poke two fingers one inch deep into the dough. If holes left by the fingers do not close up, the bread has sufficiently risen.

MORE INFORMATION FOR THE BREAD MAKER

Rising Place

Try the following possibilities:

- Gas stove: Let bread rise near the pilot light. You may place a broad pan with steaming hot tap water on the floor of the oven to add moisture.

- Electric stove: Preheat the oven to a low heat for 1–2 minutes. Turn it off. Let bread rise in oven. Repeat before the second rising.
- A closed cupboard or high shelf, warm and free from drafts
- A table in a very sunny corner, free from drafts
- A chair near a hot radiator, free from drafts
- An automatic dishwasher: After a load of dishes has been run through and removed, the steamy hot lower rack makes an excellent place for the first rising. But check the dough earlier, after just 35 minutes.

Storage of Bread

Because homemade bread lacks preservatives, it stays at peak freshness for just 2–3 days.

Here's how to get the most out of your baking:

- Let each loaf cool (and dry out slightly) by exposing it to the air for 4–8 hours. If a fresh loaf has been cut, stand it on a plate, cut side down, during this period. Place the bread in a plastic bag, then in a second bag. Seal. Refrigerate or not. It's a matter of personal preference. Either way, it will stay at peak freshness for 2–3 days.
- For longer keeping, freeze bread. Place the cooled, sliced, wrapped bread in the freezer for up to 2 weeks. Thaw in the refrigerator or heat slices in the toaster.
- For a very small number of bread eaters, mix one batch of Daily Bread and shape it into 2 small loaves. Bake them as freestanding bread (see later). Use one loaf immediately and freeze the other.

Quantity Baking

When you have a very large number of bread eaters, baking a sufficient quantity, not storage, is the challenge. Luckily you can bake 6 rectangular loaves at a time in a standard-sized oven.

The processor makes large-scale family baking practical, enabling you to save substantial amounts of money. When you are measuring out ingredients to mix into dough, use a separate bowl for each loaf. Add ingredients one at a time—all the flour, all the water, and so forth. Then, if interrupted, you can return to the kitchen and easily scan your assembly line for where you left off.

Baking for Variety

Food processor mixing is ideal for making a variety of different breads during one baking session. Just remember: one bowl (or the workbowl) per loaf. And keep different doughs separate when rising.

To Correct Consistency of Batter

Even white bread is subject to the problem of variables such as moisture content, age, and how the flour was stored. Add to that what you bring to the baking process: accuracy of measurement and baking temperature; the weather, humidity, and altitude where you bake.

With whole grain flours there is even more variability than with white flour. So how do you compensate?

Luckily for the beginner, there is a wide range of acceptable dough textures. You will be safe if you fall within the range of *dry* to *damp*. Machine kneading can actually help you judge dough textures because of less distracting mess around you and clear visibility through the plastic workbowl.

- Dough on the *dry* side can still be processed until smooth with the metal blade. When you machine mix, sometimes you see a mass of separate little doughy crumbs start to form. That signals that it is *too dry.* Stop the machine at once. Pour ⅛ cup water into the workbowl. Process 10 seconds. Check the appearance of the dough. Repeat until a smooth texture is attained.
- Dough on the *damp* side will not form a ball in the workbowl during machine kneading. However, it still is thick and elastic. This battery kind of dough can make for tender

light-textured bread. However, if you suspect that the dough may be *too liquid* to hold up as a loaf, you can hand knead in additional flour before the first or second rising.

Whenever you knead, it works best to sprinkle additional flour onto the bottom of the counter and push the dough into it. Do not put the flour directly on top of the dough. Work with a handful of flour at a time and really work it in before you add more.

To Shape Freestanding Loaves

You can bake loaves on a baking sheet, rather than in loaf pans. After you machine knead dough, knead in flour by the handful until the dough is quite stiff. After the first rising comes the time to shape the loaves. If they are not sturdy enough to hold their shape, you have another chance to knead in additional flour.

Why not just dump in an extra cup of flour and be done with it? Unnecessary flour makes for unnecessary toughness in bread.

Developing Expertise

To develop your expertise as a baker, give yourself a chance to learn from dough textures every time you bake. When preparing the dough for the first or second rising, stop for a moment and make a mental note about the texture. Later, when you taste the baked bread, again make a note. Consider the crumb, the moistness, how high the bread rose. Relate that information to what you noted about the texture of the dough.

Such comparisons will help you gain an instinct for the whole process of baking bread. Incidentally, hand kneading doesn't necessarily ensure the greatest sensitivity. Whatever method you use to do the kneading, at each step of the way you must use your senses of touch and sight. Actively pay attention to what is happening and you won't only produce better bread, you'll gain more pleasure from baking.

COLORFUL BREADS

Once you develop the knack of processor bread making, try this colorful group of recipes.

BROWN BREAD

Hearty and sweet.

1½ teaspoons yeast
¼ cup blackstrap molasses or molasses
½ cup warm water
½ cup buckwheat flour
2½ cups whole wheat flour
¼ teaspoon salt
¾ cup cool water

Follow the procedure for Daily Bread (see earlier recipe this chapter). After the loaf has baked and been removed from the pan, brush with oil or butter for a soft, shiny crust.

Yield: 1 loaf

YELLOW BREAD

The chewy, grainy crumb of this bread gives sandwiches special interest.

1½ teaspoons yeast
1 tablespoon brown sugar
½ cup warm water
2⅓ cups whole wheat flour
⅔ cup cornmeal
1 tablespoon salad oil
¼ teaspoon salt
¾ cup cool water
1 egg yolk
1 tablespoon water

Follow the procedure for Daily Bread (see earlier recipe), adding all but the last 2 ingredients. Beat the egg and water together. Remove the pan from the oven after 35 minutes of baking. Brush the top of the loaf with the egg mixture. Continue baking until done. This glaze produces a bright, shiny crust.

Yield: 1 loaf

ORANGE BREAD

This is a cakelike bread, scented with cardamom and warm with the sweetness of orange juice. Golden raisins are optional.

1½ teaspoons yeast
½ cup warm water
¼ cup brown sugar
2 tablespoons clarified butter or butter
1 teaspoon freshly crushed cardamom or 1½ teaspoons commercially ground cardamom
Orange food coloring
¼ teaspoon salt
3 cups whole wheat flour
¾ cup cool (not refrigerator cold) orange juice from concentrate
***Optional:* ½ cup golden raisins**
1 egg white + 1 tablespoon water

Proof the yeast in the warm water and brown sugar. When mixing the dough, first process in the butter and cardamom until uniform, then process in food coloring to turn the mixture orange, then add the salt, flour, and juice. Proceed as with Daily Bread (see recipe).

For raisin bread, reserve the raisins until after the first rising. When you are shaping the loaf, roll the dough out on a floured surface into a rectangle about 8 × 4 inches. Sprinkle the raisins onto the dough, leaving a 1-inch margin on all sides. Roll it up like a jelly roll. Place in the loaf pan seam side down.

Continue as with Daily Bread, adding all but the egg white and water. To make glaze, beat the egg white and water together. Remove the loaf from the oven after 35 minutes of baking at 400° F. Brush the top with the glaze. Continue baking until done (about 5 minutes longer). This glaze produces a vivid, shiny crust.

Yield: 1 loaf

SPECKLED BREAD

This loaf is chewy, speckled with sesame and millet. The toast is terrific.

1½ teaspoons yeast
2 tablespoons honey

½ cup warm water
2 cups whole wheat flour
¾ cup cool water
1 cup sesame seeds
½ cup millet
¼ teaspoon salt
Additional whole wheat flour as needed

Proof the yeast in the honey and warm water. For the first rising add only the cool water and flour—the batter is moist and sticky. Meanwhile, pan roast the sesame seeds until they brown. Process in a dried workbowl with the millet and salt for 60 seconds.

After the first rising, add about ½ the batter to the machine and process 30 seconds. Hand knead the rest of the batter into this mixture until the dough is stiff enough to shape into a loaf—add additional flour as necessary. Let rise and bake in a 400° F. oven. During baking, place a pan of water (any temperature) on the floor of the oven. The steam crisps the crust while it bakes. Check after 40 minutes.

Yield: 1 loaf

F FLEXIBLE CORN BREAD

We eat corn bread too often to want to serve it the same way every time. After you've savored the zesty basic recipe, try some of the variations.

Remember, too, the versatile uses of corn bread. Bring it to a picnic, brown bag it for a lunchtime entree, or serve it as a main course at dinner, fresh from the oven, topped with a steaming hot puree of green split peas and a sprinkling of minced Parmesan.

1¼ cups whole wheat flour, sifted
⅛ teaspoon salt
½ teaspoon baking soda
1 teaspoon baking powder
***Optional:* 1 item from Group A (see Table 13)**
***Optional:* 1 item from Group B (see Table 13)**
1 egg
¼ cup corn oil (substitute other salad oil)
1¼ cups buttermilk
1 cup cornmeal

TABLE 13: CORNBREAD CHOICES

Group A

1 cup corn kernels, cooked on the cob and scraped off
1 cup shredded zucchini (wring out after measuring; see recipe for Zucchini Lace)
1 cup shredded carrot + ¼ cup chopped parsley

My Discoveries:

Group B

Substitute Unadulterated Mayonnaise (see recipe) for corn oil
½ cup Sunflower Meal (see recipe)
½ cup sesame seeds, pan roasted and processed into a meal

My Discoveries:

Preheat oven to 425° F.

With a dry machine, processor sift whole wheat flour. Measure 1¼ cups. Return to the workbowl and processor sift again with the salt, baking soda, and baking powder. Set aside.

Prepare optional ingredients as needed. Set aside.

Process the egg for 5 seconds. Add the oil and buttermilk and process 10 seconds.

Pulse in the flour mixture until barely mixed. Pulse in any optional ingredients.

Transfer to an oiled 8- or 9-inch square pan and bake until a tester inserted in the center comes out clean (check after 20 minutes). Corn bread is best served hot, right out of the oven, but keeps for several days if necessary, well wrapped and refrigerated.

Yield: 9 servings

PASSION FOR PUMPKIN

If you didn't know a pumpkin passion was possible, see how you feel after you taste these muffins. The sweetness and characteristic flavor is a delight.

1 cup cooked pumpkin or winter squash, pureed
1¼ cups whole wheat pastry flour (substitute whole wheat flour)
¼ cup rye flour (substitute wheat germ)

1½ teaspoons baking powder
½ teaspoon baking soda
¼ cup butter, cut into 4 pieces
¼ cup honey
½ teaspoon nutmeg
½ teaspoon cinnamon
Pinch salt
1 egg
½ cup raisins

Preheat oven to 350° F.

Steam or bake enough pumpkin to measure a little less than 1 cup cooked flesh. Let it cool to room temperature.

Processor sift the whole wheat and rye flours, baking powder and soda. Set aside.

Process about ⅞ cup pumpkin into the thickest possible puree by pouring a thin stream of water through the feed tube. Scrape down often. When the mixture is smooth, measure 1 cup.

Process the puree with butter, honey, nutmeg, cinnamon, salt, and egg until smooth, scraping down as necessary.

Distribute the flour mixture and raisins over this mixture. Pulse until barely mixed.

Transfer the batter to fill oiled muffin tins ⅔ full. Bake until a tester inserted in the center comes out clean (check after 25 minutes).

Yield: 12 muffins

POPPY MUFFINS

Enjoy the contrast of poppy seeds with a fluffy-textured muffin. We prefer to use the seeds because they add nutlike savor without nutlike calories. Still, you may prefer to substitute finely chopped nuts, sesame seeds, or sunflower seeds.

1 cup brown rice flour + 1 tablespoon sesame oil (substitute 1 cup whole wheat flour)
1 cup whole wheat flour
2 teaspoons baking powder
Dash salt
1 egg
2 tablespoons corn oil (substitute other salad oil)
1 cup milk
½ teaspoon vanilla extract
¼ cup poppy seeds

Preheat oven to 400° F.
Pan roast the rice flour with the oil until it starts to brown. Let cool to room temperature. (To substitute whole wheat flour, omit roasting.)
Process the rice flour in a thoroughly dry machine for 5 seconds. Add the whole wheat flour, baking powder, and salt. Processor sift. Set aside.
Process the egg and oil for 10 seconds. Pulse in the milk and vanilla extract. Distribute the poppy seeds and flour mixture over the top and pulse until barely mixed.
Spoon into oiled muffin compartments, filling them ⅔ full. Bake until a tester inserted in the center comes out clean (check after 15 minutes).

Yield: 12 muffins

MAPLE NUT CUPCAKES

Turn muffins into a dessert treat by making 2 substitutions in the Poppy Muffin recipe. Use 3 tablespoons pure maple syrup instead of 3 tablespoons of the milk and use chopped walnuts instead of poppy seeds.
Optional: Ice the cupcakes with Malted Milk Frosting (see Index).

Yield: 12 cupcakes

CORN MUFFIN RIDDLE

What makes these muffins so luscious? The answer: apple flavoring.

¾ cup whole wheat flour
1 cup cornmeal
1½ teaspoons baking powder
½ teaspoon baking soda
1 egg
¾ cup buttermilk
¼ cup frozen apple juice concentrate, thawed enough to measure
3 tablespoons butter
¼ teaspoon cinnamon
Dash salt

Preheat oven to 400° F.
Processor sift the first 4 ingredients. Set aside.
Process the remaining ingredients until uniform. Add the flour mixture and pulse until barely mixed. Transfer to oiled muffin compartments, filling them ⅔ full. Bake until a tester inserted in the center comes out clean (check after 20 minutes).

Yield: 9 muffins

HIGH-PROTEIN CARAWAY HOTCAKES

This unusually satisfying breakfast cake incorporates soybeans inconspicuously. Mashing the well-cooked beans and teaming them up with caraway seed (notable for its digestive properties as well as piquant flavor), will help you digest all that protein first thing in the day.

¾ cup cooked soybeans
1 egg
¼ teaspoon salt
1–1½ cups milk
1 cup whole wheat flour
¼ cup wheat germ
1 teaspoon baking powder
1 teaspoon caraway seed
2 tablespoons salad oil

Drain the soybeans well. Process with the egg, salt, and lesser amount of milk, until uniform. Add more milk for thinner pancakes.

Distribute the other ingredients over the top of the mixture. Pulse twice and scrape down. Repeat until the batter is just mixed.

Heat a heavy skillet over medium heat until water dropped on the surface spatters. If well-seasoned cast iron is used, it is not necessary to oil the cooking surface.

Drop the batter onto the skillet by 1/8-cup measures. When bubbles begin to appear on the surface of the pancakes, flip them over with a metal spatula. When the bottoms brown, the pancakes are done.

Yield: 18 hotcakes

12 Desserts That Are More Than Sugar

When it comes to dessert, sweetness is what we often focus on. We choose junk food on the basis of how much, health food on the basis of how little.

I propose a different perspective. Take for granted that a dessert is going to have some sweetening (preferably the minimum needed, in an unrefined form) and look at the other ingredients. What else can a dessert have to recommend it?

Nutritious whole grain flours, fruit, even vegetables. Flavors enhanced by something even more potent than those delicious chemicals the big companies use: freshness. These are the ingredients you will find in this chapter of miscellaneous desserts. Unquestionably, for everyday eating, fresh fruit is the best dessert. When you hanker for something fancier, use the processor to create more-than-sugary sweets.

FROZEN BANANA FLAKES

Discover frozen bananas, if you haven't already. The freezer is such a happy home for brown (sugar) spotted bananas that you may even find yourself oversupplying the kitchen with them on purpose.

Peel each banana and, if desired, cut it into 2 or 3 pieces. Wrap each chunk of banana in plastic and freeze.

Frozen banana stays good for a week. However, the firmest texture lasts only 2–3 days. Make Frozen Banana Flakes, following the directions below, within that time. Frozen bananas of more advanced vintage are better used in Just About Ice Cream or Smoothies (see recipes).

Frozen bananas are especially delectable when sliced paper thin, something which would be hard to do without a food processor. In the form of frozen flakes, bananas melt on your tongue almost as quickly as snowflakes.

2 large frozen bananas

Remove the bananas from the freezer. Unwrap them, pack them together in the feed tube, and push through the slicing disc. Or use the thin slicing disc, if you have one. Serve at once.

Yield: 2 servings

E SMOOTHIES

If you're an old hand at natural food cooking, you're probably a longtime smoothie maker. If you're new to smoothies, prepare yourself for a frothy, fruity, thick and refreshing treat of a drink. Think of summertime; when fruit is abundant, smoothies can be outrageously inventive; for a good breakfast on the run try protein powder smoothies; for satisfying but light repasts try meal-in-a-glass smoothies; imagine party smoothies, where guests linger over drinks as sumptuous as the most extravagant cocktails.

Processor smoothies are denser and less fluffy than blender smoothies. Processor smoothies allow for a variety of textures. Spoon Smoothies have the density of melted ice cream. Straw Smoothies draw out the drinker's pleasure by doubling the volume of liquid flavored with the same amount of fruit.

One word of caution, though, drink smoothies in moderation. Smoothies represent a great temptation to the calorie conscious. Some do claim that fruit drinks encourage calorie consumption because they lack satisfying bulk. Fortunately, the ingredients listed here in Table 14 have a good nutrient density; remember, too, the processor allows you to drink the whole fruit, not just the juice.

So, using Table 14 as your guide, create a wide variety of smoothies.

SPOON SMOOTHIE
1 unit essential ingredient
1 unit liquid
Optional: **sweetener**
Optional: **1 flavoring unit or 1 texture changer**

Place the essential ingredient in the workbowl. Process 30 seconds. Scrape down. Repeat. If ingredient(s) have not formed a smooth mixture, add ¼ cup liquid. Process 10 seconds; scrape down. Repeat until uniform. Pulse in sweetener by the teaspoon to taste.

Yield: 1 serving

STRAW SMOOTHIE

Prepare a Spoon Smoothie. Add ¾ cup more liquid. Process 30 seconds.

Yield: 2 servings

TABLE 14: SUPREME SMOOTHIES

Essential Ingredients

Flavor	Amount	Comments
Blueberry	1 cup fresh or frozen	A touch of vanilla accentuates these delectable berries.
Blueberry + Peach	¼ cup 2 small or one large, pitted	With orange juice for the liquid, this smoothie tastes like the essence of summer.
Mango	Pulp from one ripe fruit	Mango becomes even more subtly delectable when combined with mineral water and a touch of honey.
Mango + Peach	½ cup pulp ½ cup pulp	Mix with milk and rosewater for a very exotic beverage.
Strawberry	1 cup trimmed; fresh or frozen	For a festive punch, add pineapple juice and coconut.
Apricot	Simmer ¾ cup dried apricots in 2 cups water until they plump.	To create a superb nectar, use mineral water, Grenadine (see recipe), and just a dash of cinnamon.
Cherry + Nectarine	½ cup pitted ½ cup pulp	Cherry-vanilla flavoring is the idea behind this sophisticated dessert beverage. Flavor with vanilla. Use milk for half the liquid, sparkling mineral water for the rest. Serve at once. (*Note:* Since most of us are used to brightly colored cherry desserts, you may choose to process red food coloring into the mixture.)

My Discoveries:

Smoothie Liquids

Flavor	Amount	Comment
Milk	1 cup	Do not mix milk and yogurt in the same drink.
Yogurt	1 cup	
Orange juice	1 cup	
Pineapple juice	1 cup	
Sparkling mineral water	1 cup	

My Discoveries:

Smoothie Sweeteners

Flavor

Honey

Pitted dates

Brown sugar

Maple syrup

My Discoveries:

Texture Changers

Flavor	*Amount*	*Comments*
Protein powder	⅛ cup	Process it in at the start of the recipe. Protein Powder Smoothies are great lunches for hot summer afternoons. Protein powder enhances the consistency, especially in a Spoon Smoothie.
Wheat germ	⅛ cup	Add to a Straw Smoothie along with the extra liquid. It's a pleasant way to add a little extra protein, but dispense with the straw for this drink.
Wheat bran	⅛ to ¼ cup	Add to a Straw Smoothie along with the extra liquid. The extra fiber may aid digestion. You will get a coconut-like texture without adding a lot of calories. To really fool your tongue, use ⅛ cup each of bran and coconut.
Fresh Grated Coconut (see recipe)	¼ cup	Process it in at the start of the Spoon Smoothie. Coconut works especially well with orange or pineapple juice.

My Discoveries:

Special Smoothie Flavorings

Flavor	*Amount*	*Comments*
Vanilla	¼ teaspoon	Try it especially with blueberry, peach, cherry, and date smoothies.
Rosewater	¼ teaspoon	Rosewater can be purchased at Middle Eastern or Indian stores or at a pharmacy. It subtly perfumes a Smoothie, working especially well with apricot, mango, yogurt, and milk.
Grenadine (see recipe)	Process in 1 teaspoon at a time to taste.	This pungent sweetness can really compliment a fruity taste, especially orange juice, apricot, and pear. Additional sweetener will not, in most cases, be needed.

My Discoveries:

JUST ABOUT ICE CREAM

In some ways this is better than ice cream: no preservatives, no artificial flavors, no stabilizers, no sugar, less cost. It even can be made without any dairy products.

So what is in this delightful "soft serve" style dessert? Frozen banana, processed with natural flavorings and only enough liquid to form a smooth mixture.

With frozen banana as your base, discover dozens of flavoring variations by adding small quantities of other fresh fruits or fruit concentrates to the processed bananas. Use the Essential Ingredients section of Table 14 for some flavoring suggestions if you wish, but keep the quantities small (about 1 tablespoon) to prevent a too-liquid consistency.

Here is our family favorite.

1 cup frozen banana, cut into 1-inch pieces
1 tablespoon orange juice concentrate
¼ teaspoon vanilla

Process the banana chunks for 45 seconds. Add the remaining ingredients and process 10 seconds. Scrape down. Continue to process and scrape down until smooth. Serve immediately.

Yield: 1 serving

BANANA PUDDINGS, HOT AND COLD
HOT BANANA PUDDING

This marvelous hot pudding has a remarkably subtle taste. Considering the ingredients, sole credit for this must go to this remarkable fruit.

4 ripe bananas, unpeeled

Drop the unpeeled bananas into a saucepan of boiling water (enough to cover). Boil until the banana skins turn completely black.

Drain the bananas. Carefully separate the cooked fruit from the peel—avoid splashing your fingers with boiling water. Process the fruit until smooth.

Yield: 2 servings

CHILLED BANANA CUSTARD

You'd be hard put to bake a custard with this flawless, firm consistency.

½ cup heavy cream
4 ripe bananas, unpeeled
¼ teaspoon almond extract
2 teaspoons honey

Chill the cream thoroughly in the refrigerator.

Drop the unpeeled bananas into a saucepan of boiling water to cover. Boil until the banana skins turn completely black. Drain the bananas. Carefully separate the cooked fruit from the peel and place the fruit on a plate. Let it cool to room temperature.

When the fruit has cooled, process the cream for 20 seconds. Pulse in the bananas, almond extract, and honey until smooth. Scrape down as necessary. Do not overprocess, because overwhipped cream has a way of becoming butter.

Transfer the custard to individual serving dishes. Cover and chill until set (check after 1 hour). Serve this dessert within 6 hours of preparation.

Yield: 4 servings

STRAWBERRY TINGLE

Note the high proportion of fruit. No wonder this tastes so much better than commercial yogurts flavored with preserves.

1 cup strawberries (fresh or frozen unsweetened)
1 cup yogurt, preferably made with whole milk
1 tablespoon honey
¼ cup brown sugar

Trim the strawberries. Process with the other ingredients until uniform.

Transfer the mixture to a covered container and freeze until the top of the yogurt turns icy—about 2 hours. Return the yogurt to the workbowl and process until uniform. Scrape down between 10-second processings.

Refreeze and serve within the next few days.

Yield: 2 servings

⊞Ⓣ FLEXIBLE BERRY SAUCE

During the summer you can save money by pureeing exciting fresh berries with everyday apples. And in the middle of winter you still can enjoy natural fruit sauces, flavored with unsweetened fruit delicacy.

Make the amount you want, the flavor you want, during any season of the year. And choose from a number of serving possibilities as well.

Flexible Berry Sauce is delicious on pancakes. It makes a nutritious snack or a simple dessert. Or use it in combination with other ingredients for a more elaborate dessert: turn it into Flexible Berry Whip (see recipe); serve it shortcake style, over Confidence buttermilk biscuits and topped with whipped cream; stir it into yogurt; pour it over vanilla pudding (see Cake with the Works).

Apple cider
Apples (try Golden or Red Delicious)
Fresh cherries, blueberries, or strawberries or
Hain's Fruit Concentrate in black cherry,
blackberry, or other flavors
Optional: **¼ teaspoon lemon juice**
Salt
Optional: **dash cinnamon**
Optional: **honey or brown sugar**

Pour 1–2 inches of cider into a stainless steel saucepan with cover. Heat the cider as you prepare the apples. You will need 1 large or 2 small apples per desired serving. Peel if waxed; quarter and core. Simmer in the juice until tender (check after 5 minutes).

If you will be using fresh berries, wash them and remove stems, hulls, pits, and so forth.

Transfer cooked apples to the workbowl. For best results do not work with more than 2 cups per batch. Reserve the delicious cooking liquid for other uses.

Add to the workbowl 1 tablespoon berries or concentrate plus ¼ teaspoon optional lemon juice, a dash of salt, and a dash of optional cinnamon. Process 10 seconds. Scrape down and taste.

For a stronger fruit flavor or moister texture, add more fresh fruit or fruit concentrate. For additional sweetness, add honey.

Pulse in small quantities of addition, tasting as you go, until you achieve *it*—a taste as fruity and sweet as you like.

Process the sauce into as smooth a texture as you wish. For an extrachunky texture, reserve ¼

of each cooked apple. Cut each quarter into 8 pieces and sprinkle them over the top of the puree. Pulse in until barely mixed.

Serve the sauce at room temperature, chill, or heat right before using. The exception is Strawberry Sauce, which should not be heated.

FLEXIBLE BERRY WHIP

Try serving this dessert with fresh whole berries, chopped nuts, Fresh Grated Coconut (see Index), or strawberry syrup (from the FP Fruit Salad recipe).

1 cup Flexible Berry Sauce (see preceding recipe)
1 cup heavy cream

Prepare the sauce. Chill to room temperature or refrigerate.

Whip the cream. If your food processor comes with a special whip attachment, use it according to manufacturer's directions. Otherwise processor whip, as described in the box.

> ### To Processor Whip Cream
>
> Chill the cream thoroughly. Process 10 seconds. Scrape down and repeat. The goal is fluffy cream that mounds softly—don't expect it to peak as high as it would with an electric beater. Note too that here, as with any whipping method, you must take care to stop short of producing butter. If more processing is needed, do it in 3- or 5-second pulses, inspecting the cream each time until you achieve the desired texture.

Pulse the sauce into the cream. Now you have a choice. Either refrigerate the whip and serve it when chilled or use a slightly more elaborate method for a more ice-creamy dessert.

Freeze the mixture until solid (check after 1 hour).

Distribute it evenly in the workbowl and pulse until the texture is uniform. Transfer into dessert dishes and freeze again until solid (check after 2 hours). Maximum keeping time for the frozen dessert is 2 days.

Yield: 4 servings

⊞ FLEXIBLE BROWNIES

Chocolate, white flour, white sugar—those ingredients are no nutritional bargain. Why not bake brownies using unrefined ingredients? Beyond that, you can vary these Flexible Brownies according to your mood.

1 flour option (see Table 15)
Optional: **1 teaspoon baking soda to go with texture choice**
2 or 3 eggs
⅓ cup carob flour
⅓ cup butter, cut into 6 pieces
⅔ cup brown sugar
1 teaspoon vanilla extract
1 optional chewy addition or 1 optional frosting (see Table 15)
1 texture choice (see Table 15)

Preheat oven to 350° F.
Processor sift the flour option and optional baking soda. Set aside.
Prepare 1 chewy addition or frosting option. (Frosting should have an easy-to-spread consistency.) Set aside. If necessary, rinse out the workbowl.
Process the eggs for 10 seconds. Add the carob flour, butter, brown sugar, and vanilla. Process 10 seconds. Scrape down. Repeat until smooth. Pulse in the flour option and any chewy addition.
Transfer to an oiled 8″ × 8″ × 2″ pan. Bake until an inserted tester comes out clean (check after 35 minutes). Tender-soft brownies may be spread immediately with room-temperature frosting. (Carob Fudge Frosting is especially good on hot brownies—it melts instantly to give the effect of a hot fudge sundae; see recipe.) Let gooey-dense brownies cool before frosting.

Yield: 1 dozen brownies

GINGERBEET CAKE

Far be it for me to recommend cake as a way to put vegetables into the diet. Still, see what happens when you serve this cake to someone who supposedly "hates" beets.

2 cups whole wheat flour
2 teaspoons baking powder
1 teaspoon baking soda

TABLE 15: CUSTOM-MADE BROWNIES

Flour Option

⅔ cup millet flour
⅔ cup barley flour
⅔ cup whole wheat pastry flour

Chewy Addition

½ cup coarsely chopped walnuts
⅓ cup toasted sesame seeds
½ cup Fresh Grated Coconut (see index)
⅓ cup raisins

Optional Frosting

Carob Frosting with Flexibility (see index)
Carob Fudge Frosting (see index)
Peanut Butter Frosting (see index)
Peppermint Frosting with Flexibility (see index)
Toffee Frosting with Flexibility (see index)

Texture Choice

For a tender-soft texture, add 1 teaspoon baking soda when you processor sift the flour. Serve brownies hot out of the oven.
For a gooey-dense texture, let brownies cool in the baking pan, then refrigerate until chilled.

My Discoveries:

1 cup shredded beets (2 medium)
6 tablespoons butter, cut into 6 pieces
¼ cup honey + ¼ cup dark brown sugar, packed, or ¼ cup molasses + ¼ cup light brown sugar, packed
1 cup sour cream or sour half and half
1 egg
2 teaspoons ginger
⅛ teaspoon powdered clove
½ teaspoon cinnamon
⅛ teaspoon salt

Preheat oven to 325° F.
Processor sift the flour, baking powder, and soda. Set aside in a large mixing bowl.
Drop fresh beets, with 4 or more inches of stem left on them, into boiling water. Remove after 5 minutes. Under running water, slip off the

skins. Trim the beets and push through the shredding disc. Measure 1 cup. Set aside.

Insert the metal blade and process the butter, honey, and sugar for 10 seconds. Add the sour cream, egg, ginger, clove, cinnamon, and salt. Process 5 seconds. Scrape down. Repeat until the mixture is smooth. Process an additional 15 seconds. Transfer to the mixing bowl along with the beets. Stir just until mixed.

Transfer to an oiled 8″ × 8″ × 2″ pan and bake until a tester comes out clean (check after 45 minutes).

Serve with whipped cream or Toffee Frosting with Flexibility (see Index).

HONEY PIE

This honey-sweetened dessert, like any apple pie, is easy to make with the processor. The fruit is sliced very quickly, often being sliced thinner than one would have the patience to do without the machine.

There is no pastry lid or grid on this pie to supply unnecessary fat. (To protect the uncovered apples from drying out, the pie is baked in a paper bag.)

Flexible Pastry for 1 8- or 9-inch pie (see Index)
6–7 cups sliced apples (try Jonathan, Granny Smith, or McIntosh)
1–2 tablespoons butter
2 tablespoons honey
2 tablespoons brown sugar
2 tablespoons arrowroot
½ teaspoon cinnamon
Pinch salt
Optional: **1 tablespoon lemon juice**
Optional: **sharp cheddar cheese, whipped cream, or ice cream**

Preheat oven to 400° F.

Lightly oil a pie pan and line it with pastry. Set aside.

Quarter and core fresh apples. Peel if desired. At this point you have a choice. For the most elegant appearance of this topless pie, hand cut enough gorgeous slices for a top layer. (To gauge this amount, try slices out for size in the pie pan.) Sauté the apples in the butter until lightly browned. Otherwise simply use the butter to dot the apples on the top layer when you assemble the pie.

Push apples through the slicing disc and measure a total of 6–7 cups. Set aside in a large mixing bowl.

Insert the metal blade. Process about ⅛ cup of the apples you have sliced, the honey, brown sugar, arrowroot, cinnamon, salt, and optional lemon juice. Scrape down as needed. Repeat until smooth. Pour this mixture over the apples in the mixing bowl. Stir until they are coated. Transfer this mixture to an oiled pie pan. Either add a top layer of sautéed apple slices or dot the top with butter.

Place the pie inside a large paper bag (such as a grocery sack). Fold the ends over and fasten with 2 paper clips. Bake on the middle rack for 45 minutes. Remove from the oven. Slit the bag with a knife and pull the paper away. Examine the pie. If not done, return it to the oven for as long as necessary.

The pie may be served with wedges of cheese, scoops of ice cream, or a frothy layer of whipped cream.

FAVORITE CARROT CAKE

Everyone who loves carrot cake has one favorite recipe. This is mine. I designed it to be relatively low in fat and sugar, to contain no white flour, and to be large enough to satisfy all requests for extra helpings.

2 cups walnuts
1 cup golden raisins
⅓ cup whole wheat flour
1 cup raw or toasted wheat germ
1 teaspoon baking powder
1 teaspoon baking soda
¼ teaspoon salt
3 cups whole wheat flour
2 cups shredded carrots (2 medium)
½ cup water
2 teaspoons cinnamon
1 teaspoon nutmeg
½ teaspoon ground clove
½ cup corn oil (substitute salad oil)
½ cup honey
3 eggs
1⅓ cups dark brown sugar
1½ cups buttermilk

Preheat oven to 350° F.

Optional: To bring out the flavor of the nuts,

pan roast them. See box on page 31.

With a dry machine pulse the nuts until chopped medium fine. Set them aside with the raisins in a very large mixing bowl (5-quart capacity).

Processor sift the ⅓ cup flour, wheat germ, baking powder, baking soda, and salt. Set aside in a separate bowl. Processor sift the remaining flour. Add it to the bowl.

Insert the shredding disc. Push through carrot chunks and measure 2 cups. Cook them with the water and spices over medium heat in a covered saucepan for 10 minutes. Remove from heat. Stir in the oil and honey.

Insert the metal blade. Process the eggs for 15 seconds. Process in the sugar for 15 seconds. Scrape down. Add the buttermilk. Process and scrape down until the mixture is smooth.

Combine all ingredients in the mixing bowl with clean hands or a large spoon. Do not overmix. Transfer to an oiled and floured 9" × 13" pan and bake on the middle rack until a tester comes out clean (check after 1 hour). Cool in the pan on a rack.

Frosting is optional. Try Vanilla Frosting with Flexibility or Peanut Butter Frosting (see Index).

QUINTESSENTIAL FRUIT SALAD

If only there were a word to signify "a fruit, or combination of fruits, with the quintessential taste of a season." That's the word that would really describe this poetic dessert.

Autumn has always been my favorite season. The air is so fresh, with a wistful undertone like a premonition of winter. If you know what I mean by this, maybe you'll also agree that a parallel bittersweet quality is present in persimmons and in pears, if you bring it out. Grenadine adds a superb resonance to the flavors.

1 ripe persimmon
2 or 3 ripe anjou pears
1 tablespoon honey
1 tablespoon water
Optional: Grenadine (see Index)

Peel the persimmon and cut off the stem. Push halves or quarters through the slicing disc.

Set aside in a glass jar or plastic storage container.

Trim the pears. Push through the slicing disc. Add to the jar. Add the honey and water.

If a fresh pomegranate is available, prepare Grenadine and chill separately.

Just before serving, toss the two mixtures together. Or give the plain persimmon-pear mixture a good shake, to distribute the syrup, before transferring to serving dishes.

Yield: 4 servings

HILMA'S FRUIT SALAD

This fruit salad tastes lavish and sumptuous. Thanks to the tofu-based mayonnaise, though, it tastes far richer than it actually is.

1 cup Amazing Mayonnaise (plain or curried version) (see Index)
¼ cup walnuts
2 oranges
2 ripe bananas
¼ cup Fresh Grated Coconut (see Index)

Prepare Amazing Mayonnaise. With a dry machine, pulse the nuts until minced.

Peel and section the oranges. Cut the peeled bananas into inch-long chunks. Mix with the other ingredients.

Serve at once.

Yield: 4 servings

BERRY SAUCES

We've already seen berries used in food processor recipes. Yet the best use of all may be in fresh natural sauces. Use berry sauces to top many desserts or stir them into sparkling mineral water for a sophisticated beverage. Berry sauces mean unalloyed berry sweetness, far superior to oversweetened preserves or liqueurs.

Trim cherries, blueberries, or strawberries and place 1–2 cups at a time in the workbowl.

Process into a thick juicy sauce. Process in brown sugar or honey by the teaspoon to taste. Serve at once.

To use blackberries and raspberries is a bit more complex (see recipe for Grenadine).

⊡ THE FP FRUIT SALAD

The Base
1 or more large shapes of fruit
Optional: **contrasting shapes of fruit***
Optional: **extra additions***

Note: For some of these items, the food processor is essential. See Table 16.

- Be consistent in how you cut each kind of fruit. The contrasts in the salad will be easier to appreciate. Peach wedges contrast with cantaloupe cubes and so forth.
- To prevent discoloration of cut fruit, add 1 teaspoon lemon or lime juice to 1 cup water. Dip slices of apple, banana, avocado, peach, pear, persimmon, or nectarine.
- Use a ball-shaped scoop for melons if you wish. A faster method, though, produces equally attractive shapes. For most melons, pare off the rind, scoop out the seeds, and cut the melon into cubes. With watermelon, it is not difficult to remove the seeds in an efficient way, provided that you take a systematic approach. Look for the angle at which the seeds follow a pattern and cut the fruit accordingly. Then geometrical cutting and seeding go together efficiently.
- Portions of fresh fruit that might otherwise be discarded make attractive containers for fruit salad: halved, scooped out peels of oranges, lemons, and limes; pineapples or melons, halved lengthwise and scooped out.

To Design the Fruit Salad
Start by picking out fresh compatible fruits. See what looks best at your produce market; in-season fruits are cheapest and generally the freshest. Plan the rest of the salad around that (also take into account what else will be served at the meal). When you are trying something new, give yourself a fail-safe factor by sampling a bit before you combine large quantities of

food. Stir together a spoonful of the base and morsels of other proposed ingredients. Taste to make sure that the chemistry works out as well in reality as it does in imagination.

To Assemble the Fruit Salad
If the base contains a milk product or mayonnaise, mix all other items together but combine with the base just before serving. As a precaution against summertime food poisoning, be sure to serve such salads straight from the refrigerator. Don't leave them out, to warm up in the sunshine and perhaps spoil.

With other types of base, the salad can sometimes benefit from being refrigerated for 30 minutes or longer to permit the flavors to blend and mature.

Stir the salad before serving.

TABLE 16: A GARDEN OF FRUIT SALADS

Large Shapes of Fruit

Natural or geometric shapes

apple
apricot
banana
cantaloupe or other melon
grapefruit
mango
orange
papaya
peach
pear
persimmon
pineapple
plum
tangerine

My Discoveries:

For a natural shape, cut in a way that emphasizes the natural contours of the fruit; for instance, unpeeled peach cut into slices, peeled orange separated into sections.

For a geometric shape, cut generously proportioned cubes, circles, or semicircles.

(continued on next page)

Contrasting Shapes of Fruit

Push the following through the slicing disc:

apple (pack sideways)*
nectarine (pack sideways)*
orange sections*
peach (pack sideways)*
pear*
tangerine sections*
avocado wedges (see Index):
Unless you plan to use avocado with grapefruit sections, be sure to taste test before you experiment.
raisins
grapes
persimmon cubes
berries (whole)
cooked apple, peach, or pear, diced
cranberries: Boil until soft in apple cider and drain. Sweeten to taste.

My Discoveries:

Nonfruit Additions

chopped nuts*
Fresh Grated Coconut (see recipe)*
sunflower seeds, sprouted or toasted
sesame seeds, sprouted or toasted
sprouted almonds
cooked brown rice
shredded carrot*
sweet potato: cooked, peeled, and diced

My Discoveries:

The Base

Juice gained in cutting the fruit.
Honey Water: Bring to a boil equal parts of honey and water, stirring to dissolve all the honey. Cool to room temperature.

Strawberry Syrup: Trim and slice fresh strawberries. Place them in a glass jar and cover with Honey Water at room temperature. Close the jar. Refrigerate for 6 hours, so that a syrup can form. Shake the jar occasionally.
Pureed Apricot: Soak dried fruit. Process the fruit alone. Pour the extra liquid from soaking through the feed tube until you achieve the desired consistency. Bear in mind that this base will be diluted by juices from the other fruit in the salad.
Fruit Juice: Add natural sugar with unsweetened apple, pineapple, or white grape juices.
Herbal Tea: Use a rose hips or hibiscus blend. Brew the tea strong, strain, sweeten with honey, and cool to room temperature. Other herbal blends can also be delicious, either alone or mixed with fruit juice.
Yogurt: Sweeten it to taste with honey.*
Sour Cream: Sweeten it to taste with honey, frozen orange juice concentrate, or both. A small amount of cinnamon can also be added. This mixture could also be used, instead, as a topping for the fruit salad.*
Heavy Cream: Processor whipped (see page 121),* it makes a good base or topping. Or try tossing fruit in a small amount of cream as you would mix salad greens and oil. Avoid combining heavy cream with grapefruit, orange, lemon, or lime.
Sweet Spreads: Unadulterated Mayonnaise or Amazing Mayonnaise (see recipes) processed with honey to taste.
Sweet Dressings, such as Date Nut Dressing, Sweet Curry Dressing, Gorgeous Orange Dressing, Bingo Dressing, or Pineapple Cream Dressing (see recipes).

My Discoveries:

---

*For these items, the food processor is helpful or indispensable.

13 | Frostings and Candies

Why does a nutritionally oriented cookbook include recipes for confections? Assuming that basic nutritional needs are met and obesity isn't a problem, there is no good reason to prohibit occasional sweets. Moreover, human nature being what it is, most of us would indulge anyway, whether it was good for us or not.

This chapter provides recipes for some of the healthiest candies you can make. Store-bought goodies often contain corn sweeteners, white sugar, artificial flavors, and preservatives. Homemade candies, as you'll see, can be quality controlled and produced using powdered milk, dried fruits, or carob. Sweets can and should deliver nutrients along with their calories.

The processor gives you the technical ability to create no-cook candies in seconds, to transform leftover candies into frosting, to buzz up frostings so fast that seven-minute icing seems like a slowpoke recipe.

With a processor you can do better than a store-bought frosting in every respect: quality, cost, convenience. Whether you need frosting or candy or both, you can prepare them in less time than you might spend waiting in line at the checkout counter. And when you supervise the packaging, you don't have to stock up with more than you want. A small batch can be made easily. Mix up a few ounces or a few pounds, according to what you need.

So when it's time for candy or frosting, why not let your processor show off? Pick the flavor of your choice, invest in some healthful ingredients, and your machine can deliver a helping of instant bliss.

⊞⊤ FROSTING WITH FLEXIBILITY

Choose from 3 different bases. Then the fun starts. Process in the flavor you prefer and mix up a frosting or candy. This is the only frosting recipe a cook needs to please crowds for years.

In general, a large batch of frosting will yield enough to frost the outside of a 1- or 2-layer, 8- or 9-inch, square or round cake. Small batches are useful to supply fillings for 2-layer cakes or to vary colors or flavors in one cake.

- *Do not substitute instant powdered milk for noninstant. Neither the flavor nor the texture is acceptable.*

BASE 1: PROTEIN

It wouldn't be completely accurate to claim that this frosting is made solely of milk since butter plus honey accounts for one third of the recipe volume. Bear in mind, however, that nonfat powdered milk is a concentrated food. The amount used in just one small batch, if reconstituted, would be equivalent to 2 cups of skim milk. For frosting, that isn't a bad ratio, nutritionwise.

For a small batch

½ cup noninstant nonfat powdered milk
2 tablespoons butter, cut into 1-tablespoon pieces
2 tablespoons honey
Flavoring ingredient (see Table 17)

For a large batch

2 cups noninstant nonfat powdered milk
½ cup butter, cut into 1-tablespoon pieces
½ cup honey
Flavoring ingredient (see Table 17)

BASE 2: BUTTERCREAM

As far as I'm concerned, this is one of the few instances where white sugar can be warranted. When you bake for folks who think they hate health food, you can often sneak by a rather pure whole wheat cake unrecognized under the kind of frosting they expect. Also, by using fresh flavoring ingredients you can turn this base into the most luscious buttercream your guests have ever tasted.

For a small batch

1 cup confectioner's sugar
2½ tablespoons butter, cut into 1-tablespoon pieces
1 teaspoon honey (optional except for frosting to be piped through a pastry tube)
Flavoring ingredient (see Table 17)

For a large batch

3½ cups confectioner's sugar
½ cup butter, cut into 1-tablespoon pieces
1 tablespoon honey (optional except for frosting to be piped through a pastry tube)
Flavoring ingredient (see Table 17)

TABLE 17: FRESH FLAVORS FOR FROSTING
Pick one flavoring ingredient choice from Group A, B, or C.

Group A
These are fruit flavors. Add to the base in small pieces.

Flavor	*Use*
Cherry	Pitted fresh or frozen cherries
Blueberry	Fresh or frozen blueberries
Strawberry	Fresh or frozen strawberries
Apricot	Soaked dried apricots

My Discoveries:

Group B
These are concentrated flavors. Add the measured amount. Then use milk by the tablespoon to thin the consistency. For stronger flavor, increase the measured amount to taste.

Flavor	*Ingredient*	*Small Batch*	*Large Batch*
Carob	Carob flour	1 tablespoon	¼ cup
	+ molasses or blackstrap molasses	⅛ teaspoon	½ teaspoon
Vanilla	Vanilla extract	¼ teaspoon	1 teaspoon
Mint	Peppermint extract	1–2 drops	¼ teaspoon
Toffee	Blackstrap molasses	½ teaspoon	2 teaspoons
Coffee	Powdered instant coffee	½ teaspoon	2 teaspoons
	+ vanilla extract	⅛ teaspoon	½ teaspoon
Mocha	Powdered instant coffee	⅛ teaspoon	½ teaspoon
	+ carob flour	½ teaspoon	2 teaspoons

My Discoveries:

Group C
These are liquid flavors. Add to the base by the tablespoon.

Flavor	*Use*
Apple	Frozen apple juice concentrate
Orange	Fresh orange juice or juice from concentrate—a little grated orange zest can also be used
Lemon	Frozen lemon juice—a little grated lemon zest can also be used
Pineapple	Unsweetened pineapple juice
Maple	Maple syrup

My Discoveries:

BASE 3: SYNTHESIS

This is a compromise: creamier than Buttercream, less costly than protein.

For a small batch

¾ **cup confectioner's sugar**
¼ **cup noninstant powdered milk**
2 **tablespoons butter, cut into 1-tablespoon pieces**
1 **tablespoon honey**
Flavoring ingredient (see Table 17)

For a large batch

3 **cups confectioner's sugar**
1 **cup noninstant powdered milk**
½ **cup butter, cut into 1-tablespoon pieces**
¼ **cup honey**
Flavoring ingredient (see Table 17)

To Mix Candy

Process milk or sugar or both with butter until uniform. Add the honey to the workbowl. With the machine running, drop or pour the flavoring ingredient through the feed tube. Scrape down. Repeat until the mixture barely holds together.

Shape the mixture into balls. Roll in carob flour, Fresh Grated Coconut (see Index), or finely chopped nuts until the surface is coated. Wrap and refrigerate.

The protein candy has the texture of nougat; the buttercream recipe produces buttercreams, less refined than expensive chocolates but quite acceptable; the synthesis candy has a texture halfway in between.

To Mix Frosting

Continue to add more flavoring ingredient until the desired consistency is reached. Scrape down the workbowl after each 1 or 2 additions. (If you get overenthusiastic and make the frosting too liquid, simply add more noninstant milk or confectioner's sugar to achieve the desired consistency.)

Refrigerate the protein or synthesis frostings for at least 2 hours before use. They tend to thicken when chilled, so you may wish to reprocess with additional liquid before you frost. Also store leftover cake with these frostings in the refrigerator.

⊤ CAROB FUDGE BASE

(This is the base used in Carob Fudge Frosting, Carob Fudge Rolls, and No-Fault Fudge recipes following.)

Carob or not, you couldn't ask for a more chocolaty taste. Try a chocolate mint variation too.

For a small batch

⅓ **cup carob flour**
¼ **cup honey**
2 **tablespoons butter or margarine, cut into 4 pieces**
½ **teaspoon vanilla extract or ¼ teaspoon peppermint extract**

For a large batch

⅔ **cup carob flour**
½ **cup honey**
4 **tablespoons butter or margarine, cut into 4 pieces**
1 **teaspoon vanilla extract or ½ teaspoon peppermint extract**

Process all ingredients for 10 seconds. Scrape down and repeat until you have a thick batter that forms ribbons when dripped from a spoon.

CAROB FUDGE FROSTING

For a small batch

Small batch Carob Fudge Base (see recipe)
1 **tablespoon milk**
1 **tablespoon butter or margarine**

For a large batch

Large batch Carob Fudge Base (see recipe)
2 **tablespoons milk**
2 **tablespoons butter or margarine**

Process ingredients until smooth. Add additional milk by the tablespoon until the desired consistency is reached.

Yield: ½ cup (small); 1 cup (large)

CAROB FUDGE ROLLS

Gasp! It's organic Tootsie Rolls.

For a small batch

Small batch Carob Fudge Base (see recipe)
⅓ cup noninstant powdered milk

For a large batch

Large batch Carob Fudge Base (see recipe)
⅔ cup noninstant powdered milk

Process ingredients for 10 seconds. Scrape down top, sides, and bottom of the workbowl. Repeat until the mixture is uniform—a very stiff paste. Scoop out by heaping teaspoons. Shape into logs and package in plastic wrap, then place logs in a plastic bag. Double-bagged, the candies will keep in the refrigerator for at least a week.

Yield: 2 dozen candies (small), 4 dozen candies (large)

NO-FAULT FUDGE

For a small batch

¼ cup walnuts
Small batch Carob Fudge Base (see recipe)
⅓ cup noninstant powdered milk
2 teaspoons water
Optional: 1 tablespoon malted milk powder + 1 teaspoon water

For a large batch

½ cup walnuts
Large batch Carob Fudge Base (see recipe)
⅔ cup noninstant powdered milk
4 teaspoons water
Optional: 2 tablespoons malted milk powder + 2 teaspoons water

If you're planning to make fudge, chop the nuts even before you make the base, so that you have a dry metal blade and workbowl. Chop the nuts coarsely with a few pulses. Set aside.

Process together all other ingredients until smooth, scraping down as necessary. Sprinkle the walnuts over the top of the mixture and pulse once. Transfer to the bottom of an oiled 8½″ × 4½″ × 2½″ loaf pan. A small batch fills half the pan; a large batch covers the whole length. Press into shape and wrap the pan airtight.

Refrigerate overnight. Remove with a metal spatula and cut into little squares. Wrap and refrigerate leftovers.

Yield: 2 dozen squares (small), 4 dozen squares (large)

Ⓣ PEANUT BUTTER CANDY

This chewy, nutty candy is a favorite with kids.

For a small batch

¼ cup Peanut Butter (see Index)
¼ cup noninstant powdered milk
2 tablespoons honey
1 tablespoon brown sugar
Toasted wheat germ or malted milk powder or carob flour

For a large batch

½ cup Peanut Butter (see Index)
½ cup noninstant powdered milk
¼ cup honey
2 tablespoons brown sugar
Toasted wheat germ or malted milk powder or carob flour

Process together the peanut butter, powdered milk, honey, and brown sugar. After each 15-second processing, scrape down. Repeat until you achieve a uniform, pebbly-looking texture.

Remove from the workbowl by the heaping teaspoon. Form into balls and roll in one of the three suggested toppings or the discovery of your choice.

Yield: 2 dozen candies (small), 4 dozen candies (large)

PEANUT BUTTER FROSTING

This cake topping is probably different from what you would expect peanut butter–based frosting to be. It is fresh and brightly flavorful, with the peanut aspect noticeable mostly as an aftertaste.

For a small batch

¼ cup Peanut Butter (see Index)
¼ cup noninstant powdered milk
¼ cup honey
1 tablespoon brown sugar
1 tablespoon lemon juice
Dash cinnamon
Optional: pinch lecithin granules

For a large batch

1 cup Peanut Butter (see Index)
1 cup noninstant powdered milk
1 cup honey
¼ cup brown sugar
¼ cup lemon juice
⅛ teaspoon cinnamon
Optional: ⅛ teaspoon lecithin granules

Process all ingredients until smooth. Scrape down the workbowl between 10-second processings. If a thinner frosting is desired, thin with apple cider, processed in by the teaspoon.

Chill the frosting at least ½ hour before using and adjust the consistency as needed.

Yield: ⅓ cup (small), 1⅓ cups (large)

⊡ PAPAYA DELIGHT CANDY

The candy is dried-fruit sweet and golden in color, with specks of white and vivid orange. Dried papaya is available at health food stores.

For a small batch

½ cup dried papaya, cut into ½-inch cubes
½ cup golden raisins, packed
½ cup dried apple, packed
Sections as needed of fresh orange, preferably seedless

For a large batch

1 cup dried papaya, cut into ½-inch cubes
1 cup golden raisins, packed
1 cup dried apple, packed
Sections as needed of fresh orange, preferably seedless

Measure the dried fruit and place it in the workbowl with the metal blade.

Peel the orange. Separate individual sections and remove seeds, if any. Bring them close to the processor. For a small orange you will be using whole sections at a time. For a large orange, cut sections in half.

Start the machine running. Drop pieces of orange through the feed tube until the mixture makes the change from separate particles to a paste. Stop the machine occasionally to take a closer look. Too much orange will detract from the texture of the candy. What you are aiming for is a fairly uniform mixture, speckled with orange and white.

Press the mixture into the bottom of an oiled 8½″ × 4½″ × 2½″ loaf pan. A small batch creates a thinner layer than a large batch. Allow the wrapped pan to chill overnight in the refrigerator. Then cut the candy into pieces, remove them with a metal spatula, and wrap individually. Refrigerated, the candy will keep for a week.

Yield: 1 dozen large cubes (small), 2 dozen large cubes (large)

PAPAYA DELIGHT CAKE FILLING

Small batch Papaya Delight Candy (see preceding recipe)
¾ cup apple cider

Prepare Papaya Delight Candy. Process in the apple cider. The product is thinner than the candy, but still full of chewy, sweet little morsels.

• Experiment on your own with candy and cake filling from dried fruit. To avoid overpowering sweetness, you will find it helpful to include either dried apple or nuts in the mixture.

Yield: 2¼ cups

Note: Only measurements for a small batch have been given because that amount should be sufficient for most cakes. If you have any cake filling left over, store it in a glass jar and use it as jam.

⊞ CHESTNUT FROSTING

The frosting is fluffy, wholesome, and subtly flavorful.

For a small batch

½ **cup chestnuts, peeled**
1 **tablespoon honey**
1 **tablespoon water from cooking chestnuts**
2 **tablespoons noninstant powdered milk**
Dash cinnamon
3 **tablespoons butter, cut into small pieces, or 1 ounce cream cheese**

For a large batch

1 **cup chestnuts, peeled**
2 **tablespoons honey**
2 **tablespoons water from cooking chestnuts**
¼ **cup noninstant powdered milk**
Pinch cinnamon
6 **tablespoons butter, cut into small pieces, or 2 ounces cream cheese**

Peel the chestnuts (see recipe for Celestial Chestnut Casserole). Steam them over boiling water until tender. Reserve some of this water.

Push the chestnuts through the shredding disc. Without removing them from the workbowl, insert the metal blade. Add all other ingredients and process until smooth. Scrape down as needed.

Yield: 1 cup (small), 2 cups (large)

CHESTNUT CANDY

To imagine the taste of this unusual confection, combine the best aspects of chestnuts and rice pudding.

For a small batch

2 **tablespoons cooked brown rice**
Small batch Chestnut Frosting (see recipe)
2 **tablespoons noninstant powdered milk**
¼ **teaspoon vanilla extract**
2 **tablespoons sesame seeds**

For a large batch

¼ **cup cooked brown rice**
Large batch Chestnut Frosting (see recipe)
¼ **cup noninstant powdered milk**
½ **teaspoon vanilla extract**
¼ **cup sesame seeds**

Prepare brown rice or use leftovers.

Process the frosting, powdered milk, and vanilla until uniform, scraping down the workbowl as necessary. Distribute the rice over the mixture.

Pan roast the sesame seeds until they start to brown (see box on page 31). Immediately pour into the workbowl. Pulse ingredients together until the mixture is uniform.

Turn into an oiled 8½″ × 4½″ × 2½″ loaf pan. A small batch will cover ½ the length of the pan, a large batch will cover the full length. Wrap airtight in plastic wrap and chill until set (check after 2 hours). Cut into pieces and remove with a metal spatula. Leftovers should be wrapped and refrigerated.

Yield: 2 dozen candies (small), 4 dozen candies (large)

⊞ BLOND ALMOND PASTE

(This is the base for Blond Almond Frosting and Blond Almond Candy recipes following.)
Most sophisticated—in color and taste—of all the food processor candies and frostings, this is an elegant combination of almonds and honey.

1½ cups shelled almonds
Pinch salt
¼ cup honey

Half-fill a large saucepan with water. Bring to a rolling boil. Drop in the almonds. After 2 minutes, pour into a colander. Pop the skins off the almonds and transfer the nuts to the workbowl. (The almonds should still be warm and slightly damp.)

Process 1 minute. Measure the honey. Turn on the machine and slowly pour the honey through the feed tube. A very stiff paste will form. Break it apart into a few pieces. Scrape down remaining ingredients on the sides and bottom of the workbowl and reprocess. Repeat until all the "crumbs" are incorporated.

Note: For larger amounts of almond paste, make multiple batches for most efficient functioning of the processor.

BLOND ALMOND FROSTING

When a cake has a delicate flavor, this is often the best choice of frostings.

1 batch Blond Almond Paste (see preceding recipe)
½ cup apple cider

Add the cider to the paste and process until smooth. Scrape down as needed. Enjoy the spectacle, as the paste turns from light gold to white and becomes fluffy.

Refrigerated, the frosting keeps 1 week. A cake frosted with Blond Almond Frosting should be kept in the refrigerator too.

Yield: 1⅓ cups

BLOND ALMOND CANDY

Here is marzipan without eggs, with a light golden color and a rich taste that make for understated elegance.

1 batch Blonde Almond Paste (see recipe)
4 teaspoons honey
Optional: **golden raisins or carob chips**
Optional: **food coloring**

Process the honey into the paste, scraping down the workbowl as necessary. The mixture will be very stiff.

Shape into candies by the heaping ½ teaspoon. Roll the mixture into balls between your palms. You may press a raisin or carob chip into each center.

Or, if you don't think it would be akin to gilding the lily, you can add food coloring. Pink and green both look striking. If you are considering the use of food coloring, don't worry that this sophisticated candy will take on the garish guise of a corn syrup sour ball. A small amount of food coloring, processed in drop by drop, will produce an almost translucent color. For jelly bean shapes, roll the mixture as for balls. Then make a couple of back-and-forth strokes with your hands.

Wrap candies individually or as a group and refrigerate. They will keep for 2 weeks.

Yield: about 6 dozen candies

MALTED MILK CANDY

This is fluffy-textured sweetness with a light tan color. Malted milk powder is available in supermarkets and some health food stores.

1 cup malted milk powder, or more if needed
¼ cup butter, cut into 8 pieces
¼ cup honey
2 teaspoons vanilla extract
Carob flour

Process all ingredients but the carob flour for 10 seconds. Scrape down and reprocess until every bit of the ingredients is incorporated into the mixture. The goal is a stiff paste. If it is too liquid, process in more malted milk powder by the teaspoon until the consistency becomes stiff.

Put some carob flour into a flat saucer. Take the mixture by the heaping teaspoon and shape into balls (see recipe for Blond Almond Candy).

Roll each ball in the carob. Chill before serving. Well-wrapped and refrigerated, the candy keeps about a week.

Yield: 1 dozen candies

MALTED MILK FROSTING

For a small batch

1 tablespoon milk
2 tablespoons butter, cut into several pieces
¾ teaspoon vanilla extract
⅛ teaspoon molasses
1 tablespoon honey
¼ cup malted milk powder
2 tablespoons noninstant powdered milk

For a large batch

3 tablespoons milk
6 tablespoons butter, cut into several pieces
2¼ teaspoons vanilla extract
¼ teaspoon molasses
3 tablespoons honey
¾ cup malted milk powder
⅓ cup noninstant powdered milk

Process all ingredients for 10 seconds at a time. Scrape down and reprocess until smooth. If a thinner frosting is desired, process 1 teaspoon milk at a time.

Yield: ⅓ cup (small), 1 cup (large)

Ⓣ SWEET VELVET SPREAD

The processor helps you achieve a smooth texture for this rich mixture of dried fruit. Keep it on hand as a jam, or spread it between cake layers. (Only one size batch is given here, because this is the most practical quantity to prepare at one time. If you choose to double the batch, be sure to process it separately to avoid spillage.)

1 cup water
1 tablespoon herbal tea blend made with rose hips
1 cup dried apricots
1 cup pitted prunes
1 cup pitted dates
½ cup raisins
Pinch salt

Bring the water to a rolling boil. Pour over the tea. Brew for 10 minutes. Strain and pour into a saucepan with cover.
Simmer all other ingredients with it in the covered pan until the fruit has absorbed all the liquid (check after 25 minutes).
Process until smooth, scraping down as necessary. Refrigerate after the spread cools.

Yield: about 2 cups

VELVET CANDY BARS

For a small batch

⅓ cup Sweet Velvet Spread (see preceding recipe)
⅓ cup Fresh Grated Coconut (see Index), packed
⅓ cup toasted wheat germ
½ teaspoon vanilla extract
Additional coconut

For a large batch

1 batch Sweet Velvet Spread (see preceding recipe)
2⅓ cups Fresh Grated Coconut (see Index), packed
2⅓ cups toasted wheat germ
3½ teaspoons vanilla extract
Additional coconut

Process all ingredients except the additional coconut until smooth. Scoop out 1 heaping tablespoon at a time and shape it into a bar. Gently press in coconut to cover all sides. Wrap individually and refrigerate.

Yield: 6 bars (small), 40 bars (large)

VELVET CREAM FROSTING

Smooth and rich, it tastes like a cross between icing and ice cream.

For a small batch

¼ cup Sweet Velvet Spread (see recipe)
¼ cup heavy cream

For a large batch

1 cup Sweet Velvet Spread (see recipe)
1 cup heavy cream

Chill the cream thoroughly in the refrigerator before using. Prepare the spread and let it cool.

In a dry machine, process the cream for 15 seconds. Add the spread and pulse to mix, scraping down as needed, until the mixture is smooth.

Chill at least ½ hour before using to frost a cake or cupcakes. For best results, frost right before serving. Refrigerate any leftovers.

Yield: ½ cup (small), 2 cups (large)

Ⓔ CAKE WITH THE WORKS

It used to be a cherished indulgence to order an ice cream extravaganza with "the works." Some of that feeling can be recaptured with the following approach to frosting a cake.

The Pudding Topping

2 cups whole milk
¼ cup arrowroot
½ cup brown sugar
Pinch salt
2 teaspoons vanilla extract

Start heating 1½ cups of the milk in a double boiler or well-oiled saucepan over medium heat. Process all other ingredients (including the remaining milk) until smooth and pour into the milk. Stir constantly. Bring the milk to a boil and simmer 3 minutes longer. Set aside.

The Works

Fresh Grated Coconut (see Index)
Any kind of nut meat not used in the cake,
processed until coarsely chopped
Food processor candy (see recipes in this chapter, especially No-Fault Fudge), cut with a knife into small pieces
Fresh berries, ready to eat
Freshly toasted sesame seeds

My Discoveries:

To Assemble
Either decorate the baked cake as a whole right before serving or set out many dishes of ingredients and let guests fix their own dessert combination.

Top the cake with the pudding topping, served either hot or cold (be sure to stir it before adding to the cake and lift off any skin that may have formed when the pudding cooled).

Deck the cake out with the works.

Yield: 12 servings

- For pie with the works, prepare a double batch of pudding topping. Simmer it for 5 minutes, rather than 3. Let it cool to room temperature and transfer to a fully baked pastry shell (such as Flexible Pastry with wheat germ and molasses options; see Index). Layer choices from the works in with the pudding or reserve them for a last-minute topping. Chll the pie until set.

Yield: 8 servings

14 Problem Solving with a Processor

Cheese Caché

Sunflower Meal

Pastry Scrap Cookies

Fresh Grated Coconut

Grenadine

This chapter could be considered an ode to the food processor. It may be more traditional to address odes to the muses, but in all fairness my food processor has inspired me more than any culinary muse.

Actually the Greeks didn't bother to assign a muse for cooking. Even if they had, I still would have felt pretty silly imploring her to help me solve an everyday kitchen brain teaser.

Every scrupulous cook puzzles over them: the items you wish you didn't have to buy, like packaged coconut; the tidbits you wish you knew what to do with, like the ends of broccoli; the desire to pack up a better lunch without spending a lot of time over it.

Whatever your priorities, I hope the following recipes will please you. More than that, I hope they will inspire you to make many similar discoveries. Problem solving is easier with a processor.

FRESH GRATED COCONUT

Equipped with a little know-how and a food processor, you can easily grate your own coconut. The taste is superlative; it's easy to understand why by making some comparisons. Read the label on packaged coconut: sugar, preservatives, and such adulterate the natural flavor. As for the dried coconut available at some health food stores, it comes closer to the authentic taste of freshly grated coconut but, being dried, still lacks the robust juiciness of fresh food.

The economics of do-it-yourself coconut are noteworthy too. A medium coconut will provide a generous amount of gratings, and what you don't use right away can go into the freezer.

For convenience, measure grated coconut into ½-cup or 1-cup batches. Double-bag the dry coconut in plastic. Properly frozen, it will maintain good quality for at least 2 months.

Wash a small Phillips head screwdriver or a 2-inch long nail.

Working over a sink, hammer the screwdriver into 2 or all 3 of the eyes of a fresh coconut. The punctures should be deep enough to allow for drainage of the coconut milk. Shake the coconut vigorously to remove this liquid (which should, of course, be saved for use in beverages, curry sauces, baking, and fruit salads).

Let the coconut dry out further by placing it in a preheated 300° F. oven for 25–30 minutes. Allow the coconut to cook enough for you to be able to work with it comfortably.

Break up the coconut with a hammer. Again, the kitchen sink makes a convenient work place. Pry the outer husk from the meat, using a sturdy paring knife. Also use this knife, or a swivel-blade vegetable peeler, to separate the brown skin from the white meat. If the coconut has dried out thoroughly, very little work is involved in freeing the coconut meat.

Rinse and dry each piece of coconut meat. Before you use the processor on it, assess the capability of your machine. Check its instruction manual. Does it mention that you can shred coconut with the shredding disc?

If so, pack the coconut into the feed tube and push it through. You will get at least 3 cups shredded coconut.

If not, play it safe. Avoid possible damage to your machine. Cut the coconut into 1-inch pieces and process (no more than 1 cup at a time). You'll get at least 2 cups minced coconut. True, the volume is less than with the use of a shredding disc. Otherwise, you can substitute it interchangeably with grated coconut. Minced coconut is chewier.

- For toasted coconut, spread shredded or minced coconut on a baking sheet. Bake at 350° F., stirring often, until golden brown. Cool on a plate. This most flavorful form of coconut can be used in a number of ways: in yogurt with wheat germ, as a casserole topper, in The FP Fruit Salad (see Index), wherever food processor candies require coconut. Store toasted coconut in an airtight container. Refrigerated, it will keep for a few days.

BREAD CRUMBS

Here is a prime illustration of how whole-food cooking and food processor cooking combine to accomplish things that cannot be done otherwise.

If you already have been using a processor, you know that just about any leftover bread can be transformed into crumbs. If you are a whole grain baker, you may have wished there were some convenient way to turn it into crumbs—the prepackaged stuff won't do, once you have gotten used to the flavor of whole grain bread.

Use a dry machine to process whole grain muffins, biscuits, or bread. Stop at the degree of coarseness or fineness you prefer. If desired, bread crusts may be removed before processing.

Bread crumbs may be refrigerated or even frozen successfully, when packed airtight. My preference, however, is to make small batches as needed for immediate use. With home-baked bread we never have the problem of stale leftovers—it never lasts long enough. And whole grain bread does not need to become stale in order to make excellent bread crumbs.

Some day we may look back on conventional bread crumbs as barbaric. Why use stale white bread when you can use fresh, chewy whole grain?

THE CHEESE CACHE

Hoard grated cheese for convenience, to use up leftovers, or to prevent spoilage. The food processor can be your best accomplice.

Grating cheese, you can freeze it in any quantity you like. The processor enables you to shred or mince any hard- or medium-textured cheese. Whether you've got a chunk or a snippet, it can be chopped up with dispatch. Then double-bag it in plastic and put it into the freezer.

Usually it is preferable to bag and label each type of cheese separately. Still, it can be convenient and fun to maintain an ongoing cache of assorted cheeses. It's likely to become a grab bag of serendipity, for the mixture can add up to wonderful flavors, perfect for casseroles, pasta, grains, or beans.

GENTEELRADISH

Before the food processor made it so easy, who could be bothered to grate radishes at home?

As a condiment, radishes lack the biting kick of the horseradish root. Nevertheless, when added to cooked vegetables or salads, radishes can pack a genteel wallop.

Fresh horseradish is harvested from November to April and is sold to commercial processors. In contrast, fresh radish roots, available year-round, can be sold to you at almost any supermarket.

Fresh radishes as needed

Trim fresh radishes and push them through the shredding disc. Prepare only what you need for immediate use—instant spice with unmistakable vitality.

THE EGGLESS OMELET

They say you can't make an omelet without breaking eggs. This is especially inconvenient if you don't eat eggs anymore.

Yet you don't have to forgo omelets entirely—exactly. Most people will find a cheese "omelet" made with tofu quite satisfactory.

2 tablespoons whole grain Bread Crumbs (see recipe this chapter)
¼ cup minced cheddar or other suitable cheese
½ cup cubed tofu, drained
1 tablespoon olive oil or sesame oil
⅛ teaspoon coriander
1 tablespoon whole wheat flour

Prepare bread crumbs. Set aside. Prepare the cheese and set it aside separately. Process all other ingredients together until smooth, scraping down as necessary. Pulse in the bread crumbs.

Oil a small cast-iron skillet thoroughly and heat at medium-high temperature until drops of water dance on the surface. Spread the batter over the surface of the pan. (This is tricky, because the batter has a thick consistency. The back of a spoon can help. Aim for a uniform thickness.)

Turn the heat down to medium. After 5 minutes, flip the omelet over. The mixture should hold together like a pancake. Distribute the cheese on top. Cook until the cheese melts, about 5 more minutes.

Yield: 1 main dish serving

GETTING STINGY WITH SALT

Too much salt in the diet can put you in a pickle. On the other hand, cold-turkey salt deprivation has been known to cause severe gastronomic depression.

Gomashio and Herbed Salt are two excellent compromises. Food can be served unsalted, to be adorned at the table with either of these condiments. Both taste salty, but have a low proportion of salt.

GOMASHIO

This Japanese seasoning works well on virtually everything that would otherwise be salted. It is especially delightful when fresh, so I recommend that a small batch be made at one time, then stored airtight in a jar. A small portion at a time can be transferred to a saltcellar or tiny bowl and kept on the table.

1 cup sesame seeds with hulls (always a better buy than hulled sesame seeds; the whole seeds are richer in calcium, B vitamins, and iron)
2 tablespoons salt

Pan roast the sesame seeds until they start to brown (see box on page 31). Transfer to the workbowl. Add the salt and process 60 seconds.
Before you put away the Gomashio, give yourself a minute to indulge in the fragrance.

Yield: about 1 cup

HERBED SALT

The combination of herbs given here tastes good on grains, vegetables, and beans. Once you get the hang of seasoning salts, you can vary the recipe to include other herbs and spices. Try putting up a blend especially for Italian food or chili.

⅓ cup basil
1 tablespoon marjoram
⅓ cup chervil
1 tablespoon savory
⅓ cup parsley
½ cup salt

In a dry machine, process all ingredients for 60 seconds. Stir with a rubber spatula. Reprocess for 30 seconds. While not completely uniform, the seasoned salt is sufficiently mixed to work well. Transfer a small amount to a saltshaker with large holes.

Yield: about ¾ cup

BUTTERY BUTTERMILK

These days commercial buttermilk is cultured from skim milk, rather than churned. Those of us who feel nostalgic about the more buttery variety can find solace in this approximation, which features tiny flakes of butter that melt on your tongue as you drink. Even with the added butter, the beverage still has a lower fat content than regular whole milk.

1 cup buttermilk
1 teaspoon frozen butter, cut into 6 pieces

Process for 2 minutes and serve.

Yield: 1 cup

Note: If you double the recipe, cut the butter into 12 pieces altogether. It may be tempting to skip this step, but the goal of the recipe is flakes, not little gobs of butter.

PACKING A HOT LUNCH WITH LEFTOVERS

Leftovers from our kitchen usually wind up in an evening salad or casserole or else in a lunchtime thermos. The food processor helps you recycle leftovers and even make them exciting.

Caught in a flurry of last-minute, almost-late-for-work preparations, you would otherwise have to choose between interest and instantness. Fortunately, by using the processor you can achieve both.

Here is a sample of one 10-minute lunch preparation. The leftovers available are cooked cornmeal and steamed kale; also on hand is a carrot, other salad ingredients, and butter.

Note that ingredient quantities are completely flexible. With 2 tablespoons of cornmeal and one carrot, you'll produce a sauce for the shredded carrot; 1 cup of cornmeal plus the carrot will create a stovetop grain casserole. Similarly, different quantities of kale in salads will produce different effects: ¼ cup will serve as a munchy component, while 1½ cups will turn the vegetable into the main salad ingredient.

Part of the fun of a very flexible recipe is the seasoning. The safest method is also the simplest: choose just one extra ingredient. Focus on a spice, such as pepper, ginger, or blended curry powder. Or select your favorite herb—basil, tarragon, and so forth. Don't forget that recipe ingredients also add distinctive flavors: a few drops of sesame oil, a dollop of tomato paste, lemon juice, a few minced nuts.

1. Run hot tap water into a clean thermos to preheat it.

2. Pour a little water into a saucepan with cover. Turn on high heat.

3. Push a carrot through the shredding disc. Set aside.

4. Chop the kale with the metal blade. Set it aside in a salad container.

5. Run the cornmeal through the processor to remove any lumps. Process in butter, salt, and spices to taste. Stir the mixture into the boiling water. Add more water until a smooth consistency is reached. Stir in the carrot and let the mixture cook over medium heat.

6. Turn back to the kale-based salad and add other ingredients to the container—perhaps lettuce, tomato, and sprouts. Cover the container and pack it away, along with a separate small jar of salad dressing.

7. Meanwhile, rinse out the food processor. Pack up the rest of the lunch, in this case a container of yogurt and an orange. Other meals might include a sandwich with a separate jar of homemade spread, perhaps a couple of raw vegetables to munch, dried fruit for a snack, or some roasted soybeans or nuts.

8. When the cornmeal mixture is heated thoroughly, transfer it to the thermos.

Some general ideas follow for using the processor to prepare a hot lunch in less time than it would take to wait for fast food—and to pack something that doesn't taste like yesterday's leftovers.

- Process leftover vegetables into a soup. For liquid, use milk, buttermilk, yogurt, vegetable stock, or water. Add appropriate seasonings. Either cook the soup as a uniformly textured puree or add such items as sprouts, cubes of tofu, beans, whole wheat or rye berries. (Of course, beans and grains must be cooked in advance.) If you use buttermilk or yogurt, transfer the soup to the thermos before it comes to a boil. Otherwise the soup will curdle.

- Puree leftover grains into a soup, thinning with leftover sauce, milk, or water. Add minced leftover cooked vegetables or shredded raw vegetables.

- Process leftover cooked vegetables until minced. Heat in leftover sauce.

- Push raw vegetables through the slicing or shredding disc. Heat with a Butterstretcher (see Index) or oil in a covered saucepan. Once the vegetables start to brown, moisten with a little stock or tomato juice.

- Process cooked beans into a paste and refry (see recipe for Refried Greens).

- Process cooked greens until minced and refry (see recipe for Refried Greens).

PASTRY SCRAP COOKIES FOR KIDS

With all the good ingredients that go into pastry, it seems like a waste to throw away extra dough, once you have made a piecrust or lattice top.

Instead of throwing scraps away, try throwing them into the processor. Four different alternatives are given here. Once you get started, you'll think of more.

SPECKLED SESAME SUNS

¼ cup pastry dough
1 tablespoon honey
1 tablespoon sesame seeds
2 drops Liquid Smoke

ORANGE MOONSHINE

¼ cup pastry dough
1 tablespoon brown sugar
1 teaspoon honey
⅛ teaspoon ground cardamom
1 teaspoon orange juice
Orange food coloring

VENUS VANILLA WAFERS

¼ cup pastry dough
1 tablespoon brown sugar
¼ teaspoon vanilla extract

MARTIAN GINGER SNAPS

¼ cup pastry dough
2 teaspoons molasses
1 teaspoon ginger
Dash cinnamon

Pulse ingredients for the type of cookie you choose until uniform. Avoid overprocessing.

Recipe quantities are based on a very small amount of leftover dough. Especially if you cannot make a double or triple batch at one time, check that all ingredients in the cookie dough are well distributed before shaping the batter into cookies.

Since piecrust varies in texture, the consistency of these cookies will vary. The way they are shaped should depend on that consistency. If the cookie dough is very stiff or crumbly, you may wish to add a little honey.

Shape fairly stiff dough into balls and press down with fork tines to make a pattern. Or, for an effect that children find captivating, repeatedly but gently poke fork tines *into* the dough, to create many holes. As for a very moist batter, simply drop it by the tablespoon onto an oiled baking sheet.

However you shape the batter, use about 1 tablespoon per cookie. Bake on an oiled baking sheet in a 350° F. oven until the bottoms brown (check after 8 minutes). Cool on rack.

Yield: 5 cookies

THE PROBLEM WITH BROCCOLI

Fresh broccoli is a delight but also something of an embarrassment. Everyone loves the flowerets, but what do you do with the stalk, which toughens as it gets farther from the flowerets?

A good fresh stalk of broccoli need only be trimmed slightly at the end. That leaves the cook with perhaps 2 inches of flowerets and connective stem, 2 inches of tender stem, 2 inches of less tender stem, and 2 inches of stem that is as tough as a turnip.

I've seen the noble vegetable turned into a sort of dwarfed cauliflower, with all but the top 3 inches hacked off. Other cooks ignore the problem, steaming or boiling the whole stalk.

Unfortunately, when the flowers are tender, the bottom is rocklike. Wait for the base to catch up and the flowers might as well be weeds, they overcook so badly.

One solution is to peel the outermost skin off the bottom 4 inches. That amounts to time-consuming surgery. A better choice may be to lop off each bottom 4-inch length, separate tough and tender broccoli into 2 batches, and cook them separately until done.

For the best solution, though, combine use of the food processor with knowledge of nutrition. When you push broccoli stem through the shredding disc, it comes out like shredded cabbage. Let's compare the nutrition in equal volumes of broccoli and cabbage:

Broccoli	*Cabbage*
140 mg. vitamin C	48 mg. vitamin C
3,900 IU vitamin A	190 IU vitamin A
1.2 mg. niacin	.4 mg. niacin
140 mg. calcium	64 mg. calcium

So why not set aside the bottom quarter of your broccoli? Grate it and toss it in with your salad.

As a footnote, are you wise to broccoli leaves? Although carelessly discarded by cooks who don't know any better, those delicate leaves are nutritionally first rate, comparable to other dark green leafy vegetables. Cook them along with broccoli flowerets or add them to your salad bowl.

SUNFLOWER MEAL

Sunflower seeds are delectable, as any granola fancier knows. What most of us don't realize is that seeds or nuts that are gobbled down pass right through the digestive tract. Unless you chew them properly first, you might as well throw them away. Children in particular seldom curb their enthusiasm long enough to make the seeds digestible.

Sunflower meal makes it easy to break sunflower seeds down so they don't require thorough mastication. To make it, simply process raw or toasted sunflower seeds in a dry machine. One cup of hulled seeds yields 1⅛ cups meal. Store it airtight in the refrigerator.

Exactly how do you use it? Sprinkle it onto foods that would otherwise be sprinkled with whole seeds, such as cereal. Add small amounts to pancakes, nut butters, sauces, or casseroles. In addition to a delicious taste, you'll benefit from the B vitamins and amino acids.

GRENADINE

Pomegranate seeds, like raspberries or blackberries, are beautiful to behold, flavorful to eat, and frustrating because of the tough little bits that remain after you swallow the juice. For the first few bites the fruit is so delicious it's a slight inconvenience. But as the mouthfuls accumulate, gulping the bits down or discarding them gets wearisome. So your best choice with either could be to make a syrup.

1 pomegranate
Brown sugar or honey or both to taste

Remove the fleshy red seeds from the pomegranate and process them in the workbowl for 20 seconds. A frothy liquid emerges, which is easily strained through a fine sieve. Return this liquid to the workbowl and process in sweetener.

The amount of sweetener you use should depend on the use you plan for the grenadine. If you intend to serve it undiluted as a syrup over ice cream or sherbet, sweeten it moderately (a few teaspoons of sweetener). For a syrup to be used in beverages, add a good deal more sweetener (at least ¼ cup). It's a matter of taste, but I would suggest starting with a ratio of one part Grenadine to two parts mineral water or seltzer. You also may wish to stretch the amount of syrup (about ½ cup) by diluting it with water to yield 1 cup; sweeten to taste. The tangy flavor will still go a long way.

Grenadine's most common use, of course, is as a beverage syrup. It's especially popular in France, where the term grenadine originates (the French word for pomegranate is la grenade). For a real taste awakener, compare homemade grenadine with the commercial product sold in liquor stores as a cocktail ingredient. The naturally flavored syrup makes the store-bought variety appear about as subtle as cough syrup.

- To make a syrup from blackberries or raspberries, substitute 1 cup fresh or frozen berries for pomegranate seeds. To facilitate straining after you process them, dilute the juice by processing in some apple cider, honey, or water. Sweeten as for grenadine.

15 | Meatless Meals; Meatless Menus

SOME NOTES ON VEGETARIAN COOKERY

Worldwide there are more than 4 billion vegetarians, but the term can refer to many different patterns of eating. Many people call themselves vegetarians because they choose to eat no red meat. They do eat seafood or fowl or both, either seldom or frequently.

Ovolactovegetarians allow eggs and dairy products, but no other substances of animal origin.

Lactovegetarians forgo the eggs.

Vegans dispense with the dairy products as well.

Thus even full-time vegetarians vary widely in dietary practice. People with many other eating styles enjoy an occasional meatless meal; this qualifies them as part-time vegetarians.

Whether you are eating vegetarian for a meal or a lifetime, it is essential to do some planning. Otherwise a meatless meal could be less nutritious than a fast food burger, unnecessarily costly, or simply not satisfying.

The first step in planning menus for any of these people is to ascertain their eating preferences beyond the simple label "vegetarian." In order to plan a nutritious meatless meal, though, it is essential to understand the basic principles of menu design. The information in the first part of this chapter will supply you with all the basics you need to know; it is really quite simple. The remaining problem for skilled cooks is making vegetarian meals interesting, and even some long-time vegetarians haven't gotten beyond this hurdle. Some of the menu planning questions will prove helpful, then the Situational Menus will show concrete examples of meals you can serve with pride.

PLANNING BALANCED MEATLESS MEALS

For successful meal planning, I have developed nine vital questions over the last decade. To use your full potential as a cook and to safeguard your family against boredom-inspired binges, try asking these questions while you are deciding what to prepare for lunch or dinner.

1. Where is the protein?

A two-ounce cube of natural cheese, a cup of yogurt, a cup of milk, or an egg if you eat eggs, taken with each meal will assure most individuals of getting sufficient protein. But eating from a wide selection of grains and beans adds important variety to your diet, a better diet than you would have by depending on meat, fish, eggs, or dairy products for all your protein.

2. Where are the complex carbohydrates?

Complex carbohydrates come from unrefined starches, such as grains and legumes. Because of their role in producing blood sugar, they are essential sources of energy. These satisfying foods also contribute fiber to the diet.

Each meal should contain one or two servings, for a total of at least 6 servings daily. Vegans require more: a minimum of 8 portions of grain, and 3 of beans. Bread is especially good to eat as part of that grain requirement since the yeast rising process fights phytic acid, which can block absorption of calcium and iron.

Refined carbohydrates, on the other hand, are entirely dispensable. White flour, alcohol, and white sugar are the three most prevalent

(continued on page 146)

144

CLEARING UP SOME MISCONCEPTIONS ABOUT PROTEIN AND PROTEIN COMBINING

Myth Number 1: Basically, protein comes from meat. Grains and legumes are starchy foods.

Although meat is high in protein, it is generally high in fat too. A 3-ounce hamburger furnishes 17 grams of fat along with its 21 grams of protein. The calorie-protein ratio for that hamburger thus amounts to 12 calories for each gram of protein.

Meanwhile, a cup of cooked wheat berries yields 9.4 grams of protein. The calorie-protein ratio is 24 to 1—just about half the amount of protein per calorie that hamburger has. That's not bad for a food that is supposed to be pure "starch."

Beans offer even more concentrated protein. A cup of cooked soybeans supplies 20 grams of protein, creating a calorie-protein ratio of 9 to 1. That's 25 percent fewer calories per gram of protein than hamburger has.

Incidentally, I leave it to you to compare the cost-protein ratios for hamburgers, wheat, and soybeans.

Myth Number 2: Protein combining is difficult to master and, frankly, a pain in the neck.

Nonsense. In the first place, anyone who cares about nutrition (whether a meat eater or not) ought to learn about protein combining. That knowledge enables you to get the best possible mileage out of food. A small portion of meat can multiply in protein value manyfold, depending on how it is served.

In the second place, the practical basics of protein combining are exceedingly simple. Here they are, in 25 words or less:

FOR A COMPLETE PROTEIN, COMBINE:

A GRAIN OR BEAN WITH { DAIRY PRODUCTS EGGS FISH FOWL MEAT } OR COMBINE BEAN + GRAIN

Yes, there are finer points to protein combining. You can also make use of the protein in nuts, seeds, sprouts, sea vegetables, nutritional yeast, and other foods. It helps to consult a chart that details the amino acid makeup of foods. One good reference source is the table on "Protein and Calorie Content of Protein Source Foods" in Appendix III (reprinted by permission from Laurel's Kitchen: A Handbook for Vegetarian Cookery and Nutrition by Laurel Robertson, Carol Flinders, and Bronwen Godfrey, copyright 1976, Nilgiri Press, Petaluma, CA 94953).

Careful protein combining is mandatory for vegans. For anyone else, a small amount of any animal protein taken at each meal will balance the protein in other foods sufficiently. A snack of some crackers will supply a complete protein if it includes a snippet of cheese or a Butterstretcher made with powdered milk (see Index).

Now let's look more closely at the theory behind these practical suggestions. What is the significance of protein combining?

Basically, there is a difference between protein elements in food and protein the human body can digest and use. Protein for our bodies is a combination of components, individually known as amino acids. These acids fit together chemically. You could compare this to using letters to form a word. In terms of this analogy, every time you have enough letters to spell the biochemical word for protein, your body registers usable protein. Thus, you could be getting an ample *quantity* of protein, but if the *quality* were off, due to the lack of just one amino acid, your body would register *no protein.*

Altogether there are nine essential amino acids. When you analyze their distribution in different foods, some interesting patterns emerge. Most grains lack only lysine. Most beans lack methionine and tryptophan. However, beans do have lysine, and grains supply tryptophan and methionine. So when you eat them together (in a ratio of as little as 1 part bean to 6 parts grain), you have it—protein your body can use.

Most animal products (including dairy products) supply enough amino acid "letters" to complete any vegetable protein. The notable exceptions for dairy products are cream and cream cheese (which are predominantly fat, not protein) and ice cream, of course (which in many cases is barely a dairy product at all).

Throughout the world traditional menus take advantage of protein combining for maximum value. Corn tacos with refried beans, rice and dahl, hummus on a pita.

A grilled cheese or egg salad sandwich works too. The protein value is not only in the filling; it's in the bread—and that's no myth.

carbohydrates in the American diet today. We don't need these substances and they throw the digestive system out of kilter. Refined flour is hard to digest, because it lacks fiber. Alcohol irritates the lining of the gastrointestinal tract and interferes with the digestion of other foods. White sugar has been linked to hypoglycemia and heart disease (sugar will be discussed in more detail later).

3. Where are the vegetables?

Twice a day, meals should include fresh vegetables. They contribute vitamins, minerals, protein, and fiber. At least 4 daily servings are recommended for the vegan, 3 for other vegetarians. Of this, one serving should come from the supernutritious vegetables: kale, spinach, collards, turnip greens, mustard greens, swiss chard, carrot, sweet potato, and winter squash.

4. Where is the source of vitamin C?

We do require a rich source of vitamin C daily, but that need not appear at every meal or in the form of orange juice.

When you plan your meals or snacks each day, simply include somewhere one serving of a food rich in vitamin C; it can come from an orange or a grapefruit, fresh strawberries, papaya, guava, mango, or cantaloupe. A raw green pepper, or even better a sweet red one, a serving of cooked broccoli, brussels sprouts, or collard greens all supply adequate vitamin C. Should you get marooned without fresh produce, you still need not reach for a vitamin pill. Boost your intake of vitamin C by drinking several cups of rose hips tea.

5. Where is the fat?

You've heard the statistic already. Fat amounts to 40 percent of the calories in the typical American diet. Where does it come from? Some fats are hidden, such as those in fried foods or whole milk. Other fats are added as a matter of habit—and then forgotten—such as butter on vegetables, grains, and legumes.

As a conscientious meal planner, you can and should limit the fat in meals. If baked potatoes are served with sour cream, don't compound it with an oily salad dressing. Try some of the low-fat dressings in this book or serve raw vegetables as crudités.

Less can be more with fats. By using good-quality products with discretion, you won't only be safeguarding health. You will often be enhancing the taste of the food.

6. Where is the sugar? Why?

Again, I don't have to tell you about the amount of sugar in the typical American diet. It's notorious. So be ruthless in cutting sweeteners out of meals. Be sneaky in substituting for white sugar (see How to Adapt Recipes to Natural Food Standards, Chapter 16). Be generous in supplying fresh fruit. Most important, emphasize the natural goodness of the ingredients through your cooking skills so that food will tempt without the inducement of extra sweetening.

7. How about the B vitamins? Where are they?

Make sure you get the full set of B vitamins, either directly (raw wheat germ, nutritional yeast, or food supplements) or indirectly (uncooked yogurt with live cultures enables your body to manufacture B vitamins on its own). At least once daily, preferably twice or three times, a rich B-vitamin source should be part of your meal.

An adequate supply can make a tremendous difference in your well-being.

Over the years I've found that sometimes vegetarians are afflicted with an unquenchable sweet tooth. When they make it their business to get more B vitamins and protein, the cravings stop.

8. What is the main dish?

When you serve meat, there's no question about this. The star of the meal, the protein dish, may also be the main B-vitamin source: meat is the summit of the eater's expectations.

We always expect a recognizable main dish. When we forgo meat, that doesn't change. That special dish need not necessarily be the main protein source. Here is a list of some of the items that people find satisfying as entrees:

a loaf
a stuffed vegetable
a burger

a pie or casserole
anything topped with melted cheese
pizza
a high-protein spread
something served with a sauce

9. Is there duplication?

Your judgment is essential to answer this question. Every meal can be planned to be a work of art.

Contrast fancy dishes with something plain. Balance spicy food with moderately seasoned recipes. Set off hot food with something cold, preferably something raw. It is wise to eat both raw and cooked foods to provide variety, and even the same food can vary in nutrient content, depending on whether it is eaten raw or cooked. For instance, consider 45 calories' worth of carrots, which can come from 1 cup raw gratings or 1 cup cooked pieces. The cooked version provides 15,000 units of vitamin A instead of 12,000. Yet the raw version supplies .16 milligrams of vitamin B_6, compared to none in the cooked carrots.

All of us have prepared or eaten ambitious meals that didn't work—meals with tomatoes or cream sauce in everything, carbohydrate feasts of bread, potatoes, and beans; creations by herb fanciers, with greenery as thick as a forest.

Common sense decrees that one thick sauce per meal, at most two, is enough for variety.

One entree with a very stylized shape is sufficient—a pie, a burger, a stuffed vegetable— not all of them together.

And especially relevant to those of us who get good use out of our food processors: something should be more or less whole (unchopped). Otherwise there is an unsettling impression that all of the food has been predigested.

NATURAL FLEXIBILITY

Last but not least, I want to emphasize the importance of flexibility in diet. It's unnatural to be rigid about anything, even natural food. In particular, I recommend that if you keep craving meat, eat some. It isn't such a heinous crime, especially if you keep in mind that a little fish or fowl won't be as hard to digest as beef or pork.

SITUATIONAL MENUS

I always find it fun to read sample menus. I can fantasize about a gracious occasion, with leisurely dining and an ample budget. Every food is in season, preparation time is unlimited, and guests are invariably thrilled with whatever is served.

In reality, though, I have found that such menus often leave out the critical, situational element. A cook is actually something of a juggler. In addition to the judgment required to plan a nutritious meal, there are many other factors to balance:

- How much can you afford to spend on the meal?
- What is the agenda for the evening? How much time will everyone have to eat?
- How formal should the meal be?
- When will you have to start cooking? How can you make sure everything is done at the right time? What can be fixed in advance?
- What food looks good at the store?

The following menus take questions like these into consideration. In addition, they often allow for a factor of deeper concern for a cook: the likes, dislikes, and needs of each guest.

Just as everyone loves some kind of music, each of us responds to our own kind of soul food. By inviting a guest to dinner, a cook has a wonderful opportunity to make that person happy.

I believe that cooking has its greatest significance when it is an expression of friendship or love. To express your awareness of what one particular individual—and a whole group of individuals—will enjoy is truly to cook with love.

Note: Through these menus you will see flexible recipes put to use. For details of preparation, look in the Index under the name of the recipe (given in italics). With flexible recipes, suggested options are listed in parentheses.

Situation 1: Meat Eating Company

For substance, the avocado entree. For balance, fairly plain vegetables and a light dessert.

Grated Spinach Salad
Avocado Halves Stuffed with Sweet and Sour
  Pintos
Flexible Corn Bread (corn)
Steamed Cauliflower
Strawberry Tingle

Situation 2: Vegan Company

Vegans get feasts all too seldom, so make this one a leisurely banquet. Add cheese to one side of the pie only: the pie works well without cheese, but nonvegans attending will be more satisfied with it. The dessert is a must. Vegans go wild over it; they often miss ice cream more than anything else.

Grenadine with sparkling mineral water
Simply Carrot Soup
Black Eyed Pie
Brown Bread with *Peanut Butter* (extra B and
    soy nuts)
Steamed Kale
*Just About Ice Cream (orange juice
    concentrate, vanilla)*
Choice of herbal tea

Situation 3: Dinner for an Avowed Vegetable Hater

Start reassuringly, with fruit rather than a vegetable salad. Tomato soup is a sneaky choice; many don't consider tomatoes a bona fide vegetable. Other vegetable choices are sneaky, too: the parsley won't be noticed amid the macaroni and cheese, and the dressing makes carrots seem like a dessert.

The FP Fruit Salad (pineapple juice base,
    sliced orange, white grapes)
Oomphy Tomato Soup (chick-peas, whole
    green beans, barley)
Creme Du Jardin Casserole
Shredded Carrots with *Date Nut Dressing*
Flexible Brownies (tender soft) with *Carob
    Fudge Frosting*
Choice of milk, herbal tea, or coffee

Situation 4: Dinner for an Unadventurous Eater

Nothing here will scare the guest; the only exotic item is the cake.

Fresh apple juice
Romaine and salad bowl lettuce with *Olives
    Plus Dressing*
Crusty Italian Pizza
Steamed Summer Squash
Confidence Cake (carrot, chestnut, and
    vanilla) with *The Works*
Choice of peppermint tea or coffee

Situation 5: Dinner for an Adventurous Eater

A delicious, balanced adventure.

Fresh carrot juice
Lima Wiggle
Juicy Turnips
Steamed Chard
Corn Muffin Riddle with *Butter for the Table*
Smoothie (apricot)

Situation 6: Dinner for a Guest with a Sweet Tooth

This entire meal plays a variation on the theme of sweetness.

Grapefruit halves
FP Salad (red leaf lettuce, Boston lettuce,
    marinated tofu, shredded broccoli) with
    Zesty Dressing
Artipoppy Casserole
Black Beans
Passion for Pumpkin with *Breakfast Butter*
Assorted food processor candies: *No-Fault
    Fudge, Malted Milk Candy, Strawberry
    Protein Candy*
Chamomile tea

Situation 7: Dinner for an Artist

A delicate pink soup, a white-highlighted kohlrabi casserole, green-tinted egg salad, brown bread, and a dessert vivid with red and orange; beautiful color combinations offered to someone who will appreciate them.

Flexible Cream Soup
Kohlrabi for Artists
Best Egg Salad
Daily Bread
Quintessential Fruit Salad
Choice of herbal tea

Situation 8: Dinner for a Business Associate

This formal meal will feature many familiar tastes, upgraded.

White grape juice
Tender Crackers (wheat) with *Stroganoff
    Spread* and Fontina
Fresh French Beans
Chick-Pea Sausage

Baked Potatoes and *Butter for the Table*
Crudités
Confidence Cake (coffee and date) with
   Vanilla Synthesis Frosting
Choice of herbal tea or coffee

Situation 9: Dinner for a Gourmet

After carrot juice refreshes the palate, the
guest can enjoy a progression of subtle tastes,
carefully balanced.

Fresh carrot juice
Dramatic Cucumber Salad
Avocado Casserole
Steamed Cauliflower
Speckled Bread with *Cashew Butter*
*The FP Fruit Salad (Gorgeous Orange
   Dressing,* pears, peaches, and blueberries)
Blond Almond Candy
Choice of herbal tea

Situation 10: A Romantic Dinner

A leisurely meal, with exquisite, sensuous
dishes.

Cheddar Cheese Soup
FP Salad (salad bowl lettuce, red leaf lettuce,
   sliced cucumber) with *Bingo Dressing*
Lemon Vegetable Showcase
Butternut Squash, Baked Whole
Honey Pie
Herbal tea

Situation 11: A Dinner of Conspicuous Consumption

This meal appears suitably expensive: each
item on the menu includes at least one
extravagant or exotic ingredient.

The FP Fruit Salad (coconut milk base, cubed
   pineapple and papaya, *Fresh Grated
   Coconut*)
FP Salad (Boston lettuce, marinated artichoke
   hearts, marinated chick-peas)
Cauliflower Waltz
Kasha Supreme
Gingerbeet Cake with *Velvet Cream Frosting*
Herbal tea

Situation 12: An Economical but Festive Dinner

The contrasting textures and forthright flavors
should please the guest.

Apple cider
Barley
Down Home Greens
Baked Acorn Squash
Yogurt
Alfalfa sprouts
Confidence Quickbread (ginger) with
   Breakfast Butter
Herbal tea

Situation 13: 30 Minutes to Fix Dinner— Leftovers Available (Soybeans, Rice, Avocado Spread)

Start preparing the soybean dish, then the
rice, salad last. Play the pacing of the meal itself
by ear; serve it in four courses or two.

FP Salad (green leaf lettuce, sliced cucumber,
   sunflower seed sprouts) with *Avocado
   Dressing*
Favorite Soybeans
Jeweled Rice
Yogurt
Fresh fruit
Herbal tea

Situation 14: 30 Minutes to Fix Dinner—No Leftovers Available

Begin with the beets, then the buckwheat.
Next prepare the mustard butter and the salad
dressing. The main course will be on the table in
no time. For dessert, why not let the guests wait
while you boil the bananas? Better yet, bring
them into the kitchen and let them watch you
make the pudding. Food processor magic.

FP Salad (romaine, alfalfa sprouts, cherry
   tomatoes) with *Spreadable Cheddar
   Dressing 1*
Tofu Sautéed in Mustard Butter
Buckwheat Groats
Steamed Beets and Beet Greens
Hot Banana Pudding
Herbal tea

Situation 15: A Meal to Prepare the Night Before

Everything can keep overnight except the
apple slices. Next day you'll have an instant
formal meal, with a still-fresh taste.

A Perfect Marriage Spread with *Tender*

Crackers (buckwheat) and *Apple Slices*
Swiss Bean Pie
Platter of cherry tomatoes, *Marinated
 Artichoke Hearts,* green pepper rings
Yellow Bread with *Butter for the Table*
Flexible Berry Whip (frozen, blueberry)
Herbal tea

Situation 16: An Autumn Dinner

Linger over this seasonal meal with favorite friends. End informally, popping the corn and brewing the tea together as you settle in for a long evening.

Steamed Artichoke with clarified butter
Autumn Almond Casserole
Confidence Buttermilk Biscuits
Crudités
Popcorn
Rose hips blend tea

Situation 17: A Winter Dinner

Transform the inexpensive winter staples (cabbage, potatoes, split peas, carrots, bananas) by using these simple ingredients as the basis for a memorably tasty dinner.

Amazing Green Soup
Shredded Carrots and alfalfa sprouts with
 Stroganoff Dressing
California Cabbage
Baked Potatoes with *Zesty Spread*
Frozen Banana Flakes
Herbal tea

Situation 18: A Spring Dinner

Fresh asparagus—a spring delight. Other flavors are chosen to complement that delicacy, vitality, and freshness.

The FP Fruit Salad (Amazing Mayonnaise
 base, pears, white grapes)
Steamed Asparagus with clarified butter
Cauliflower Steaks
Celery Jumble
Maple Nut Cupcakes

Situation 19: A Summer Dinner

Celebrate the summer with portable picnic food, including two distinctive salads that guests will be sure to remember.

Sparkling Potato Salad
Smiling Succotash
Sliced tomatoes
Chick Chip Bars (hot)
Yogurt with nectarines, strawberries, and
 honey

Situation 20: Dinner for One

Recycle yesterday's avocado sauce into a warming soup. The rest of the menu comes together quickly, yet is quite tasty.

Avocado Cream Soup
Tomatoes
Tender Crackers (wheat) with Brie
Chilled Banana Custard

Situation 21: Dinner for 10

Simultaneously substantial and festive—that's the aim of this summertime menu.

Grape juice garnished with strawberries
Oomphy Tomato Casserole
Summertime Salad
Confidence Cake (sunflower meal, vanilla)
 with *Synthesis Frosting* (blueberry)

Situation 22: Dinner for 25

Here's a good formal meal, suitable for those with more conventional tastes. Each item on the menu reminds guests of familiar foods, yet is distinctive enough to be appreciated as something special.

Crudités with *Garlic Spread*
Assorted *Confidence Muffins (Grape Nuts;
 Cinnamon, Nutmeg, and Allspice; Carob)*
 with *Butter for the Table*
Blonde Beans
Minted Carrots
Creamy Broccoli Pie
Favorite Carrot Cake with *Pineapple
 Buttercream Frosting*
Peppermint tea

Situation 23: Sunday Brunch

Prepare everything in advance so you can spend maximum time with your company. As guests straggle in, pop more frozen waffles into the toaster. By offering a variety of waffle toppings, you enhance the sense of an informal party.

Confidence Waffles (prepare in advance and
   freeze) with choice of *Blueberry Sauce,
   Raspberry Sauce,* or *Breakfast Butter*
Yogurt
Crispest Cole Slaw
Fruit juice, herbal tea, or coffee

Situation 24: Thanksgiving Dinner

This menu for America's biggest eating
holiday is designed in keeping with the
traditional magnificent diversity of Thanksgiving
dinner. Yet, the food here is relatively light and
easy to digest. For an elaborate meal, this feast
is surprisingly inexpensive.

Hilma's Fruit Salad
The Loaf for Special Occasions
Sumptuous Sweet Potatoes
Steamed Summer Squash with *Herbed Salt*
Alfalfa sprouts and green pepper rings
Assorted nuts
Chestnut Candy
Assorted *Confidence Cupcakes:* apricot,
   frosted with *Synthesis Frosting* (orange);
   pecan, frosted with *Carob Fudge Frosting;*
   spice, frosted with *Protein Frosting* (toffee)
Herbal tea

Situation 25: Christmas Dinner

Harmony and fulfillment are the gastronomic
themes, signaled by the cider and soup and
climaxed with the casserole.

Hot spiced apple cider
Crème du Jardin Soup
Cherry tomatoes and black olives
*Cucumbers Stuffed with Licorice Lover's
   Spread,* served over red leaf lettuce
Celestial Chestnut Casserole
Baked Sweet Potato
Daily Bread with *Duxelles* and *Butter for the
   Table*
Confidence Layer Cake (vanilla and poppy)
   filled with *Maple Nut Butter,* frosted with
   Synthesis Frosting (mocha)
Papaya Delight Candy
Herbal tea

16 | Keeping a Natural Kitchen

HOW TO ADAPT RECIPES TO NATURAL FOOD STANDARDS

Just as some old favorite recipes need to be adapted to the food processor, some of the ingredients need to be changed as you become more conscientious about nutrition and natural foods. Substitutions and changes won't necessarily produce identical results but can contribute additional nutritional value without drastically altering flavor.

I invite you to record the substitutions you use in a particular recipe and look critically at the product. Experiment further if necessary. That's the key to successful adaptation and to systematic learning about the properties of different foods. The following tips on substituting for particular ingredients are based on my own experience.

Sugar

- Consider whether the recipe really requires it; you may be able to eliminate sugar entirely.
- For cakes and other desserts, sugar can often be cut by ⅓ or even ½. To wean resistant family members from sugar without arousing resentment, try decreasing the proportion of sugar gradually, over a long period of time.
- To cut down on the amount of sugar used in a recipe, replace milk with unsweetened apple cider. You may then be able to cut the sugar to less than ½ of what it was in the original recipe.
- Replace white sugar with an equal amount of light brown (always pack brown sugar to measure it). The difference in taste will be less than with dark brown sugar, and you

still will be adding a little supplement of iron and B vitamins.
- To replace white sugar with molasses, use ¾ cup molasses for each cup of sugar. Remember to reduce liquids by ¼ cup for each ¾ cup addition of molasses. The variation in taste is a little more noticeable than with using light brown sugar, and the amount of iron and B vitamins is increased.
- To replace white sugar with honey:

1. Use ¾ cup honey for each cup of sugar.
2. Remember to reduce liquids by ¼ cup for each ¾-cup addition of honey.
3. If baking, neutralize the acidity of honey by using Instantly Soured Milk (see Index) in the recipe instead of sweet milk. Otherwise add ½ teaspoon baking soda.
4. Reduce baking temperature by 25 degrees and allow extra time for baking.

Oil and Butter

These can often be decreased or eliminated from recipes. Soups, breads, and legumes are frequently laced with unnecessary grease. Avoid it and you will gain cleaner flavors as well as healthier food.

As with sugar, tastes can change. With baked goods, many people are used to greasy food as a matter of texture, rather than flavor. For such people, the cake and cookie recipes in this book may seem dry. A more gradual reduction in fats may be necessary for such people.

If you are driven to sneakiness, initially slightly increase the amount of oil and butter in these recipes. Decrease over time to the minimal amounts used in the recipes. Don't worry; you have plenty of leeway. The proportions for a typical cake are at least ¼ cup of shortening and

¾ cup of white sugar for each cup of sifted white flour.

The best solution, though, lies in the quality of the fats, not just the amount. Try real butter and cold-pressed corn oil. Or, for a treat, try fresh corn germ or wheat germ oil. Delightful tastes!

Flour

- In baking, substitute 1 cup Confidence for 1 cup white flour. Eliminate the baking powder in the recipe. In a sour milk recipe, do not eliminate the baking soda.
- In baking, replace 1 cup white flour with ⅞ cup whole wheat flour. Replace 1 cup white cake flour with ⅞ cup whole wheat pastry flour. White flour being presifted, always sift the whole wheat replacement before you measure it.
- As a sauce thickener, replace 2 tablespoons white flour with 3 tablespoons whole wheat flour, 3 tablespoons barley flour, 3 tablespoons oat flour, 2 tablespoons brown rice flour, 3 tablespoons chick-pea flour, or 6 teaspoons buckwheat flour + 2 tablespoons whole wheat flour.

Eggs

Traditionally, *1 egg* means 1 large egg.

- To replace eggs in baked goods (as a binding agent), you can substitute for each egg 1 teaspoon soy flour + 2 teaspoons arrowroot + 1 tablespoon water. Don't expect this to provide the lift of egg whites or the richness of yolks. In general, the newcomer to eggless baking will have some adjusting to do.
- To replace eggs in a casserole, first analyze the function of the eggs in the recipe. Stick-to-itselfness (as in loaf recipes)? You can use soy flour as a binding agent (see above), or simply eliminate the eggs and enjoy a different texture.
- To replace eggs as a sauce or soup enricher, use small amounts of butter or flour or both.

Milk

According to tradition, *milk* means whole milk. However, most recipes will not suffer from the substitution of 2-percent-fat milk.

- Replace buttermilk in baking with Instantly Soured Milk (see Index).
- To replace 1 cup fresh milk in a recipe with buttermilk, use ½ teaspoon baking soda with each cup of buttermilk.
- To replace light cream in a recipe, use 1 cup whole milk + 2 tablespoons noninstant nonfat powdered milk.
- Sometimes milk can be replaced with apple cider, soy milk, or stock—use your judgment.

Leavening

- Replace double-acting baking powder (which contains aluminum) with an equal amount of single-acting baking powder (available at health food stores). Bake the batter right after it is mixed.
- If you can't locate single-acting baking powder, replace 1 teaspoon double-acting baking powder with ¼ teaspoon double-acting baking soda plus the use of ½ cup buttermilk as a substitute for other liquid in the recipe.
- You can also replace 1 teaspoon double-acting baking powder with ¼ teaspoon double-acting baking soda + ½ teaspoon cream of tartar. Mix immediately before use—it doesn't keep. Bake the batter right after it is mixed.
- Cut down on the amount of baking powder in recipes if it exceeds 1 teaspoon per cup of flour. This is a safeguard against loss of B vitamins through excessive browning and other chemical reactions.

Grains

- When you use whole grains to replace refined foods (hulled barley for pearled, etc.) substitute according to the volume of cooked grain. Be aware that liquid proportions and cooking times vary for raw grains. Unless the grain can be cooked separately and then assembled toward the end of the recipe, you may be better off with a different recipe.
- Dried white flour pasta can be replaced with an equal amount of whole wheat pasta. If you cannot get whole wheat pasta, supplement the digestibility and protein content by adding 1 tablespoon wheat bran and 1 tablespoon wheat germ per cup of

cooked pasta. Toss it into the drained pasta or stir it into the accompanying sauce.

- Commercial bran cereals should not be confused with genuine wheat bran. Read the labels. The commercial cereals are often heavily sugared.

Meat

Especially when dealing with meat, it is important to think in terms of replacing, not duplicating. The search for imitation versions of meat is probably responsible for the worst cooking perpetrated by or for vegetarians.

- The following can be used to replace meat in some recipes:
    Cubed tofu, sautéed in oil and soy sauce
    Cooked chick-peas or other beans
    Cooked burgers, such as Chick-Pea Sausage (see Index)
    Some spreads, such as Stroganoff (see Index)
    Duxelles (see Index)
    Sautéed sliced mushrooms
    Sautéed sliced summer squash
    Cubed cooked eggplant, broiled (see page 82) or sautéed
- Replace chicken stock with soy stock
- Replace beef gravy with another sauce, stock, or sometimes a nut butter processed into stock.

Chocolate

- When using carob in place of chocolate, again do not expect to duplicate the taste automatically. You are eating a more wholesome, digestible food—that is all you can consider a certainty. Carob contains calcium and fiber. Chocolate contains caffeine, and in the process of digestion robs the body of B vitamins. Chocolate has that caffeine zing and a richness of flavor. Carob, on the other hand, is sweeter, so less sugar is necessary.
- Replace 1 square (1 ounce) baking chocolate with 3 tablespoons carob flour + 1 tablespoon water. Process it until smooth with the fats or liquids in the recipe to avoid mixing problems later on.
- Replace 1 tablespoon cocoa with 1 tablespoon carob flour. Again, process until smooth to avoid mixing problems.

Herbs and Spices

- Taste is the best gauge when using herbs or substituting fresh for dried. A general guideline, though, is to replace 1 teaspoon dried herbs with 1 tablespoon fresh.

Vegetables

Replace frozen or canned vegetables with fresh ones. You may be able to substitute a vegetable from what I call the same group.

Interestingly, related vegetables do not only stand in for each other creditably; they also combine well. I explain it in terms of resonance: the differences are small enough to reverberate well together, perhaps analogous to major thirds in music. For this reason, you can often enliven a recipe by substituting ½ the quantity of one vegetable with another one from the same group. The exceptions are Groups X and Y—combining seems to muddy flavors.

Miscellaneous Interchangeables

- Unsweetened apple cider and unsweetened apple juice
- Arrowroot (natural) and cornstarch (not natural, but cheap and actually does a better job of thickening very acidic foods)
- Tahini and sesame butter (Nutritionally, the difference between the two products is significant. Sesame butter is made from the whole sesame seed, tahini from hulled. The former contains substantially more calcium and B vitamins. The latter is easier to find in some parts of the country. Being a more refined food, the taste is a little milder, the consistency smoother.)

RECIPE FOR A NATURAL COOK'S ROUTINE

How do you do it? Can you really run an all-natural kitchen without having it turn into a full-time job?

Certainly. That's the promise of natural food processor cooking. Yet the proposition may still seem overwhelming at first. If you are new to natural food—or the processor—where do you get started? How do you organize your time?

The following schedule may help you sort out your own routine. It has evolved over the years to meet my personal requirements and should help you to design a schedule of your own.

TABLE 18: VEGETABLE FAMILIES

Group A

green squash
yellow squash
green beans
wax beans
green pepper
sometimes brussels sprouts

Group B

broccoli
cauliflower
green cabbage
kohlrabi
brussels sprouts

Group C

fresh peas
mung bean sprouts
green pea sprouts
lentil sprouts
corn kernels

Group D

spinach
chard
kale
collards
turnip greens
dandelion greens
beet greens
mustard greens

Group E

turnip
rutabaga
sometimes onion

Group F

carrot
beet
parsnip

Group X

winter squash
pumpkin
sweet potato
yam

Group Y

eggplant
mushroom

The routine also demonstrates how essential the processor can be—not only for company cooking, but for everyday uses often neglected by the food processor owner.

Every Day

Cook a whole grain, enough to use some for dinner that day and have leftovers the next day for lunch or breakfast.

Prepare fresh vegetables—sometimes plain, sometimes fancy. Fix enough to use some for dinner that day and have leftovers the next day for lunch or dinner.

Prepare a salad (see The FP Salad as well as individual recipes for salads and dressings).

Use up all cooked leftovers within 24 hours (see Index for recycling leftovers).

Every Second Day

Cook a legume. They are especially versatile with the processor (see Index).

Prepare a sauce—enough to use some for the main meal that day and have leftovers the next day as a base for a soup or casserole.

Twice a Week

Start a batch of sprouts.
Make yogurt.
Shop for fresh vegetables, fruit, and dairy products.
Use the processor to bring variety to the fresh fruit served daily (see recipe for The FP Fruit Salad).

Once a Week

Bake bread.
Prepare a Butterstretcher (see Index).
Prepare a spread to use on sandwiches (after four days, any leftovers are turned into a dressing).
Bake a special dessert or make a candy.
Dine sumptuously, with a special meal (a good time to invite company).

Once a Month

Cook a big potful of soybeans or chick-peas. Freeze most of the beans and stock for convenience (see Chapter 7).

Process plenty of Confidence for use in instant muffins, quickbreads, pancakes, etc.

Prepare homemade condiments and convenience items, according to what the family favors at the time: Herbed Salts, Gomashio, Unadulterated Mayonnaise, Duxelles, Fresh Grated Coconut (see Index). Stock up The Cheese Cache (see Index). Prepare a nut butter to use as a spread, in casseroles, or as a base for frosting or candy.

Stock up on bananas, especially versatile with the processor (see Index).

Shop at a discount supermarket for common legumes, fruit juices, tomato juice, and so forth.

A Few Times a Year

A new crop of nuts comes out, inexpensive and fresh. Stock up. Store whole nuts in a cool place, shelled nuts in the refrigerator. Either way they will keep for many months. (For multifarious uses for nuts, made convenient with the processor, see Index.)

Shop at the co-op for natural food staples (grains, special flours, cold-pressed oils, herbs, and so forth).

INVITATION TO READERS

After so many pages of sharing recipes with you, I invite your feedback. Send any comments, reactions, or questions to me care of Contemporary Books, 180 North Michigan Avenue, Chicago, IL 60601. If you enclose a stamped, self-addressed envelope with your letter, I'll do my best to reply.

Appendix I:

A Cook's Guide to Nutrient Conservation

A COOK'S GUIDE TO NUTRIENT CONSERVATION

Do you boil vegetables as a matter of habit or a matter of convenience? Do you assume that fresh supermarket produce will always be more nutritious than frozen vegetables, no matter what cooking method you use?

Assumptions like this can cause problems when it comes to nutrition. Everyday culinary practices are far more wasteful than many cooks imagine. Has any one cooking method been proven to be clearly superior? No, it's neither that simple nor that rigid. Several methods of cooking, detailed in Table 6, happen to be acceptable. Here I would like to offer some general insight into the nutritional side of vegetable cookery. Put this knowledge into practice and you will boost the value of the food you prepare for yourself and your family.

In preparing the following list of pointers, Dr. Barbara P. Klein, of the Department of Foods and Nutrition at the University of Illinois, was particularly helpful. The paper she wrote with Dr. John W. Erdman, Jr. on *Harvesting, Processing, and Cooking Influences on Vitamin C in Foods* proved invaluable to me. This and other research material plus my own experimentation helped me draw conclusions that are listed here in bold type as general principles of nutrient conservation in cooking.

I would like to commend Dr. Klein and her colleagues for their research in this area. Among the hundreds of papers on nutrition published annually in the United States, a surprisingly small fraction concern the methods and materials of everyday cooking.

1. A substantial amount of the vitamins in vegetables (and fruits) is concentrated in the outer leaves or layers. Removal of these portions may result in considerable nutrient loss.

As specific examples, let's consider potato peelings, the outermost leaves on green cabbage, and other tough green leaves.

Many people find that potato peel is not unappealing once they have gotten used to it. In fact, the skins on baked potatoes taste delicious. Potato salad can gain enhanced color and elegance when the peels are visible; the pink skins of new potatoes look especially attractive.

What about mashed potatoes, perhaps the most popular use for peeled potatoes? The food processor helps considerably. If you have ever tried to use a potato masher on unpeeled spuds, you know that the skin tends to clump in a rather unappetizing manner. When you use the shredding disc (see Potato Mashterpiece), the peel shreds with the rest of the potato; in terms of texture, it is scarcely noticeable.

Many produce dealers do you the "favor" of discarding the greenest portions of cabbage (iceberg lettuce too). Chemical sprays do represent a potential problem, so such leaves ought to be quickly but thoroughly washed before use. The real hazard with these leaves is that they are often considered less desirable than the often more delicately flavored hearts of vegetables. You can make use of these useful leaves by processing the outermost leaves of cabbage along with the softer white ones when you are making coleslaw. For heated cabbage dishes, such as California Cabbage, you may prefer to mince the outermost leaves. Set them aside and reserve them for the last 15 minutes or so of casserole baking. Otherwise the minced leaves can be added to soups (especially good in cream soups). Again, it is worthwhile to take care in cooking—add the tiny leaf fragments close to serving time to prevent overcooking.

More vivid color in green and yellow vegetables signals higher vitamin content. It would be a shame to discard those bright green leaves, even if they appear to be tough.

You have probably read in gourmet cookbooks: "Use the leaves, if tender," regarding beet greens, for instance. The metal blade helps make these greens palatable. First steam them until tender over a minimum of water. Next drain the greens thoroughly. Finally, process the leaves until minced. Sometimes you can get good results by stacking up several leaves, rolling them into a tube, and pushing the tube through the slicing disc. In either case, the cut vegetable can be served, at once, steaming hot. Or you can add it at the last minute to a sauce or soup.

Many vegetables have a tough texture before being cooked. This is no disgrace and no reason for discarding them. Healthy green leaves on a head of cauliflower are another example. These leaves gain more palatability when steamed until fork tender, then pushed through the slicing disc and cut across the grain into bite-sized pieces.

2. The amount of water used in cooking is proportional to the amount of nutrient loss. It is very important to use minimal quantities of water when cooking vegetables.

To corroborate this bit of common sense, consider a study by researchers Krehl and Winters. They found that vegetables retained vitamins and minerals best with waterless cooking (see Chapter 8). Of the three methods they studied, pressure cooking came in second best. Old-fashioned boiling was the worst.

As far as less cooking liquid is concerned, the best methods are obviously baking, waterless cooking, and microwave. Stir frying is also good if you don't mind adding some more oil to your diet.

A drawback to stir frying, however, is that vegetables must be cut into small pieces to promote quick, uniform cooking. And vegetables cut into pieces lose nutrients through exposure to air. If you are stir frying, therefore, it makes sense to cut the vegetables immediately before cooking. The slicing disc is unsurpassed for convenient, quick cutting. If, in addition, you make sure that the oil in your cooking pan is well heated before you add the vegetables (for most rapid cooking), you can feel confident about the nutritional value of stir frying.

How different are the amounts of nutrient loss in steaming and boiling? Look at one experiment with broccoli. A raw 3½-ounce portion contained 123 milligrams of vitamin C. After steaming, 79 milligrams remained; after boiling, the broccoli contained only 35 milligrams of the same vitamin.

One reason why Dr. Klein and others have emphasized vitamin C in their research is that it may be the best overall indicator of how other nutrients are retained in cooking. The broccoli study showed similar differences for protein, calcium, iron, and other nutrients when boiling was compared to steaming. The conclusion which can be drawn from this study is that, given equal amounts of cooking time and liquid, a steamed vegetable is at least twice as nutritious as a boiled one.

3. When liquid is used for cooking vegetables, it also should be used for eating.

Since vegetables are shown to contain fewer nutrients after cooking, it might be expected that many of the lost items could be found in the cooking liquid. Where would be a better place to locate water-soluble vitamins? In a study by researchers Gordon and Noble, it was found that when larger proportions of water were used a higher percentage of the ascorbic acid was found in the cooking liquid. In other words, the more liquid used, the more likely it is to become vitamin rich and the more likely the vegetable is to become nutrient poor.

What is the best way to use cooking liquid from pressure cooking, steaming, or microwave preparation? If the liquid tastes pleasant, save it for stock.

What about the liquid residues that taste downright awful? They still do not need to be thrown away. Use them as cooking liquid for legumes and the legumes will just taste heartier.

Artichokes are a major exception to the policy of conserving cooking liquid. In the first place, due to their size and the length of cooking time required, artichokes demand preparation with a good deal of water, sometimes even boiling (depending on your availability of cookware). Second, artichokes contain few vitamins to begin with. And third, but by no means least, the cooking liquid tastes unbelievably bitter. As far as I'm concerned, artichoke liquid can and should be discarded without remorse.

4. Longer cooking time means greater cooking loss. To conserve nutrients, cooking time should be kept to a minimum.

Here is one happy coincidence for fine cooking and nutritional conscientiousness. Let your nose be your guide. When a vegetable begins to perfume the air, it is usually done. At least it pays to check.

A major disadvantage of pressure cooking or microwave preparation is how easily you can overdo it. The inconvenient truth is that cooking times for vegetables cannot be standardized. The shape and freshness of the vegetable, among other factors, varies the cooking time. Although the timetables supplied with these appliances can serve you better than nothing, beware.

All cooks should appreciate what a difference overcooking makes for taste as well as nutrients. Certain vegetables, such as cauliflower, change drastically in taste once they are overcooked.

5. The more whole a vegetable can remain while it cooks, the better. Sliced vegetables have a greater surface area exposed. The smaller the pieces, the greater the exposure, and the greater the nutrient loss.

The problem is that many vegetables seem more appetizing when chopped, even when served plain. To many people, broccoli or greens have more appeal when chopped. In fact, I suspect that cute little shapes of food help to sell the commercially processed products available today.

With the food processor's help, you have a healthy alternative to serving whole vegetables. After the vegetable has been cooked, right before you serve it, let the processor slice it or chop it. The machine handles hot food easily. Moreover, the speed of processing ensures that you can bring the food to the table piping hot.

Because of the vitamin loss with small pieces of food, I advocate steaming vegetables first,

then processing them, and finally reheating them in a sauce. Since the sauce gets eaten, waste of leaked-out nutrients is kept to a minimum. The nutritional content is higher than it would be if the vegetables were cut up, then boiled, and later warmed in the sauce.

6. To maximize nutrients, eat your vegetables freshly cooked from the pan.

As far as good health is concerned, it pays to cook just what you need for a particular meal. When you reheat vegetables, the vitamin loss can be substantial. Even refrigerated vegetables lose a surprising portion of their nutritive value.

Table 19 shows some of the figures Dr. Klein reports for vitamin C retention in one study.

For taste, as for vitamins, reheating follows the law of diminishing returns. If you do have leftover vegetables, try using them cold in a salad. The processor can help you cut the leftovers into finer pieces, which may be more appealing. Or in some cases you can process bits of vegetable into dressings or spreads—vegetables disguised but not discarded.

A GUIDE TO COOKWARE

If you are what you eat, by the same token you are what you cook in. Cookware affects nutrition considerably.

Iron Cookware

Ever hear of iron-deficiency anemia? It's the most common disease in our country caused by nutritional deficiency. Many cases go undiagnosed.

As the family cook, you can do a great deal to prevent this problem. Remember to include iron-rich foods (such as eggs and black beans) in your menus. For best utilization of the iron in these foods, serve them along with foods that are high in vitamin C such as green pepper and

TABLE 19: VITAMIN C RETENTION IN SOME VEGETABLES

The Vegetable	Freshly Cooked	Refrigerated 1 Day, Not Heated	Refrigerated 2 days, Then Reheated
Broccoli	88% retained	68% retained	60% retained
Snap beans	83% retained	41% retained	29% retained
Shredded cabbage	73% retained	44% retained	33% retained
Spinach	52% retained	48% retained	32% retained

brussels sprouts (during digestion, the chemical reaction will ensure better iron absorption). And use cast-iron cookware on a regular basis.

How much metal transfers to the food when you cook in cast iron? A surprisingly large amount. Eggs scrambled in a cast-iron skillet double their iron content. Simmer your spaghetti sauce in iron for a few hours and the difference becomes even more dramatic: the number of micrograms of iron per 100 grams of sauce jumps from 3 to 87.

By cooking a couple of dishes in iron each day, you can increase your family's iron intake substantially. It may also help you become aware of the three major factors in the use of cookware as a dietary iron supplement:

1. Longer cooking time means more iron.
2. Acid ingredients in the pot (such as tomatoes or vinegar) mean more iron.
3. A pot that is too well seasoned transfers less iron to food. With too little pot seasoning, food can acquire dark coloration and an unpleasant metallic taste. For a happy medium, keep iron cookware moderately well seasoned.

One final note: We've mentioned that the body will make better use of iron if some vitamin C is also eaten at the meal. Ironically, foods that are cooked in iron tend to lose their vitamin C. For best results, then, cook those brussels sprouts in a noniron pot.

Aluminum Cookware

Aluminum cookware has an impact on food that parallels that of iron cookware. It's an undesirable effect, unfortunately.

According to Gary Null, "Studies have proven aluminum to be a toxic, highly reactive metal which combines with various elements in food, especially when the food has been cooked in or left to stand in aluminum for a long time."

Whether the saucepan is a costly item from the fanciest store in town or a cheap model from the nearest dime store, aluminum is aluminum. The heat conduction may be magnificent, but the fact remains that aluminum in your food can rob you of vitamins. Moreover, the overall effect of routine use of aluminum consumption can be to irritate, even damage, the digestive system.

Presumably aluminum foil produces comparable effects. Foil is a convenient household item, but you can find better methods to heat or store foods. In my opinion the best thing you can do with aluminum foil is to use it for gift wrap.

Tin

Tin is not recommended. If you own one of those fancy copper pans lined with tin, you should be aware that tin leeches onto food in a way that parallels that of aluminum. High levels of dietary tin have been associated with gastrointestinal distress, and have been found to disrupt the metabolism of calcium and zinc.

It may take some time before research on tin is done, and the reason why is not hard to imagine. If I were a researching nutritionist, I would be quite leery of studying tin. Who wants to incur the wrath of the entire canning industry and their conglomerate affiliates throughout the United States?

Fine Choices for Healthful Cooking

Stainless steel, glass, and good-quality enamel have been the choice of discriminating cooks for generations. These materials heat with food unobtrusively. They do not react with ingredients to discolor the food, or alter the taste or nutritional value.

Appendix II:
Vital Statistics for Grains and Beans

VITAL STATISTICS FOR GRAINS

Properly cooked natural grains are a delight: flavorful, chewy, nutritious. However, grains also require fairly precise cooking. We're used to thinking of cakes as demanding a certain degree of precision for success. That's only because they are made out of grain. Other cooked grains similarly demand that we measure proportions and cooking time.

Add too much water and most grains cook into a goo. Yet leaving water out can be even worse, because if more water must be stirred in while cooking, disaster is almost certain. (The exception is flaked grains, which produce lumps, if not disaster, unless they are stirred intermittently.)

With practice, of course, it becomes easy. And the statistics in Table 20 can help you enjoy getting practice. You will want to fine-tune the statistics according to the cookware you use, your stove, the characteristics of the grains you buy, and, most important, personal taste.

To prepare this table, I cooked one cup of each grain in stainless steel cookware. Please note that cooking times are conservative. Really they signify a time when it is safe for you to check how the grain is doing. Probably it will be done, but not necessarily.

TABLE 20: VITAL STATISTICS FOR GRAINS

Type of Grain	Amount of Water (cups)	Cooking Time (minutes)	Yield (cups)
Barley (hulled)*	2	75	2½
Brown Rice (short-grain)*	2¾–3	45	3
Brown Rice (long-grain)*	2¼	50	3½
Buckwheat Groats**	2¼	12	4
Bulgur**	2	15	2¾
Cornmeal***	3½	40	3½
Cracked Wheat**	2	15	2¼
Rolled Oats*	2	5	1½
Rolled Rye*	2	5	1½
Rolled Wheat*	2	5	1½
Millet**	3	35	4
Rye Berries*	2½	60	2½
Oats (steel-cut)*	2	45	1½
Wheat Berries*	2½	60	2½

   *Prepared by the fluffy boil method.
  **Prepared by the toast and boil method.
***Steamed.

TABLE 21: VITAL STATISTICS FOR BEANS

Each type of dried bean is unique. It pays to know how long various beans need to be cooked, how much water should be added, and the final yield. Inevitably, statistics are approximate. In each case, 1 cup of bean was measured, then sorted through. Except for lentils and split peas, all beans were quick-soaked in the cooking water. Next, beans and water were brought to a boil in a stainless steel saucepan. Heat was turned to a simmer, and the pan covered. Then timing began.

Type of Bean	Amount of Water (cups)	Cooking Time (hours)	Yield (cups)
Adzuki	2¼	1½	2½
Black	4	1½	2
Black-Eyed Pea	2½	½	2¼
Chickpea	4	3	3
Great Northern	2¼	1¼	3
Kidney	3	1½	2½
Lentil (green)	2¾	1	3
Lima (baby)	2½	1¼	2⅓
Mung	2¼	1	3
Navy	2	2	2½
Pinto	3	2½	2⅔
Red	2½	2	2½
Soy	4	5	2½
Split Pea (either green or yellow)	2½	1	2¼

Appendix III:

Protein and Calorie Content of Protein Source Foods

TABLE 22: PROTEIN & CALORIE CONTENT OF PROTEIN SOURCE FOODS

	% Protein in edible portion	Calories per gram of protein	Limiting amino acids (% of ideal pattern)‡
Dairy Products & Eggs			
Nonfat dry milk	35.9	10	*
Whole dry milk	26.4	19	*
Cheddar cheese, ripened	25.0	16	*
Cottage cheese, uncreamed	17.0	5	*
creamed	13.6	8	*
Egg, whole (hen's)	12.9	13	*
Egg white	10.9	5	*
Cream cheese	8.0	47	**T** 86
Skim milk or buttermilk	3.6	10	*
Whole milk (cow's)	3.5	19	*
Yogurt, low-fat	3.4	15	*
Goat's milk	3.2	21	**M**†
Whey, fluid	0.9	29	*
Grains (raw)			
Oatmeal	14.2	27	**L** 73
Wheat: hard red spring	14.0	24	**L** 56
white bread flour (80% extraction)	12.0	30	**L** 41
gluten	88.9	4	**L** 28, **T** 95
germ	26.6	14	*
bran	16.0	13	**L** 85
Triticale	14.0	†	**L** 60, **T**†, **M**†
Rye, whole-meal	12.1	28	**L** 67, **T** 69
Buckwheat	11.7	29	**L** 75
Bulgur wheat (parboiled)	11.2	32	**L** 51
Sorghum	11.0	30	**L** 40, **T** 95
Millet	9.9	33	**L** 67
Barley, pot	9.6	36	**L** 68
Cornmeal, whole-ground	9.2	39	**L** 53, **T** 57
Rice, brown	7.5	48	**L** 75
parboiled, "converted"	7.4	50	**L** 69
polished (white)	6.7	54	**L** 71

*No limiting amino acids   †Values not available   ‡**T** = tryptophan, **L** = lysine, **M** = total methionine and cystine

	% Protein in edible portion	Calories per gram of protein	Limiting amino acids (% of ideal pattern)‡
Legumes (Raw)			
Soybeans	34.1	12	M 99
fermented (tempeh)	16.9	10	*
cake or curd (tofu)	7.8	9	*
Soy milk	3.4	10	*
Peanuts	26.0	22	L 70, M 92, T 96
Fava beans (broad beans)	25.1	13	M 58, T 81
Lentils	24.7	14	M 65, T 90
Mung beans	24.2	14	M 47, T 75
Peas	24.1	14	M 77, T 84
Black-Eyed peas	22.8	15	M 86
Common (red, white, pinto, black)	22.5	15	M 73, T 95
Garbanzos (chickpeas)	20.5	18	T 81, M 85
Limas	20.4	17	T 75, M 86
Nuts & Seeds			
Pumpkin seeds	29.0	19	L 76, M†
Sunflower seeds	24.0	23	L 71
Walnuts, black	20.5	31	*
Pistachios	19.3	31	T 95, L 96
Sesame seeds	18.6	30	L 54
Almonds	18.6	32	L 44, T 80
Cashews	17.2	33	L 91
Cocoa (high-fat)	16.8	18	L 97, M†
Walnuts (English or Persian)	14.8	44	L 30, T 95
Brazil nuts	14.3	46	L 55, T 90
Filberts (hazelnuts)	12.6	50	M 47, L 58
Pecans	9.2	75	L 89
Coconut (dried kernel)	7.2	92	L 69
Carob flour	4.5	40	T 57
Vegetables (Raw)			
Immature seeds			
Limas, green	8.4	15	M 83
Peas	6.3	13	M 72, T 95
Corn	3.5	27	T 59, L 73
Black-Eyed peas (in pods)	3.3	13	T 95, M†
Green leaves			
Kale (without stems)	6.0	9	L 61, M 69
Brussels sprouts	4.9	9	M 58
Collards (without stems)	4.8	9	*
Pigweed and lambsquarters	4.2	10	*
Parsley	3.6	12	M†
Spinach	3.2	8	*
Turnip greens	3.0	9	M 69
Mustard greens	3.0	10	L 95, M 96

---

*No limiting amino acids   †Values not available   ‡T = tryptophan, L = lysine, M = total methionine and cystine

	% Protein in edible portion	Calories per gram of protein	Limiting amino acids (% of ideal pattern)‡
Swiss chard	2.4	10	L 78, T 96, M†
Beet greens	2.2	11	L 56, M 67, T 95
Watercress	2.2	9	M†
Other vegetables			
Red pepper (hot)	3.7	25	T 93, M†
Broccoli	3.6	9	M 96
Mushrooms	2.7	10	M 38, L 88, T 96
Cauliflower	2.7	10	M†
Asparagus	2.5	10	M 84, L 89
Okra	2.4	15	T 54, L 65, M 87
Beans, snap	1.9	17	M 82
Roots			
Potato	2.1	36	M 72, L 94
Yam	2.1	48	L 81
Sweet potato	1.7	67	L 67
Cassava	1.1	†	M 66, L 82
Yeast			
Brewer's	38.8	7	M 95
Torula	38.6	7	T 42
Active dry	36.9	8	T 87

*No limiting amino acids †Values not available ‡ = tryptophan, **L** = lysine, **M** = total methionine and cystine
Adapted from Watt and Merrill 1964 (Ag. Handbook no. 8), FAO/WHO 1970, and Orr & Watt 1957

Appendix IV:

Bibliography

COOKING

Like other cooks of my generation, I owe a great deal to Irma Rombauer and Marion Rombauer Becker, James Beard, and Julia Child. I would like to include in the following list some lesser-known authors. Their superb cookbooks have taught me a great deal, and I am happy to recommend them to you.

Anderson, Jean. *Jean Anderson's Processor Cooking.* New York: William Morrow, 1979.

Brown, Edward Espe. *Tassajara Cooking.* Boulder, CO: Shambala Publications, Inc., 1980.

Jaffrey, Madhur. *Madhur Jaffrey's World-of-the-East Vegetarian Cooking.* New York: Knopf, 1981.

Kasin, Miriam. *The Age of Enlightenment Cookbook.* New York: Arco, 1980.

Newman, Marcea. *The Sweet Life, Marcea Newman's Natural Food Dessert Cookbook.* New York: Houghton Mifflin, 1974.

Pinkwater, Jill. *The Natural Snack Cookbook.* New York: Four Winds Press, 1975.

Robertson, Laurel, Carol Flinders, and Bronwen Godfrey. *Laurel's Kitchen, a Handbook for Vegetarian Cookery and Nutrition.* Berkeley, CA: Nilgiri Press, 1976.

Townsend, Doris McFerran. *The Cook's Companion.* New York: Crown Publications, 1978.

Whyte, Karen Cross. *The Complete Sprouting Cookbook.* San Francisco: Troubador Press, 1973.

NUTRITION

Anyone can do research on the nutritional contents of food. You need no special degree or educational background. In fact, if you read labels before you buy food, you already are doing a form of nutritional research.

Both Adelle Davis and Lelord Kordel have done an exemplary job of making practical points about good nutrition intelligible to the lay reader. The following sources of information have also been useful to me, both personally and in the preparation of this book.

Null, Gary, with Steve Null. *The New Vegetarian, Building Your Health Through Natural Eating.* New York: William Morrow and Company, Inc., 1978.

Watt, K., and Annabel L. Merrill. *The Handbook of the Nutritional Contents of Foods.* Prepared for the U.S. Department of Agriculture. New York: Dover Publications, 1975.

Journal of Food Science, 221 N. LaSalle, Chicago, IL.

Prevention Magazine. Emmaus, PA: Rodale Press.

Acknowledgments

I consider that I have studied with the greatest cooking teacher of our time: His Holiness Maharishi Mahesh Yogi. Although he never taught me a single recipe, he instructed me in a method to systematically develop refined sensory perception, creativity, and other abilities that would make any chef thrive. My inexpressible gratitude goes to Maharishi for the Transcendental Meditation and TM-Sidhi programs, my teacher training and advanced courses with him, and the inspiration of his personal example.

Thanks also to the hundreds of people who enabled me to make the discoveries that led to this book, most notably David Ramsay, Ernest and Sue Rosenbaum, Amy Patton, Sylvia Burnes, Hilma Hawkins, Carol Paley, Art Boucher, Lynne Ambrosini, Mitch Weber, Frances Kerridge, Mary England, and Ellen Hausknecht. Thanks also to Merinda Obeirne and the Springfield, Illinois YMCA.

Special appreciation goes to Steven M. Royce, who edited the manuscript of this book while a doctoral candidate at the Department of Food Science, University of Illinois. I also want to acknowledge the generous help of Dr. Barbara W. Klein, of the Department of Foods and Nutrition at the University of Illinois.

All those who worked on the production of *Food Processor Cooking—Naturally* have earned my gratitude, particularly Jody Rein.

Index